THE
COMPACT
DISC

THE
COMPACT
DISC

Erik S. Schetina

 PRENTICE HALL, Englewood Cliffs, New Jersey 07632

Library of Congress Cataloging-in-Publication Data

Schetina, Erik S.
  The compact disc / by Erik S. Schetina.
    p.   cm.
  Includes index.
  1. Compact discs.   2. Compact disc players.   I. Title.
TK7882.C56S34 1989
621.389'32–dc19

88-18671
CIP

Editorial/production supervision and
  interior design: Anthony Calcara
Cover design: Ben Santora
Manufacturing buyer: Mary Ann Gloriande

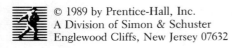
© 1989 by Prentice-Hall, Inc.
A Division of Simon & Schuster
Englewood Cliffs, New Jersey 07632

Printed in the United States of America

10 9 8 7 6 5 4 3 2 1

ISBN 0-13-154429-2

Prentice-Hall International (UK) Limited, *London*
Prentice-Hall of Australia Pty. Limited, *Sydney*
Prentice-Hall Canada Inc., *Toronto*
Prentice-Hall Hispanoamericana, S.A., *Mexico*
Prentice-Hall of India Private Limited, *New Delhi*
Prentice-Hall of Japan, Inc., *Tokyo*
Simon & Schuster Asia Pte. Ltd., *Singapore*
Editora Prentice-Hall do Brasil, Ltda., *Rio de Janeiro*

To my parents, thanks for the investment.

CONTENTS

PREFACE

The audio recorder has been around for quite a few years. At the turn of the century, Thomas Edison demonstrated the first audio recorder, the record player. Since then there have been numerous advances in the art of sound reproduction. Tape recorders appeared in many forms. The reel-to-reel deck, eight-track player, Elcast system, and cassette are but a few of these. New decks feature special alloy tape heads for greater performance, and magnetic tape is constantly being improved to yield greater reproductive latitudes. Turntables, too, have gone from archaic to high tech; many now feature low-weight graphite tonearms and vacuum suction platters. Unfortunately, these systems have one basic flaw. The media they use to record and play back sound, vinyl or tape, are limited in both life expectancy and performance. Tapes wear and break, melt and stretch, can be demagnetized unwittingly, and loose their punch after a number of playings. Records accumulate dirt, scratches, and warps, and lose their musical highs after only a few playings. Even worse, the average LP or cassette is not of very high quality from a high-fidelity standpoint, and to obtain true high-fidelity recordings, one must often purchase special-edition pressings or recordings, both rare and expensive items.

Enter the compact disc. This high-technology system promises a tough, wear-resistant medium which also provides true high-fidelity sound. Stereo components, once limited by their sound sources, are now able to realize their full musical potential. In fact, a compact disc player can be so musically accurate that it will often outperform conventional speakers and amplifiers, and can warrant a reevaluation of one's current stereo components.

What is this system that has gained so much attention in the audio community? How does it work, and what are its strong points and limitations? How does one choose a disc player? Which features contribute to a better-sounding machine, and in fact, do they all really sound the same? The compact disc player is so new that almost everyone has his or her own idea of the answers to these questions, yet many people have little idea of what makes a player work. That is the purpose of this book—to explain the technology behind the machine. You will learn some of the basics of digital electronics and understand how music can be transformed into bumps on the surface of a plastic disc. We take a look at some of the features that are available on players, whether intended for home, car, or portable use. We will also learn how to choose a disc player from among the many models and brands on the market, and how to perform some quick tests to separate the good players from the bad. In short, if you are thinking of buying a player and want to know what to look for, or if you already own a player and want to learn how to care for it or what makes it work, you will find that information in the following pages. You need not hold a doctorate in electrical engineering to understand the disc player or how it does what it does. In fact, most of the concepts involved in the digitization of sound can be related to everyday items and events. So read on, and welcome yourself to the digital world.

Acknowledgments

I would like to extend my sincere thanks to Martin Clifford, who first prompted me to write this book, and without whom I may never have become an author. I would also like to thank Matthew Fox for his help and guidance, as well as Paul Becker and Anthony Calcara for their immense parts in the preparation of this book.

Erik S. Schetina

INTRODUCTION

The compact disc systems on today's market embody a technology known as *digital signal processing*. Unlike record or tape players, which employ electronics to control the mechanical aspects of their operation, the compact disc system uses digital electronics to store, recover, and process musical information. This is the first time that such a process has been used for this type of consumer product, and it differs from the conventional means of recording in several ways. But before examining the compact disc system, a synopsis of other recording means is in order.

ANALOG RECORDING: RECORDS AND TAPES

A record player may use modern electronic circuits to control the rotational speed of its platter or even to control the positioning of its tonearm. But the means of sound reproduction is based on a diamond-tipped stylus scraping along a groove in a vinyl record. This groove is formed when sound vibrations cause a microphone's surface to vibrate, thereby converting the sound into electrical impulses. These impulses travel along a wire and excite another magnet, which is connected to a cutting stylus, thereby forming grooves in the record which correspond to the original sound wave. It is this physical contact of diamond against vinyl that is the link between your ears and the sound contained on the record (Figure 1.1). This is the same basic

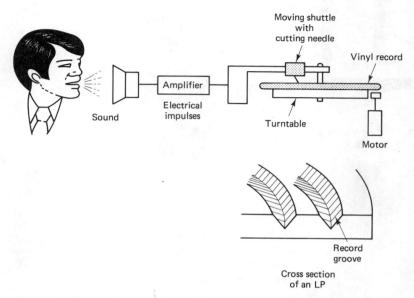

Figure 1.1 Sound is transformed from vibrations in the air to ripples in the groove of a vinyl record.

method as that first used by Thomas Edison around the turn of the century to record and play back sound (Figure 1.1).

The tape deck uses a more modern concept to achieve sound reproduction—the fact that the orientation of the particles that reside on a magnetic tape can be changed by a magnetic field so that their orientation is proportional to the applied field. The value of the magnetic field transmitted through the tape recorder's head is dictated by the same audio impulses as those used to cut a record's groove, so the audio impulses are transferred to tape in this manner. The orientation of magnetic particles, called *polarization*, can later be read from the tape and converted back into sound. Tape players may use electronic memory and controlling circuits to find particular songs on a tape, automatically replay a selection, or automatically reverse direction when the end of a tape is encountered. Still, the actual reproduction of sound is achieved by a magnetic head contacting and scanning a moving tape (Figure 1.2).

In each of these cases, sound reproduction is achieved through both mechanical and analog techniques, yet both systems have several serious drawbacks. For the case of the LP record, there are many. To begin, the bandwidth, or range of musical highs and lows that can be recorded on a vinyl disc, is severely limited by its physical parameters. This is because the groove can be cut only so accurately and can retain only a limited amount of audio information. There is simply a limit to the fidelity of such a recording. And even if extremely high fidelity recordings are made, the high-frequency components of the recording, such as cymbals, strings, and the like, will deteriorate after a few playings. This is because the stylus that tracks the groove also wears it down, removing some vinyl with each playing. So the more a record is listened to, the worse it will sound. Dirt and dust find havens in the record's groove and are ground into its surface by the stylus. Even the act of cleaning a record can damage it, for harsh chemicals may dry out the vinyl, and a badly designed cleaning pad can grind old dirt into a new record's grooves. Stereo separation, the ability to distinguish the left channel from the right, is limited by the design of the vinyl record, as is the dynamic range, the record's ability to capture both soft and loud noises. Also, LPs are far from suited for portable use, and may warp with age if not stored correctly. In short, they are a medium that deteriorates with use.

Tapes are a more versatile and durable means of recording sound, but they, too, have several shortcomings. Like LPs, their bandwidth is limited in all but the most esoteric of players. They are portable and require little maintenance, but like records, the magnetic head that reads the tape must also contact it physically. This causes tape particles to rub off the tape's surface, creating wear to both the tape head and the tape itself. After a large number of playings, a tape will lose some of the audio information stored on it. This degrades the quality of sound that can be reproduced by a stereo system's amplifiers and speakers. It is also difficult to find prerecorded tapes whose quality can match even those of LPs.

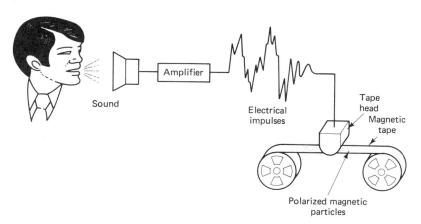

Figure 1.2   Sound is transformed into electrical impulses and then transferred to magnetic tape.

DIGITAL RECORDING: SOUND REPRODUCTION
IN THE COMPUTER AGE

The compact disc system differs from both LPs and tape in that the circuitry which controls and processes the recorded music, as well as the medium of recording itself, is based on the cornerstone of electronic microcircuit technology—the binary bit. Unlike records or tapes, disc recording and playback involve an almost completely digital process. Audio information, sound and music, is converted into a digital code, then stored on a digital medium that is mass produced and sold to you, the consumer. The discs are then read by a beam of light (which causes no wear), digitally processed, and then restored as music. The compact disc is rugged, portable, and resistant to dirt and the elements. The act of playing the disc in no way causes any type of wear, and dirt or nicks that would cause a record to skip or a tape to break have little effect on a CD. Sound, which is essentially physically transferred to the groove of a record, is not present on a compact disc. There exist only reflective depressions in a plastic disc which are translated into the sounds of a guitar, piano, organ, or whatever. The compact disc's fidelity is unmatched by that of any previous medium and has many possible avenues of expansion. It is as much an innovation as was the first cylindrical phonograph, and has been both praised and condemned by members of the audio community. What is this technology that uses lasers and computers to bring sound into our homes, forsaking analog for digital and magnets for lasers?

THE COMPACT DISC: ITS ORIGINS

The roots of the compact disc are found decades back in time. The concepts that are employed to make this system work are far from new, yet it was only in the mid-1970s when the idea of using digital signal processing for a consumer item dawned on the corporate minds of the world. Two companies, N.V. Philips of the Netherlands and Sony Corporation, combined resources to produce a product aimed at the masses, a product embodying advanced technology with a simple purpose. That purpose was to create a medium for high-fidelity sound reproduction which would far outperform conventional audio products. The fruit of that labor was the compact disc system, a system that has borrowed technology from the microchip manufacturing arena as well as that of physics, optics, signaling theory, and a host of others. Digital audio is new and exciting and challenges the limits of conventional stereo equipment—amplifiers, receivers, speakers and so on. As LPs forced 78s out of existence and cassettes spelled the end of eight-track tapes, so digital audio may have its sights set on the domain of analog reproduction. But before we write off analog as an antique system, we want to learn how digital audio works and why it can achieve such impressive results. That is the aim of this book—to educate you in the practice of digital sound reproduction.

In this chapter we examine some of the basic terms and ideas that you must master before you can begin to understand this most magical of processes, the digitization of sound.

ANALOG SIGNALS: THE BASICS OF SOUND REPRODUCTION

The reproduction of sound is the final aim of digital recording. So to understand how to reproduce sound, we must first be aware of its nature. The average person does not think of sound in terms of its electrical characteristics or modes of behavior, but simply as an audible stimulus to the ear, something that can be felt if loud enough, and shut out with earplugs when annoying. There is another side to sound which we uncover in this chapter—the side that describes its properties. What does sound look like when it is converted into electrical impulses, such as when it is captured by a microphone and displayed on laboratory equipment such as an oscilloscope or spectrum analyzer? How does recording sound change its characteristics, and how can it be faithfully recorded and reproduced? To answer these questions, we must first understand some of the fundamentals.

For the special case of music, there are several factors that give a particular instrument its unique voice. A flute may play the same note as a pipe organ, but there can be no doubt when you listen to them which instrument produced which sound. This is due to the effects of amplitude, timbre, and harmonic interaction produced by each instrument as it is played. Let's look first at the simplest of waveforms, the sine wave, to see how these effects can change it.

The Sine Wave: A Musical Building Block

A *sine wave* is a product of a mathematical function which, as it happens, describes a pure, single tone. To generate a sine wave for inspection, a musician might play a sustained note on an instrument. To view this tone, we could place a microphone next to the instrument and connect it to an *oscilloscope*, a device that displays a signal's amplitude as it varies with time. Sine waves can also be produced by a device called a *function generator*, which, as its name suggests, outputs various mathematical functions in electrical form.

A typical sine wave is depicted in Figure 1.3. Notice that it has a minimum and maximum amplitude, $\pm A$, which in this case is 1 volt (V). It also has a frequency, f, which is determined by the time it takes the sine

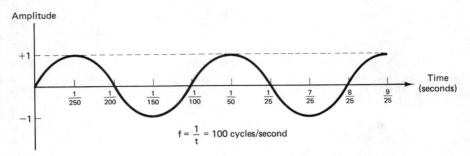

Figure 1.3   A 100-Hz sine wave.

wave to complete one full cycle. Frequency is defined as 1 over the time for one cycle. Since the sine waves takes $\frac{1}{100}$ of a second to complete one cycle, f for this sine wave is 100 cycles per second, or 100 hertz (Hz).

Harmonics: Combining Sine Waves to Make Music

If we listened to this sine wave through a loudspeaker, all that we would hear would be a single, constant, boring tone. To make the sound interesting and give it a special voice, such as that produced by a musical instrument, harmonics would have to be introduced into the tone. A *harmonic* is simply a multiple of the fundamental frequency of an instrument. Although the *fundamental*, or lowest and strongest frequency, that a flute produces may be at 1000 Hz, it would also produce weaker tones at 2000 Hz, 3000 Hz, 4000 Hz, and so on. These harmonics are attenuated, that is, their amplitude is diminished, the farther out they extend. The first harmonic is just the fundamental frequency, 1000 Hz. The second harmonic, 2000 Hz, might be at only half the amplitude of the fundamental frequency. The seventh harmonic, in this case 7000 Hz, might be so attenuated that it would be inaudible. Sometimes an instrument may produce only odd or even harmonics, depending on its design and how it is played. All the harmonics combine with the fundamental frequency to change the appearance of the signal and give it a particular look and sound. Figure 1.4 shows a sine wave after the second and third harmonics have been added. Notice that its *period*, that is, the time for one cycle, does not change regardless of how many harmonics are added.

Harmonics are usually referred to as being either odd or even. An *odd harmonic* is an odd multiple of the fundamental frequency. The third, fifth, and seventh harmonics, for instance, are odd. Similarly, the second, fourth, and sixth harmonics would be referred to as *even*. Musical instruments produce odd and even harmonics in different quantities and strengths. This is what gives a particular instrument its unique sound. These harmonics, referred to as *overtones*, vary not only with the type of instrument, but also

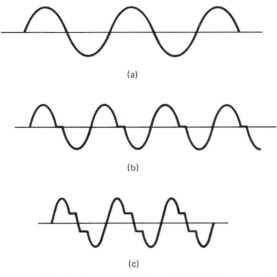

(a)

(b)

(c)

Figure 1.4 Sine wave (a) after the second (b) and third (c) harmonics have been added.

with the manner in which it is played. If an instrument is played softly, it may produce only a few weak overtones, and the sound emanating from it may appear much like a pure sine wave. The same note played loudly may result in the production of added harmonics of greater strength which will color the fundamental frequency. If played too loudly, the harmonics may overpower the fundamental frequency and produce distortion.

The Spectrum of Sound: A Graphical Representation

There are many ways to represent sound graphically. Figure 1.3 represented a sine wave by plotting the amplitude of the signal as it varied with time. We also saw how sine waves of different frequencies combined to alter the shape of the initial wave. In some cases, however, the shape of a wave may not interest us. We may be more interested in how many different waves occupy a spectrum that we wish to observe. Suppose that we play an instrument and wish to plot all the different frequencies that it produces and see how their strengths, that is, amplitudes, vary. We can use the plot of Figure 1.5 to do just this. This graph plots the strength of a wave as a function of its frequency. You can see from this graph that this particular musical instrument has a fundamental frequency of 1 kilohertz (kHz) and harmonics spaced 1 kHz apart up to about 6 kHz, where they drop off dramatically. In general, when we refer to a *spectrum* of sound we mean all the frequencies that occupy a particular range, and the graph of Figure 1.5 is referred to as a *graph* of that spectrum.

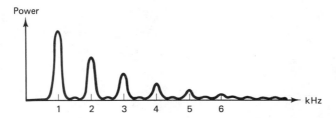

Figure 1.5 Spectrum of a typical musical instrument. Harmonics after the sixth are severely attenuated.

Bandwidth: The Scope of an Analog Signal

Often, a signal will be referred to as being *bandlimited*, or having a finite bandwidth. This means that the range of possible frequencies associated with this signal is limited to a known range. Telephone lines can transmit frequencies that span the range from 100 to 3000 Hz. Any sound of greater than 3000 Hz is cut off and not transmitted, as is any whose frequency is less than 100 Hz. We would refer to phone lines as being bandlimited, with a bandwidth of 2900 Hz.

Transfer Functions: Visualizing Frequency Response

Another type of graph is called a *transfer function*. The human ear, as an example, can register sounds from about 20 Hz to 18 kHz. This equates to a *bandwidth* of a little less than 18 kHz. Some animals, such as dogs, can hear sounds of significantly higher frequency than those that can be heard by human beings. This is due to the difference in construction between human and animal ears. This difference results in the human ear filtering out high frequencies. How, graphically, can this filter be represented? It is done with the graph in Figure 1.6, called a *filter transfer function*. This plots the gain of a human ear against frequency. We see that for ultralow frequencies our ear is relatively insensitive, since it attenuates, or diminishes the intensity of, sound in the low-frequency bands. For frequencies between 20 Hz and 18 kHz, the gain is 1, meaning that it passes all frequencies without changing their intensity. From 18 to 20 kHz sensitivity again decreases, or rolls off, and above 20 kHz there is almost total attenuation. There are several ways to determine the transfer function of a particular device. If we wished to produce one for a microphone, we could play tones of equal intensity and plot their intensity when they exited the microphone. This is essentially the same process that doctors go through when they administer a hearing test. Both these graphs, the transfer function and the spectrum, will become very useful in later chapters when we discuss how a digital recorder works.

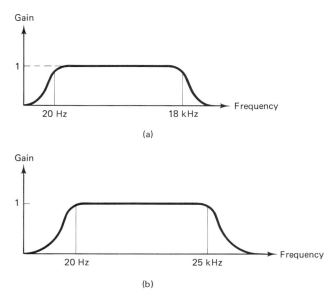

Figure 1.6 The frequency response of a human ear (a) shows its limited bandwidth; the response of an animal's ear (b) shows an extended range.

Decibels: A Way to Compare Quantities

The functioning of the human ear leads us to the discussion of decibels. The *decibel* is a unit of comparison that is often misinterpreted as a unit of measure. It is useful because it allows us to map broad changes in the size of various parameters down to a more understandable scale.

For the human ear to perceive a doubling in the intensity of a sound, the power used to generate that sound must be increased by a factor of 10. If you set your stereo set at an arbitrary sound level that requires it to produce 10 watts (W) per channel and then wish to double the intensity of the sound, you must increase the power not to 20 W but to 100 W. Because these changes require exponential rather than linear increases in power, we often use decibels to express their value. The decibel is perhaps the most misunderstood and incorrectly used term in the audio industry. The decibel (dB), unlike the watt or volt, is not an absolute unit of measure. You cannot have 15 dB of sound or 30 dB of sugar. Rather, it is a relative unit of measure. When someone says that a sound is at a level of 30 dB, they mean that it is 30 dB greater than the threshold of human hearing. Decibels always express how one value relates to another value. Sometimes when a benchmark of comparison is established, we tend to forget that we are indeed comparing one level to another. The formula for computing decibels is fairly straightforward. Simply take the log of the ratio of the numbers that

TABLE   1.1   Decibel Values and Corresponding Ratios

Decibels	Power Ratio, $10 \log_{10}$	S/N Ratio, $20 \log_{10}$
0	1.00	
1	1.26	
2	1.58	
3	2.00	
4	2.51	
5	3.16	
6	3.98	
7	5.01	
8	6.31	
9	7.94	
10	10.00	3.16
20	100	10.00
30	1000	31.62
40	10,000	100.00
50	100,000	316.23
60	1,000,000	1,000
70	10,000,000	3,162
80	100,000,000	10,000
90	1,000,000,000	31,622
100	10,000,000,000	100,000
110	100,000,000,000	316,227

you are comparing and multiply that value by 10 [$10 \log(x)$]. Fortunately, most pocket calculators have a log button that frees us from using look-up tables or doing hand calculations. If you wish to know how many decibels greater 100 W is than 10 W, divide 100 by 10 and then take the logarithm. This gives a 10-dB power ratio. To figure the difference between 10 W and 1000 W, we perform the same function to realize a 20-dB gain in power. Sometimes, the actual decibel value is multiplied by a constant before quoting its value. The popular specification of *signal-to-noise ratio* (*S/N*) is defined as $20 \log(x)$. Some tables of decibels and their corresponding power ratios are listed in Table 1.1. You may wonder why decibels are quoted when the actual ratio is available. It is certainly as easy to say 1000 times greater as it is to say 30 dB. But if you have to discuss a 90-dB difference in the intensity of two function, you will agree that its preferable to use the decibel value rather than the actual ratio, 1,000,000,000:1.

Crossing Over from Analog to Digital

These, then, are the basics of sound and some of the ways in which it is expressed and interpreted. Yet compact discs contain no reference to transfer functions, sine waves, or decibels! The only mars in the mirrored surface of a CD are the bumps and indentations, which somehow represent all the electrical impulses and relations that constitute the audio signal. This representation is accomplished by encoding sounds and music into binary codes, and in later chapters we examine just how this is done. For now, let's cross into the digital world and examine how it differs from the one which we are familiar.

BINARY NUMBERS: THE BASIS OF ALL DIGITAL SYSTEMS

Why Binary?: A Case for Digital Electronics

As noted previously, the compact disc system employs a great deal of digital circuitry, called *hardware*, to perform its function. This circuitry is the same type as that used in computers, video games, calculators, and in fact, in virtually every consumer product on the market that runs on electricity. The reason that digital circuits are so prolific in the modern world is that it is quite easy to combine them so that they can perform a complex task, be it adding numbers or controlling a spaceship. Part of the power behind digital circuits is the binary number system. *Binary numbers* are strings of 1's and 0's used to represent decimal numbers, the type that we use every day. In one binary system, the number 1 0 1 0 represents the decimal number 10. Before you can understand digital recording, you must be familiar with this number system and digital circuitry in general. The reason for this is simple. You often hear of compact disc players using 14-, 16-, or 18-bit digital-to-analog converters, or of using noise-shaping and error-correcting circuits. In fact, the basic unit of storage on the compact disc itself is the binary digit. So compact discs and the binary number system are intricately intertwined concepts. Just as it is impossible to read a book without knowing the alphabet, so it is difficult to discuss digital audio without understanding the binary number system and a bit of digital electronics. Luckily, these are relatively easy concepts to understand on a simple level, and that is the only level you need worry about.

A Binary Beginning: The Basics

At first the binary system seems illogical. After all, how can you represent information by strings of 1's and 0's? In truth, the binary system is as easy to understand as the one we use every day if you simply think of it as another language. For just as German or French is unintelligible until you speak it, so is the binary system a mystery until you understand it.

To begin, let's take a look at how numbers are represented in the base 10 number system, the one we use every day. In particular, let's examine the number one thousand nine hundred and thirty-nine (1939). It is composed of a string of four digits, and each digit's value depends on its position in the string. The nine, for instance, means nine hundred when it is in the second position from the right, but only nine in the rightmost position. To compute the value of a digit, we multiply the digit by 10 to the power of that position. The 1 in the third position becomes 1×10^3, or $1 \times 10 \times 10 \times 10 = 1000$. Similarly, the 9 becomes $9 \times 10 \times 10$, or 900. The 3 takes on the value of 3×10, or 30, and the final 9 becomes 9×10^0 or, simply, 9. We then add up all these values, $1000 + 900 + 30 + 9$, to get the value of this string of four numbers, one thousand nine hundred and thirty-nine (Figure 1.7). Of course, you learned all this in elementary school, but this little refresher should help you to understand how the binary number system functions.

Notice that all that is done to compute a digit's value in the string is to multiply it by 10 to the power of its position. This is called the *base 10*, or *decimal, number system.* In the *binary*, or *base 2, number system,* we multiply a number by 2 to the power of its position. In the decimal, or base 10, system, there are 10 possible digits that make up a number: 0, 1, 2, 3, 4, 5, 6, 7, 8, and 9. For the binary system there are only two possible values for each digit: 0 or 1. A typical binary number containing four positions might look like this: 1011. How do we compute the value of this number? Easily. In fact, it is done the same way as for a base 10 number. Let's number the positions of each digit 0 to 3 starting from the right. Each digit is called a *bit*. As you can see, the value of any bit is either 1 or 0. Now, to compute the value of 1011, we start at the right and multiply the 1 by 2 to the power of 0, or 1 (Figure 1.8). This yields a value of 1 for the first bit. Taking the second bit and multiplying it by 2 to the power of 1, or 2, gives the value of the second position. For the third bit, we multiply 0 by 2 to the power of 2, or 4, which gives us 0. The final bit yields 1 times 2 to the third power, or 8. These four values are now added up. 8 plus 0 plus 2 plus 1 yields a sum of 11. 1011, then, is the binary equivalent of 11. That was easy enough! To represent a larger number, we would add more bits to the left of the third position (remember: that is the leftmost bit). Note that any bit can take on only two values, either 0 or 2, to the power of its position. This is different from the base 10 system, where there are many possible values for each position.

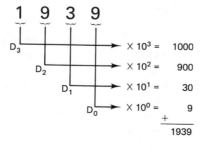

Figure 1.7 Breakdown of a decimal number into its components. Each digit is multiplied by 2 to the power of its position.

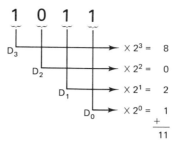

Figure 1.8 Breakdown of a binary number into its components. Each binary digit is multiplied by 2 to the power of its position, then added together to get the resultant value.

A string of eight binary numbers is called a *byte*. This length is special because it has been adopted as the unit length of information for many microprocessors and other electronic circuits. The American Standard Code for Information Interchange (ASCII) uses 8-bit bytes to represent anything from the alphabet to special characters such as asterisks (*) and ampersands (&) (Table 1.2). Some microprocessors use one word consisting of two 8-bit bytes as their basic unit of transmission. Other devices may use 32-bit words as their unit. All, however, are based on a multiple of the 8-bit byte.

Adding Numbers in the Binary System

Now that we understand the basics of the binary number system, we can inquire as to how numbers are added, subtracted, multiplied, and divided. Obviously, 0001 and 0001 cannot be added to come up with 0002, even though 0001 and 0001 do add up to 2 in the decimal system. How, then, is binary addition accomplished? Let us begin by adding two single bits, 1 and 1. Both binary and decimal 1 have the same value, so they should add up to the same value, 2. Two is represented by the binary number 10.

TABLE 1.2 Partial Table of ASCII
Conversion Characters

ASCII	Character
00100001	!
00100010	”
00100011	#
00100100	$
00100101	%
00100110	&
01000001	A
01000010	B
01000011	C
01000100	D

Just like decimal addition, if the sum of two numbers is greater than can be represented by one digit, that digit is carried to the next position. 01 + 01 add up to a binary 10. We simply carry a binary 1 from the first position to the second. 10 + 01 would add to 11, or 3. Again, this makes sense because 10 is a decimal 2 and 01 is a decimal 1. In this case there is no carry generated in either position.

Let's try to add the binary equivalent of 1 plus 3. The numbers are positioned as is done for decimal addition:

$$0011 \quad \text{three}$$
$$0001 \quad \text{one}$$

The first thing that you should see is that the sum of the first two digits cannot be represented by a single digit. Since 1 and 1 add to 10, we carry a 1 over to the next position and put a 0 in the first column of the sum:

$$10 \quad \text{carry}$$
$$0011$$
$$0001$$
$$\overline{0} \quad \text{sum}$$

Now add the second bits, with carry, to obtain this result:

$$110 \quad \text{carry}$$
$$0011$$
$$0001$$
$$\overline{00} \quad \text{sum}$$

See how the first carry added to the 1 in the second position to produce a second carry. Finishing up the next two steps yields this result:

$$0011$$
$$0001$$
$$\overline{0100} \quad \text{result}$$

Note that the sum is the binary representation of a four, the correct result of adding one and three.

If a triple addition was encountered in any of the columns, that would produce a sum bit as well as a carry bit. 1 + 1 + 1 = 11. Adding 0011 and 0011 gives this result:

$$11 \quad \text{carry}$$
$$0011$$
$$0011$$
$$\overline{0110} \quad \text{sum}$$

LOGIC GATES: THE BUILDING BLOCKS OF DIGITAL ELECTRONIC CIRCUITRY

Well, all of this binary number stuff is fine, but why is it important to us? It is important because it is very simple to implement binary operations (addition, subtraction, etc.) in digital electronic circuits. Using transistors as a basis for construction, scientists have developed several devices which are the building blocks of everything from digital watches to supercomputers. These devices are called *digital logic gates.*

AND Gates

The most basic gate is the *AND gate,* represented by the symbol shown in Figure 1.9. This gate has two inputs, A and B, and an output, Z. The AND gate is used to implement 1-bit binary addition. If both inputs are 1, called a *logical high,* the output Z, is 1. If either input is 0, called a *logical low,* the output is 0. For the output to be high, both A and B must be high—thus this gate's name, the AND gate. This gate's functioning is described by a truth table, also shown in Figure 1.9. To understand the physical operation of an AND gate, just picture it as two switches connected in series to a light bulb. In order for the circuit to conduct electricity and turn the light on, both switches A and B must be closed. If either switch is off, the bulb stays dark.

OR Gates

Another building block is the *OR gate,* depicted in Figure 1.10. Here, for Z to be high, either A or B must be high. Using the analogy of switches, we come up with a circuit similar to that of the AND gate. In this case it is obvious that if either switch is turned on, the bulb will light.

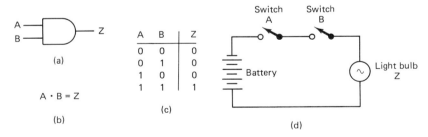

Figure 1.9 Symbol for an AND gate (a), the algebraic expression (b), and the truth table (c). (d) The light lights only if switches A and B are both closed.

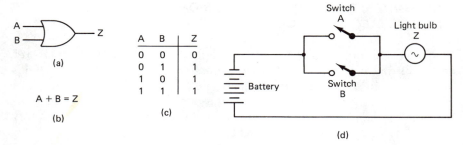

Figure 1.10   Symbol for an OR gate (a), the algebraic expression (b), and the truth table (c). (d) If either switch A or B is closed, the light will light.

NOT Gates

A final logic gate is depicted in Figure 1.11. It is called a NOT *gate*, or *inverter*. Here Z is the opposite of the input, A. If A is 1, Z is 0, and vice versa. An inverter can be realized using a single transistor.

Combinations of Gates

These simple gates can be used to implement most of the functions required for any digital system. They are called *decision-making circuits* because their outputs control various aspects of an electronic device, depending on the values of the input. These gates can also be configured to realize very complex functions such as oscillators, frequency counters, adders, and a host of others. Figure 1.12 shows how to implement a 2-bit adder using AND and OR gates. An adder such as this is used regularly in the design of everything from pocket calculators to the most sophisticated microprocessor. You can see that if one but not both inputs to the first set of AND gates is a 1, the SUM output will be a 1 and the CARRY will be 0. If both inputs are 1, the SUM output remains low while the CARRY output goes high. This is consistent with our notion of binary addition. The set of three logic gates that produce the sum are so common that they are given the name

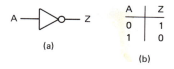

A	Z
0	1
1	0

(b)

(a)

$Z = \overline{A}$

(c)

Figure 1.11   Symbol for an inverter, or NOT, gate (a), the algebraic expression (b), and the truth table (c).

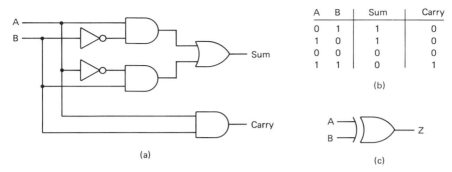

A	B	Sum	Carry
0	1	1	0
1	0	1	0
0	0	0	0
1	1	0	1

(b)

(a)

(c)

Figure 1.12 Realization of a 2-bit adder using AND, OR, and NOT gates (a), and the associated truth table (b) and (c). The symbol for an Exclusive-OR, or XOR gate, which replaces the five summing gates.

Exclusive-OR, or XOR. The process of binary addition may take as little as 4 nanoseconds (0.000000000004 second) when implemented in digital circuits. An addition of two 16-bit numbers can take as little as 40 nanoseconds. The speed at which digital logic implements its function allows us to perform many operations on a signal in a very short period, thereby facilitating the processing and filtering of audio signals in the digital domain.

All these concepts and systems—binary numbers, bandwidth, frequency, decibels, transfer functions, and graphs—will be essential when we begin to discuss the how and why of digital recording and playback. Be sure that you have a clear understanding of these concepts before you go on, as without them you could become lost in a sea of technical terms.

2

DIGITAL BASICS

The difference between analog and digital recording is as great as that between night and day. Although the aims of both techniques are the same—to record and reproduce audio information—the way that each accomplishes its task is radically different. Analog recorders attempt to make an image of sound in a medium such as magnetic tape or vinyl, and then reproduce that image through mechanical means. The digital system converts this same audio information into binary data and then encodes the data many times before placing them on a medium for storage.

In this chapter we see just how and why digital recording works, as well as how different parts of a digital recorder function. Understanding the compact disc system involves not only examining the hardware that performs the conversions, but also delving into the theory behind the practice. The theory behind digital audio involves many mathematically complex theorems which, fortunately, can be related to everyday phenomena. As we probe these theorems and algorithms, we will touch on both abstract and concrete examples of signaling theory. There are many complexities that we omit in this chapter but which are treated in later chapters. We explore the hardware side of digital audio, the electrical devices that implement various algorithms and processes. These are the building blocks of a digital system, and have some very real limitations and advantages.

THE SAMPLING THEOREM: THE BASIS OF DIGITIZATION

The basis for all of digital recording is a mathematical theorem first posed by a French mathematician named Joseph Fourier. The *Fourier theorem* states that we can take discrete samples of a continuous waveform, such as a tone produced by a musical instrument, and by taking enough samples, can reproduce the original waveform exactly. That is a lot of theorem for one sentence, so let's see just what it all means. To begin with, what is a discrete sample? Recall the sine wave from Chapter 1. It is depicted in Figure 2.1. If we wished to record this sine wave for future reproduction, an analog recording could be made which would, in effect, record the value of the waveform at every moment in time. Alternatively, the sine wave could be examined at particular points in time spaced at regular intervals, and the value, that is, amplitude, of the wave at each point could be recorded. The latter process is called *sampling*, and the values that are recorded are called *discrete samples*. We start off with a continuous waveform, the sine wave, and end up with discrete samples, a set of numbers. What Fourier said is that with the information contained in these samples, the entire waveform can be reproduced exactly. Notice that this does not say that this will be an approximate reproduction, but an exact one, including all the points in between the samples. This is perhaps the most important concept of digital recording and reproduction and is the most difficult to understand fundamentally. After all, how can a waveform be reproduced completely if the values at every point in time are not recorded? The answer to this question lies in the fact that more than just the information contained in the points sampled is used to reconstruct the wave. In fact, if we start with some information about the type of signal to be captured, such as its frequency,

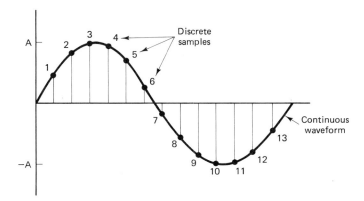

Figure 2.1   Sampled sine wave. The points labeled 1 through 13 have discrete values that can be recorded and later reproduced.

number and strength of harmonics, and so on, then when the signal is reproduced, this information can be combined with that contained in the samples. It is the combination of all this information that allows us to reconstruct the signal.

SAMPLING RATE: A RULE FOR DIGITIZING SOUND

The first quantity that must be determined is how many samples to take of a particular signal. This can be done by consulting the *Nyquist sampling theorem*. Simply stated, Nyquist says that if the highest-frequency component of the signal that you wish to capture is known, then by taking twice as many samples per second as that frequency, you will have enough samples to reconstruct the signal. The Nyquist frequency is denoted by F_s, and is called the *Nyquist sampling frequency*. Since the average person can hear frequencies up to about 20 kHz, a sampling frequency that could be used to reproduce all the sound up to 20 kHz would be $F_s = 40$ kHz. This means that for every second of sound that we wish to capture and reproduce, we must take 40,000 samples. Just why does the Nyquist theorem hold true? A mathematical proof of this theorem would be beyond the scope of this book, but there is an intuitive analogy that illustrates Nyquist's main point.

Suppose that a scientist wishes to record fluctuations of the outside air temperature as it varies during the day (Figure 2.2). Suppose also that she has an accurate thermometer and some means of automatically recording its reading at regular intervals. If the scientist does not know anything about how the temperature fluctuates, she may set the apparatus to record a reading once every second. Although the temperature variations occur continuously, she would have only discrete values, or samples, with which to trace the variations. As you may know, variations in air temperature do not occur as quickly as 1°F per second. In fact, by recording one reading per second, the scientist will end up with a great deal of redundant data. This means that there will be little or no change between the values of

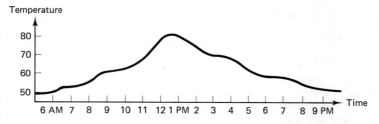

Figure 2.2 Graph of air temperature as it varies throughout the day.

consecutive data points. That is, the temperature at 12:05:00 A.M. is probably the same as that at 12:05:01 A.M. She will still have an accurate record, but will have wasted a lot of effort in taking so many unnecessary readings. In this case she would have taken too many readings per second, or oversampled. Suppose that upon realizing this the scientist changed the sampling rate to one sample every 2 hours. This time, she would end up with some samples with very different values, but since she had taken only a few per day, she would not have enough information to deduce correctly the fluctuations of temperature between readings. If the temperature at noon is 70°F and the temperature at 2 o'clock is 83°F, how can she extrapolate the temperature that occurred at 12:30? She cannot. By decreasing the sampling rate she has lost too much information, or undersampled. If, however, she knows something about the rate at which the temperature changes during the day, she can intelligently choose a satisfactory sampling rate. If the most that the temperature changes is 1°F per minute, then by taking two samples per minute she can catch every change. Of course, she can only make this choice if she has some previous knowledge about the phenomenon that she is attempting to record, in this case temperature fluctuations.

This is the basic message of the Nyquist sampling theorem. With some knowledge about the signal that we are trying to record, a satisfactory sampling rate can be chosen. Again, the sampling theorem does not at first seem to be a logical proposition. By sampling a waveform it would seem that all the information between samples is lost, yet these data can be recovered by some mystical mathematical process. Even after all the mathematical proofs are laid out before you and proven down to the last decimal point, the sampling theorem still requires some measure of belief before it can be accepted.

ALIASING: THE BIG PROBLEM WITH SAMPLING

Unfortunately, there are some problems with the analogy of the scientist and temperature fluctuations. For unlike temperature fluctuations, one can never be exactly certain of the properties of the sound that is to be recorded. This uncertainty has an impact on recording in many forms, one of which is the phenomenon of aliasing.

Aliasing: What is it?

Remember from Chapter 1 that a musical instrument creates a unique sound by producing tones of a fundamental frequency along with harmonics. These harmonics may extend far beyond the range of the fundamental frequency into the hundreds of kilohertz. A 10-kHz note played on a musical instrument will provide overtones at 20 kHz, 30 kHz, 40 kHz, and so on. The problem encountered is that if the signal is sampled at $F_s = 40$ kHz, the highest frequency that can be captured (according to Nyquist) will be 20 kHz. What happens to all those harmonics that lie above the 20 kHz maximum? One might think that they are cut out of the signal and lost forever. If that were indeed the case, the lives of a great many digital designers would be simplified immensely. After all, these frequencies are inaudible to the human ear, so losing them should pose no acoustic difficulties. Unfortunately, these upper frequencies are not cut out, but rather work to distort the sound in the lower-frequency bands. This is the phenomenon of *folding*, also called *aliasing*. What is observed is that the frequencies above $F_s/2$, the maximum allowable frequency according to Nyquist, mix with the frequencies below $F_s/2$. Given the example of $F_s = 40$ kHz, we would observe that a harmonic at 22 kHz would move down to the same point as an 18-kHz component. There it would mix with the 18-kHz component of the signal and introduce unwanted distortion into the recording. Similarly, a 28-kHz tone would fold down to 12 kHz and there introduce more unwanted distortion. You can think of these frequencies as folding over across the critical $F_s/2$ point. Folding is a problem because even though we may not be interested in frequencies above $F_s/2$ and do not want to record them, they still affect the sampled data in a destructive manner.

The reason for folding can be traced back to the digitization process. Before digitization there exists an analog waveform of some bandwidth whose spectrum can be represented graphically. When dealing with an audio signal, the bandwidth can be taken to be about 20 kHz, as depicted in Figure 2.3a. The process of digitization changes the spectrum of the analog signal. This is significant because rather than a single spectrum, digitization produces many copies of the spectrum at multiples of the sampling frequency. This is a side effect of digitization that can be proven mathematically and observed on laboratory equipment. If the sampling frequency is greater than twice the bandwidth of the original signal, the graph of Figure 2.3b arises. This type of spectrum would pose little problem, since the unwanted extra spectra could easily be filtered out in later stages. But suppose that F_s is less than twice the bandwidth of the original signal. Then the multiple spectra overlap the original spectrum and add to it to produce distortion. Now the added spectra cannot be filtered out because they are indistinguishable from the original spectrum that was digitized and recorded. If the original spectrum is bandlimited, that is, has a finite bandwidth, we can easily select the correct sampling frequency that will prevent aliasing. It's quite simple to make certain that F_s is high enough to produce a guard band around the original spectrum. The guard band is a kind of digital no man's land that safeguards the integrity of the original spectrum. If, however, the signal contains harmonics that extend far out into the audio band, there will inevitably be some aliasing because regard-

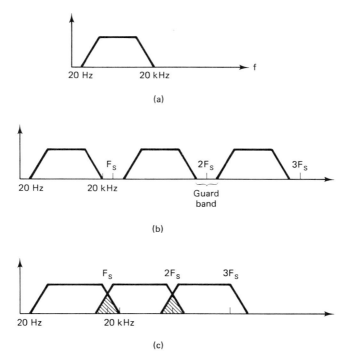

Figure 2.3 An audio signal has a limited bandwidth before sampling (a). Sampling causes multiples of the original spectrum to be reproduced at multiples of the sampling frequency (b). If the sampling frequency is too low, the spectra will overlap (c).

less of the sampling frequency, there will always be harmonics that it cannot encompass.

Another way to view aliasing is to examine a sampled sine wave, as in Figure 2.4. Here, a 1-kHz sine wave is sampled at a sampling frequency of 2 kHz. Notice that a sine wave of a lower frequency, such as 500 Hz, does not pass through all of the same points as the 1-kHz wave. However, a sine wave of a higher frequency, such as 3 kHz, can be drawn so that it passes through the same points as the 1-kHz wave. It folds across the sampling frequency down to 1 kHz. If we were looking at this 3-kHz wave from the point of view of samples, there would be no way to distinguish it from the 1-kHz sine wave. A 6-kHz wave could be drawn through the same points, and there is no way to distinguish it or any other high-frequency component from the 1-kHz wave. Only if it is known that there are no frequency components above 1 kHz can the true identity of the wave that produced such a pattern of points be established. This is one reason that a signal must be bandlimited before it can be sampled, to ensure the uniqueness of a wave with a particular pattern of sampled amplitudes.

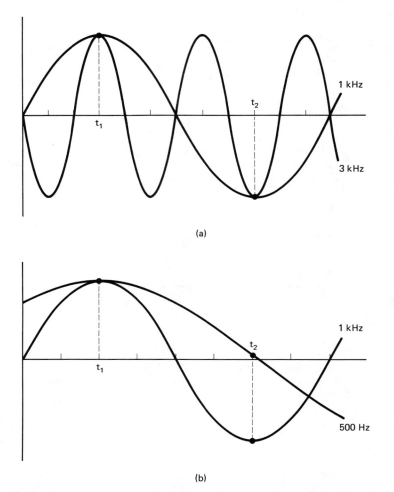

(a)

(b)

Figure 2.4   A 1-kHz sine wave sampled at $F_s = 2$ kHz. A 3-kHz wave passes through the same points as the 1-kHz (a), but a 500-Hz wave does not (b).

If you have ever watched a western movie, you have witnessed the phenomenon of aliasing. Often, the wheels of a wagon appear to slow their rotation and then reverse direction as the wagon accelerates from a stop. That appears to occur because motion pictures take 30 frames of film per second to capture action. In effect, they sample at 30 Hz. As the wheels pick up speed, the high-speed rotation of the spokes folds down across the 16-Hz point into the lower frequencies. Optically, the spokes of the wheel appear to slow down. As the rotational speed passes through exactly 30 Hz, the wheels look as if they are standing still. For moviemakers to eradicate this phenomenon, they would have to increase the number of frames per second which their cameras take. This would necessitate a redesign of the cameras and a drastic increase in the amount of film used. Since aliasing does not seem to affect the quality of such movies, moviemakers choose the more economically attractive alternative and live with this phenomenon.

Solutions to the Aliasing Dilemna

One possible solution to aliasing is to sample at a higher frequency so that all the harmonics are included in the band below $F_s/2$. There are, however, two problems with this method. The first is that as the sampling speed of a system is increased, so its complexity is increased, and it becomes more difficult and expensive to produce. It also seems wasteful to capture and record data that contain information which holds no interest, that is, information pertaining to the high-frequency harmonics. Why record a 30-kHz sound component when the only ears that can enjoy it belong to the family dog? The second problem is that regardless of how high the sampling rate of choice is, there will almost always be frequencies above $F_s/2$ that will alias down below $F_s/2$. This problem is not critical if F_s is chosen high enough so that the harmonics that do alias down do not contain very much energy, and so do not cause significant amounts of distortion. If we want to record a frequency range from 0 to 20 kHz and choose our sampling frequency as 80 kHz, the harmonics that alias down into the audio band will lie at 60 kHz and above. In most cases these harmonics do not have sufficient amplitudes to effect an audible change in the quality of sound below 20 kHz. Still, there should be some way of sampling at the most efficient frequency, 40 kHz, without incurring the penalty of aliasing. In fact, this can be accomplished with the help of a device called, appropriately enough, an antialiasing filter.

Antialiasing Filters: Screening Out Distortion

Because of the cost and complexity of oversampling, the general practice is to filter out all the harmonics above the audio-frequency band before it is digitized by using analog devices. These devices, called *antialiasing filters*, strip off the high-frequency components of a signal before it is sampled so that there is nothing left to alias down. This process is called *low-pass filtering* and is described in Figure 2.5.

The Ideal Filter: A Perfect Example

The low-pass filter has two areas of interest. The first is called the passband, and the second is called the stopband. In the *passband*, all frequencies are passed without distortion or changes in amplitude. In the

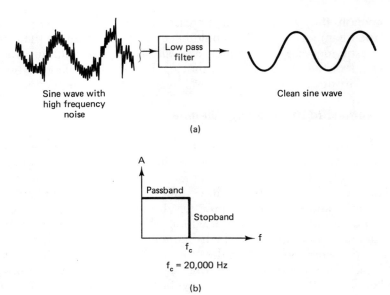

Figure 2.5 A low-pass filter strips off the high-frequency components of a signal (a). The transfer function of a low-pass filter (b) showing the passband, stopband, and cutoff frequency.

stopband, all the frequencies are attenuated down to a zero-amplitude level and are wiped out. The filter passes the low frequencies without change, hence its name. The point that separates the passband from the stopband is known as the *cutoff frequency.* In Figure 2.5, the cutoff frequency occurs at 20 kHz. Any component above this frequency is completely attenuated and cut out of the spectrum so that it will not alias down into the passband when the signal is sampled. A low-pass filter operates in much the same way as the tone control on a stereo. As the tone is turned down, high-frequency components are attenuated and low-frequency components are boosted. Turn the tone up, and the opposite occurs.

Analog Filters: Implementations in the Real World

Surprise: The filter described in Figure 2.6 cannot be implemented in the real world. It is called an *ideal filter* and serves as a model after which we pattern filters that can be realized in hardware. Such filters serve as models that designers can attempt to approximate and judge their products by. The graph of Figure 2.6 more accurately describes a real-world filter. Notice that the passband is not completely flat. It attenuates some frequencies slightly, amplifies some slightly, and passes some unchanged. This is called *ripple* because there are ripples in the otherwise flat passband of the ideal filter.

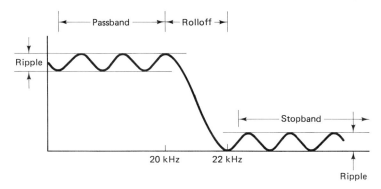

Figure 2.6 Transfer function of a realizable low-pass filter showing ripple in the stopband and passband and its gradual roll-off from band to band.

The drop from passband to stopband is not a straight vertical line. Rather, there is a more gradual drop called *roll-off* which occurs over the span of several hundred hertz. In this area one small frequency band may be almost wholly passed while its neighbor may be significantly attenuated. Finally, the stopband does not completely attenuate the high-frequency range. There is always some remnant of the high frequencies that is not filtered out in the stopband. Like the passband, the stopband has associated with it some amount of ripple. Because the ideal filter can never be constructed, a small amount of aliasing will always occur, and there is added distortion due to the ripple in both the stop- and passbands. You might also surmise that the roll-off region can cause some problems of its own, which manifest themselves in the form of distortion. Regardless of these facts, low-pass filtering is preferable to aliasing since the filtering process will create far less audible distortion than that caused by aliasing. Although there are many "brickwall" filters available on the market, so called because of their steep drop-off from passband to stopband, which could effectively eliminate aliasing, they are prohibitively expensive, ranging into the thousands of dollars, and introduce a severe form of distortion in their roll-off regions.

Analog Filters: Some Guidelines for their Design

All these parameters—stopband and passband ripple, roll-off, attenuation in the stopband, and cutoff frequency—must be considered when a filter is designed, since they are all somewhat interdependent. As we endeavor to approximate the ideal filter, the complexity of our filter is increased dramatically—to the point where a very small gain in filter performance comes at the cost of substantially more components. In the world of digital recording, components and complexity translate into money, so a designer is ultimately limited by the final cost of the product. Fortunately, there are other, smarter ways to combat aliasing, some of which we discuss later.

ANALOG-TO-DIGITAL CONVERSION: A WAY TO GO FROM MUSIC TO BITS

Now that we know at what rate to sample our signal and what type of antialiasing filter to use, there remains only one problem. How can the physical conversion from analog sound to digital data be accomplished? For this task we can employ, appropriately enough, an *analog-to-digital converter* (A/D). An A/D usually comes in the form of an integrated circuit, which combined with some peripheral circuitry does the entire job of conversion. There are literally dozens of manufacturers of A/D microchips, some of whose products can perform millions of conversions per second. The A/Ds vary in their accuracy, maximum sampling speed, and cost and are the heart of any digital audio system.

The Analog-to-Digital Converter

The input to an A/D is a sampled analog signal, such as the output from a microphone. The A/D takes this signal and converts the analog amplitudes to binary values. The hardware that accomplishes this task consists of hundreds and sometimes thousands of transistors contained on a single chip, but the actual strategy used to implement the conversion is quite simple. There are many types of A/D converters, but the two most popular are the successive-approximation converter and the integrating converter.

The Successive-Approximation Converter: The Fast Way to A/D

The *successive-approximation converter* has several components, as outlined in Figure 2.7. Initially, the converter assumes that an incoming signal's value is half of the converters full-scale value. For an 8-bit converter with a maximum range of 10 V, the full-scale value is 11111111, the highest binary value that it can output. The half-scale signal is then 00001111, or 5 V. This digital value is passed to a digital-to-analog converter, which converts this binary number back into an analog voltage. This is next compared to the original analog input voltage by a device whose output is proportional to the difference between the two voltages. The output of this device, called a *comparator*, is used to modify the next value applied to the D/A. If the converter's guess is less than the actual value, the next guess will

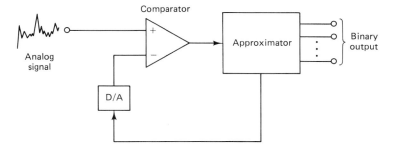

Figure 2.7 Successive-approximation converter.

be higher. If the comparison of the two analog voltages shows that the first guess was too high, the next approximation will be lower. After a number of cycles, the output will match the input to within a specified limit, and the A/D will signal that its binary output is correct.

The Integrating Converter: A Simpler A/D

An *integrating* A/D compares the time taken to perform a mathematical operation on the analog input to that required to perform the same operation on a known value. In its simplest form, the integrating A/D simply charges up a capacitor to the value of the input voltage and then counts the time necessary to discharge the capacitor to a value of zero volts. The discharge time is kept track of by a binary counter, and the value of the counter after the capacitor has been discharged is converted to a suitable binary output by some digital logic. This converter can be likened to a person who measures the amount of liquid in a bucket by poking a hole in the bucket and timing how long it takes for all the water to drain. If he knows the number of gallons that can drain through the hole in a single minute, he can multiply the time taken for the water to drain out of the bucket by the number of gallons per minute that can pass through the hole to obtain the volume of water. The integrating A/D uses a capacitor, a kind of electrical leaky bucket, to time how long it takes voltage, rather than water, to drain at a known rate. It then converts this time to a binary value by a similar method (Figure 2.8).

A Comparison of A/Ds

Generally, the successive-approximation converter is faster than the integrating converter, but the integrating A/D is simpler to implement and therefore cheaper and easier to produce. This arises from the fact that to be constructed, an approximating converter requires a digital-to-analog converter, itself an expensive device. The integrating A/D requires only a few

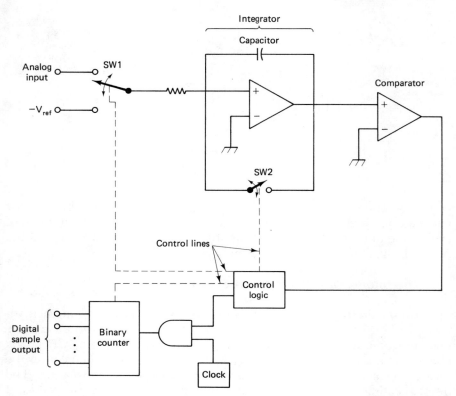

Figure 2.8 Integrating converter. Initially, the control section clears the binary counter and closes SW2 to discharge the integrator. When a sample is to be converted, SW1 is switched to the anolog input so that the capacitor will charge to that voltage. This sends the output of the comparator high. The binary counter is also cleared. The control section then switches SW1 to $-V_{ref}$, which begins to discharge the capacitor. At the same time, the control section allows the clock to increment the binary counter at a fixed rate. When the capacitor has been discharged, the comparator goes low and the clock is no longer able to increment the counter. The output of the counter is now the correct digital value.

cheap components, such as a capacitor and a counter. The successive-approximation converter is faster because approximation takes very little time to perform, so the sum of all the conversions takes little time. The integrating A/D is constrained by the time required to discharge its capacitor, which varies depending on the voltage that appears at the capacitor's input. Regardless of how the operation is done, after the analog-to-digital conversion has taken place, the wave will no longer be analog but digital in form. Whereas there was but one input to the A/D converter, there are now several digital bits which are output for every conversion.

Quantization: A Side Effect of the A/D Process

A/Ds for use in compact disc recording must produce digital outputs 16 bits wide. The number of bits is significant since it limits the accuracy of the digital samples. This is because only a finite number of values of an incoming signal can be represented, and values that have no representation must be rounded to either the next-higher or next-lower value. Using 16 bits, we can represent 2^{16}, or 65,536, discrete levels. That is quite a few levels. You might think that there are so many discrete values that almost every analog value could be quite closely approximated by a binary number. Consider, however, the case of a 2-bit A/D. This device could represent 2^2, or four, levels. Suppose also that at the moment the sample is taken, the value of the analog signal lies between two of these values. Then the A/D must decide which binary value the analog value is closest to, and represent that analog value by a 2-bit number. Regardless of which value it chooses, it will be incorrect, since in fact the analog value does not lie exactly at either digital value. The act of choosing a binary number to represent an analog voltage is called *quantization*, and the difference between the analog value and its digital representation is called *quantization error*. The quantization error introduces noise and distortion into a system but is inevitable, since regardless of how many bits are used for quantization, there will always be some unfilled space between quantization levels into which an analog value may fall. This is akin to the mathematical theorem which says that an infinite number of points can fit between any two points in space. Even if enough bits are used to represent every whole number from zero to 1 million, there will always be some intermediate value that will fit between two adjacent numbers and cannot be represented exactly. So an A/D converter, regardless of its quality, always introduces errors which manifest themselves later as noise. This is not bad if the noise is small enough that it does not significantly affect the quality of the recorded music. If, however, the noise is large enough, it can become an audible factor when the signal is reproduced.

The Sampling Frequency for Compact Disc Recording

The standard sampling frequency used in the digital recording of compact discs is 44.1 kHz. This rate is sufficient to record accurate frequencies up to 20 kHz as well as to compensate for frequencies in the low-pass roll-off area, which may alias down a few hundred hertz. This frequency was picked not only for aesthetic reasons, but also to keep down the price of compact disc players. As the sampling rate of a system goes up, so does the cost of its components.

Inside an A/D: An in-Depth Explanation of its Workings

The inner workings of an A/D are relatively complex when one looks at the level of discrete transistors. A given device may consist of many electronic networks, each of which may in turn be made up of hundreds of individual transistors. The transistors can be miniaturized and etched into the surface of a silicon chip. The dimensions of such transistors are infinitesimal compared to the dimensions of even a human hair, and the characteristics of each network are governed by laws of electromagnetics which are themselves the epitome of intricacy. An explanation of the A/D at this level would prove both fruitless and boring. Luckily, all but the most devoted design engineers can get by by understanding the innards of an A/D at a much higher level. It is at this higher level, with the help of block diagrams, that we will begin to delve into the electrical characteristics of an analog-to-digital converter.

The sampling frequency is a parameter that is often changed from signal to signal. A/Ds have a range of sampling frequencys at which they can operate, usually from dc, that is, zero samples per second, to as many as several million samples per second, depending on the particular device. To vary this rate, the A/D must be told at which rate to sample. The rate at which an A/D sample is controlled by a signal known as a *clock*. An integrated circuit called a *clock generator* takes the frequency produced by an oscillating quartz crystal and derives from it the clock frequency. Since quartz crystals oscillate at very stable frequencies, the clock output is inherently stable. Each clock pulse triggers a *sample-and-hold circuit* in the A/D. This circuit captures the current value of the analog input and holds that value so that the A/D has time to perform its conversion. Since the clock is periodic, each sample will be held for the same amount of time, so the analog signal will indeed be sampled at regular intervals. A sample-and-hold is necessary for several reasons. A successive-approximation converter requires a sample to be present at its input while it performs the functions necessary to generate a digital output. If the analog value constantly changes at the A/D's input, the converter will be unable to choose a binary value correctly. After the A/D decides on the appropriate value for its 16-bit output, it places and holds that value in an output register. The output register is actually a small electronic memory. Once a value has been placed into it, the A/D can begin another conversion without losing the value output previously. The register holds the output of the A/D until it can be sensed and used by whatever device is recording the samples. The A/D also provides a signal called *end of conversion*, which tells the recording device when the data at the output register are valid. This signal is important

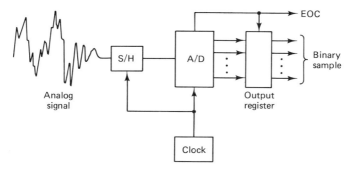

Figure 2.9 Block diagram of an A/D subsystem showing the sample-and-hold, converter, clock, and output register.

because when the A/D changes its output, there will be a period between the time the old value is erased and the time the new value appears. During this period, data at the output will consist of random bits, so the recording device must be told when it can fetch a new, valid value from the A/D. Some A/Ds even contain their own antialiasing filters whose parameters can be set with some external circuitry. They may also contain circuitry which scales down the analog input so that it can be represented accurately by the A/D (Figure 2.9).

DIGITAL-TO-ANALOG CONVERSION: TURNING SAMPLES INTO SOUNDS

Sampling, digitizing, and storing analog data are all quite useless if you cannot convert the bits back to an analog form. This task falls on a device called a *digital-to-analog converter* (D/A). The D/A works much as an A/D, only in reverse. Digital data are applied to its inputs, and after a short delay an analog value is presented at the output. Just like the A/D, a sample-and-hold circuit takes the analog outputs of the D/A and holds them for one sample period.

The Digital-to-Analog Converter

The operation of a D/A converter is much simpler than that of an A/D. To perform the conversion, the device simply weights each binary digit by an appropriate amount and then adds all the weighted values to achieve the analog result. In Figure 2.10 we see the realization of such a circuit. From Chapter 1 you know that binary 0's and 1's are represented by 0 and 5 V, respectively, in most digital electronic circuits. The summer simply weights these voltages by passing them through resistors of varying

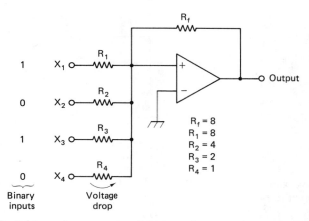

Figure 2.10 Digital-to-analog converter. Resistor values are chosen so that their values progress in powers of 2.

values. The output of the summer is then dependent on both how many bits are high (5 V) or low (0 V) and the value of the resistors they pass through. As their name implies, resistors resist the flow of electricity, called *current*. The higher the resistance, the less the amount of current that the resistor lets pass. The current that is not passed is converted to heat and dissipated in the body of the resistor. These current reductions assert themselves in the form of drops in the voltage which appear across the resistor's two terminals. A higher resistance has a higher voltage drop than that of a less resistance. If the resistors are chosen in the correct proportions and the same voltage is applied to all of them, the voltages at their outputs will be of the same proportions as the resistor values. The summer merely combines these values into a single voltage whose value is proportional to the inputs. For the 4-bit D/A shown, the output of the summer is $[(R_1 \cdot X_1) + (R_2 \cdot X_2) + (R_3 \cdot X_3) + (R_4 \cdot X_4)]/R_f$. If each resistor value is chosen to be twice the previous resistor's value, and the scaling factor, R_f, is chosen correctly, the output will be an analog value which corresponds to that of the binary representation. As an example, suppose that the input to our D/A is 1010. Using the resistor values listed, the output would be $[(8 \cdot 5) + (4 \cdot 0) + (2 \cdot 5) + (1 \cdot 0)]/8$, or $50/8 = 6.2$ V. The full-scale output of this D/A would be 1111, or 10 V. Note that the spacing between values is 5/8, or 0.62 V. This is not a sufficiently small step size to resolve an audio signal. A 16-bit device covering the same 10-V range would have a spacing between levels of 0.00015 V, which is more than sufficient for the reproduction of quality sound. If the A/D and D/A are paired correctly, the output of the digital-to-analog converter will be extremely close to the original input of the analog-to-digital converter. In the next chapters we take a look at how the step size, that is, the distance between binary values, affects the quality of sound when it is reproduced.

The Sample-and-Hold Circuit: Saving the Output of the D/A

Once a binary number is transformed to an analog value and exits the D/A converter, it is still not ready to be amplified and sent to a speaker. A string of analog values coming out of the D/A will look like the graph of Figure 2.11a, a series of spikes. These spikes occur because a D/A, unlike an A/D, has no facility such as an output register, which can hold its analog outputs while it works on another conversion. It merely outputs a value, turns on a signal to signal the end of this conversion, and proceeds with another conversion. Nothing remains at its output while the new conversion proceeds. A sample-and-hold circuit is tagged onto the output of the D/A to remedy this situation. It is triggered by the end-of-conversion pulse provided by the D/A. The sample-and-hold is sometimes a simple capacitive

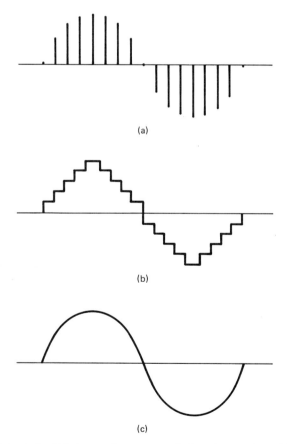

(a)

(b)

(c)

Figure 2.11 Output of a digital-to-analog converter before the sample-and-hold (a), after the sample-and-hold (b), and after low-pass filtering (c).

circuit which is charged up to the output voltage of the D/A and then isolated so that it cannot discharge once that voltage is taken away. It performs the same function as a measuring stick on the scale in a doctor's office. Once the scale's height is matched to the patient, the patient is free to walk away while the doctor reads the height. The capacitor performs the same function with voltage.

The Staircase Waveform and Smoothing Filter: Tidying up the D/A's Output

At the output of the sample-and-hold, spikes are stretched out in time so that they look like those of Figure 2.11b. This is called a *staircase waveform* because of the resemblance to its namesake. You will notice that this output does not exactly resemble the analog waveform that went into our digital recorder. It contains instantaneous jumps in amplitude, called *discontinuities*. These discontinuities occur when the sample-and-hold changes its value. Indeed, if the signal was applied to an amplifier and speaker at this point, the resulting sound would be of very poor quality. The sharp steps of the staircase function must be smoothed out before the signal can be said to have been accurately reproduced. The smoothing process is handled by something called a *smoothing filter*. This is nothing but an analog low-pass filter of the type we saw previously. Its cutoff frequency is set at roughly the same point as that of the antialiasing filter on the A/D's side of the operation. This filter is insensitive to high-frequency changes in amplitude and so smooths the staircase function until it looks like the one in Figure 2.11c. The speaker this signal is eventually played through, as well as your eardrums, tend to filter out these discontinuities, although without the smoothing filter several other distortion-causing side effects would arise. These side effects are discussed later.

DIGITAL RECORDING AND PLAYBACK: PUTTING ALL THE PIECES TOGETHER

The complete analog-to-digital-to-analog conversion scheme looks something like the block diagram of Figure 2.12. As you might expect, the A/D portion is a mirror image of the D/A portion. This diagram does not address the way digital information is stored and then submitted for conversion back to analog. We examine this storage process in more detail in Chapter 5. Also not discussed are the myriad gremlins that pop up in every phase of D/A and A/D conversion, and the solutions, which make digital recording a possibility. The following chapters address these subjects in depth.

These few devices—the analog-to-digital converter, digital-to-analog converter, low-pass filters, and sample-and-hold—are the basis on which

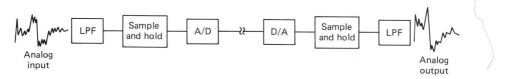

Figure 2.12 Block diagram of the digital conversion and reproduction process.

many refinements have been made. Designers play with mathematical manipulations of the encoded information and utilize some of the peculiarities of the sampled data to increase a digital audio system's performance beyond what one might at first consider possible. Digital encoding has many benefits, only some of which have been taken advantage of fully in the average disc player. From your newly developed base of knowledge we can now explore these benefits.

3

ANALOG-TO-DIGITAL AND DIGITAL-TO-ANALOG CONVERSION

CONVERSION: ITS SIDE EFFECTS AND SOLUTIONS

Based on the information presented in Chapter 2, we can now examine some of the problems that digitization creates, as well as study the techniques that manufacturers have chosen to use to solve these problems. Although by this point you should know the basics of digitization and digital-to-analog conversion, there are many side effects of these processes to which you have not yet been exposed. These side effects arise because although digitization is intended to preserve the integrity of music, the act of digitizing changes composition of the original sound. This is obvious in one respect, for sound starts off as a vibrating surface causing vibrations in the surrounding air, and ends up as depressions on the surface of a plastic optical disc. Each aspect of digitization—filtering, analog-to-digital conversion, storage onto a disc or tape, retrieval from that medium, processing, and finally, digital-to-analog conversion, more filtering, and amplification—introduces errors and distortion. These changes are not peculiar to compact discs, for both tape and phonograph media add their own types of distortion. It is important that you come to understand, for the special case of the compact disc player, how these oddities are handled. Indeed, many tricks are played with the digitization and the playback process so that the sound you hear is as close to perfect as allowed by the parameters of the compact disc standard.

Quantization and Quantization Error:
Rounding Off the Signal

One of the most important parameters of a digital system is the number of bits employed by its analog-to-digital converter. This, in turn, determines the effects of quantization. We touched on the concept of quantization in our discussion of analog-to-digital converters. Since the number of possible levels that an A/D can assign are limited by the number of bits in its output, there is inevitably some small error when an analog signal is transferred into a digital form.

Let's examine the case of a 4-bit A/D converter. This has 2^4, or 16, values, that it can use to represent an input. Let's also assume that the maximum value that is to be represented is 10 V. This range must then be divided into 16 separate levels in order to determine the voltage spacing between consecutive binary numbers (Table 3.1). This turns out to be about 0.67 V per level. If at some time the analog value of 3.1 V appears at the A/D's input, it will have to be represented by either 0100 or 0101, depending on which is closer. Since 0101 represents 3.33 V and 0100 represents 2.67 V, the A/D would choose 0101 as the digital value for its output. Although this number does not represent the exact value, it is the closest approximation that the A/D can make. By digitizing, the analog value has been changed by 0.13 V. The worst case occurs when an input falls right between two digital values. Then, for an A/D using any number of bits, the maximum error will be one-half a level. This is the maximum error due to quantization, and it

TABLE 3.1 Analog Voltages and Their
Digital Representations for
a 4-bit A/D Converter

Digital	Analog
1 1 1 1	10.00
1 1 1 0	9.33
1 1 0 1	8.67
1 1 0 0	8.00
1 0 1 1	7.33
1 0 1 0	6.67
1 0 0 1	6.00
1 0 0 0	5.33
0 1 1 1	4.67
0 1 1 0	4.02
0 1 0 1	3.33
0 1 0 0	2.67
0 0 1 1	2.01
0 0 1 0	1.33
0 0 0 1	0.67
0 0 0 0	0.00

manifests itself in the form of noise when the analog signal is reconstructed. In actual practice, a signal never falls exactly between two steps, for there will always be some small difference that will push the converter to choose one value or the other.

For the foregoing A/D, maximum noise due to quantization is one-half of the quantization unit, or 0.335 V. From this example it is seen that if a signal such as a sine wave whose maximum amplitude is less than 0.335 V appears at the A/D converter's input, it will be converted to 0000 for every point in time (Figure 3.1). It will be effectively wiped out because of quantization! If the signal's value is greater than 0.335 V but varies by less than 0.67 V, it will again be converted to a single binary value and will again be destroyed because of quantization (Figure 3.2). This is the case for a complex waveform that has a minimum value of 0.34 V and a maximum value of 0.98 V. This signal is always mapped to 0.67 V, 0001, even though it varies by 0.64 V from peak to peak. The amount of information that is lost due to quantization can be expressed as a signal-to-noise ratio, denoted S/N.

Signal-to-Noise Ratio: A Measure of the A/D's Quality

It is possible to measure the noise that is added by quantization and express it in the form of a signal-to-noise ratio. The signal-to-noise ratio measures the greatest possible amount of noise at the peak signal excursion, that is, when the input is at its maximum value. To calculate this ratio, we first compute the number of levels that the A/D has available. For the case of a 16-bit A/D, this is 2^{16}, or 65,536. Also, in the worst case, the most that a binary representation can differ from the original analog value is one-half of a level. It can be less, but the signal-to-noise ratio is an average of all the worst-case possibilities. From these the signal-to-noise ratio is determined to be 65,536/0.5, or 131,072. This means that the error when a full-scale analog input is digitized will be 131,072 times smaller than the signal's actual value. When this ratio is expressed in decibels, it equals 102 dB. For an A/D with an N-bit-wide output, the signal-to-noise ratio is $(6.02N) + 6.02$, expressed in decibels. As a rule of thumb, the signal-to-noise ratio in decibels can be calculated by multiplying the number of bits in the A/D's output by 6 (Table 3.2).

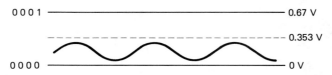

Figure 3.1 A sine wave whose value is less than half of the least significant bit of an A/D is always converted to 0000, and so is lost to quantization.

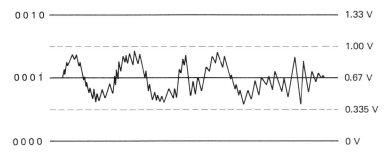

Figure 3.2 A complex wave that varies by less than one quantization level and is centered about 0001 is always converted to 0001.

A 14-bit system's exact signal-to-noise ratio (due to quantization) is 16,384/0.5, or 90 dB. The 4-bit system we discussed previously has a S/N ratio of 16/0.5 = 32, or 30.1 dB. Using the rule of thumb, these work out to 84 and 24 dB, respectively, reasonable approximations. The S/N ratio is important because it gives us a feeling for how close the reproduced signal will be to the actual signal. Larger S/N values are more desirable than smaller ones, but at some point the signal-to-noise ratio will become so large that any increase will be virtually inaudible, and so unnecessary. Indeed, the S/N ratio of the digital section of a compact disc player could be made extremely high, but the gains from the increased ratio would be negated because its output would have to pass through an analog amplifier whose S/N is greatly limited. It is for this reason, along with others, that a 16-bit converter was chosen as the compact disc standard.

Obviously, there exists a trade-off between the number of bits that are used to represent a number and the accuracy of that representation. One might think that the only way to increase the accuracy of a system is to

TABLE   3.2   *S/N* Ratio of A/D Converters
with Varying Word Lengths

Bits,[n]	S/N Ratio[a]
1	12.04
2	18.10
4	30.10
6	42.14
8	54.19
10	66.23
12	78.27
14	90.31
16	102.35

[a] $S/N = 20 \log (2^n/0.5)$.

increase the number of bits and therefore the complexity and cost of the system. This is not necessarily true. There are several tricks that designers use to circumvent the restrictions imposed by digitization and quantization.

Companding: Compressing More Sound Detail into Fewer Bits

Remember that the S/N ratio defines the maximum amount of noise at the maximum signal excursion. What happens when a signal is very small, say on the order of a few quantization levels? If this signal falls exactly between two possible binary values, we would expect that the quantization error would be significantly greater than the S/N ratio calculated for the system. In fact, for a signal whose value is one-half of a quantization level, the quantization error must be as great as the signal itself, yielding a signal-to-noise ratio of 1, or 0 dB! If a 0.99-V signal appeared at the input of our 4-bit A/D, it would be mapped to the closest value, which is 0001, or 0.67 V. The amount by which this binary value differs from the actual voltage is 0.32 V, and the signal-to-noise ratio is computed as 0.99/0.32, or 9.81 dB. This is hardly the 28-dB S/N ratio that is expected from a 4-bit A/D. In a 16-bit system the quantization errors are not as gross, but you can see that as a signal's level diminishes, the relative signal-to-noise ratio increases. This occurs because the relative error due to quantization becomes larger as the signal's size approaches that of one quantization level. This is particularly important in audio applications, where the dynamic range, the range of a signal's amplitudes, may vary from that of a whisper to a bone-shaking cymbal crash. The loud signal may be accurately produced, while the whisper might be distorted beyond recognizable limits. Increasing the number of quantization levels is both expensive and difficult, yet it seems unthinkable that important audio details be left out simply because their amplitudes are not as large as that of others.

There is a method, called *companding*, whereby low-level signals can be as finely reproduced as high-level ones. Companding implies that the total number of quantization levels are not divided into equally sized steps. Rather, they are bunched into steps that are close together for small values and far apart for larger values. More steps are then available for small signals, and there are correspondingly lower errors due to quantization. The quantization error for larger signals increases, but since the signals themselves are larger, the errors are not as noticeable. In effect, we try to keep the average error the same for every signal amplitude.

As an example, suppose that, as before, we are dealing with a 4-bit A/D system. Again, there are 2^4, or 16, distinct levels. If this system does not use companding, then as calculated before, a 0.99-V signal yields a 9.81-dB S/N ratio. The actual error in volts is 0.32. A large-scale signal of 8.99 V which falls between two quantization levels is in error by the same 0.32 V, but computes to a S/N ratio of 28.9 dB, a significantly greater value than before. If this distribution of levels is rearranged to that of Figure 3.3, the overall signal-to-noise ratio will be changed substantially. For the same analog values we obtain an error of only 0.01 V for the 0.99-V signal and 0.98 V for the large signal. These equate to a 40-dB and a 20-dB S/N ratio, respectively. Although the large-signal S/N ratio decreased somewhat, the small-signal ratio increased dramatically. Overall, the S/N ratio of the uncompanded A/D will be different from that of a companded system. Our companding scheme will resolve small signals with a higher S/N ratio than larger ones. For some applications this is a desirable trade-off. When the time comes to reconstruct the original signal, we simply rotate the companding graph on its side so that it maps binary numbers to analog values. We then make sure that whatever scheme is used to convert the binary numbers back into analog voltages makes use of this companded scale.

Companding gets its name from the process of compressing small-scale signal levels and expanding the large-scale ones. There are several standards for companding, many of which can be implemented through the use of off-the-shelf electronic parts. μ-Law companding is one such

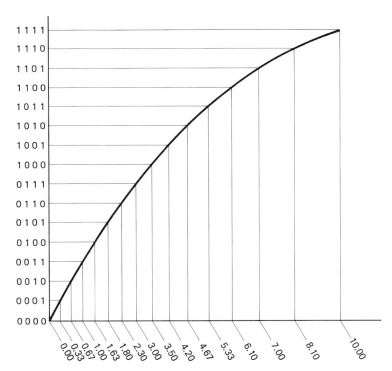

Figure 3.3 Companding graph for a 4-bit D/A converter. Spacings for small values are closer together than those for large values.

algorithm which is used widely in commercial applications, such as telephone communications. This is necessary to accommodate the wide range of levels at which people speak, so that those of us who speak softly are not less intelligible than a booming speaker.

Dithering: Adding Noise to Get Rid of Distortion

Quantization error normally does not manifest itself in the form of destructive distortion if the signal levels are constantly changing and of large amplitude. The sound of traffic on a busy city street probably would not be altered significantly because of quantization error, even in an uncompanded system. Suppose, though, that a signal's amplitude were small and changed on the order of a little less than one quantization level, as suggested in Figure 3.4. This condition might occur in a concert hall during a solo performance of an instrument such as a flute or violin. If the signal is centered about one quantization level, it will assume a constant value associated with that level. If, however, it is centered between two quantization levels, it will continuously vary between two adjacent values and

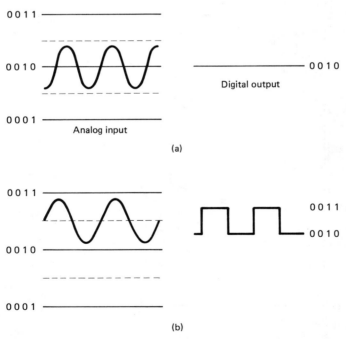

(a)

(b)

Figure 3.4 A small sine wave is converted to a dc value if centered about a single quantization level (a), but is converted into a square wave if centered between two levels (b).

produce a square wave. This occurs because the signal constantly crosses a decision region between the two quantization levels. One might imagine that the square-wave output would be preferable to a constant dc output, since the square wave resembles, if only remotely, a sine wave. In fact, just the opposite is true. The square wave can be very destructive to the quality of overall sound because it produces harmonics out beyond the Nyquist sampling frequency. If our theoretical low-amplitude signal is at 1.65 kHz, it will produce a square wave of the same frequency. Since square waves are composed of odd harmonics, there will be strong components at 4.95 kHz, 8.25 kHz, 11.55 kHz, and so on, all the way out beyond the sampling rate (Figure 3.5). In particular, the fifteenth harmonic will produce a 24.75-kHz tone. This will alias down about the 22.05-kHz point down to 2.70 kHz. This frequency is completely unrelated to any harmonics of the original sine wave. This is especially important since the human ear is more tolerant of distortion that is similar in frequency to the naturally appearing overtones than it is of completely uncorrelated harmonics. When the artificially introduced harmonics fall at the same points as larger, naturally occurring overtones, they can be masked because of their small size. But if they are introduced as new components that are not related to any other frequencies, they will be completely unmasked. An antialiasing filter does nothing to change this situation because the distortion leaks in after the filtering stage. Of course, the initial assumption was that this signal was of very low level, so you might think that its effects on the overall signal quality would be insignificant. Unfortunately, the effects are audible, and have been described as gritty or granular sounding. This is especially true for pure tones, as opposed to complex waveforms.

How, short of increasing the number of quantization levels, can the effects of quantization noise be diminished? It can be done by a process

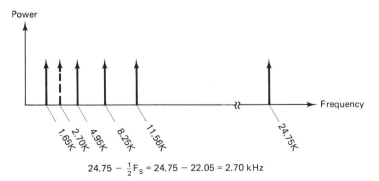

$$24.75 - \tfrac{1}{2}F_s = 24.75 - 22.05 = 2.70 \text{ kHz}$$

Figure 3.5 Harmonics caused by a squared-off sine wave whose fundamental frequency is 1.65 kHz. The thirteenth harmonic, 24.74 kHz, will alias down to 2.70 kHz.

called *dithering*. Dithering is accomplished by adding noise to an input signal. Its purpose is to decrease the harmful effects of quantization noise. If adding noise to a signal seems illogical to you, read on, for it is actually a very elegant solution to the quantization dilemma. Remember that it was the square-wave product of a low-level signal that produced the unwanted harmonics. The periodic nature of the input caused a similarly periodic square wave. Suppose that to the clean sine-wave input of Figure 3.4a we added some random noise on the order of one-third of a quantization level. Random noise takes on an unpredictable value at every moment, and so is statistically uncorrelated to the sine-wave input. Now the input to the A/D is a composite of a sine wave plus noise. But since this composite waveform has an average value greater than that of the least significant bit of the A/D, it will boost the value of the sine wave so that it crosses more than one quantization threshold. You can see how in Figure 3.6 the composite waveform looks like noise being modulated by a sine wave. The A/D now toggles between two decision regions rather than one. This output looks like that of Figure 3.7b, but it still does not appear that it will do us any good. But notice what happens when we average the value of many of these traces. Figure 3.7c is the average value of 32 traces, and Figure 3.7d is the same wave after 960 averages. This is a virtually undistorted sine wave which has been faithfully reproduced even though its value is less than one quantization level. It has been rescued from beneath the noise floor of the A/D system. The truly interesting part of this is not, however, that the waveform can be recovered by averaging. That type of process would take more time and processing capability than is available in disc players. The real benefit is that the harmonics arising from the square-wave output are nearly completely obliterated, so there is nothing to alias down into the audio band and distort the sound. Figure 3.8 shows the spectrum arising from a 1-kHz sine wave before and after dithering. Although the average power of both graphs is about the same, the dithered signal contains only the third harmonic as

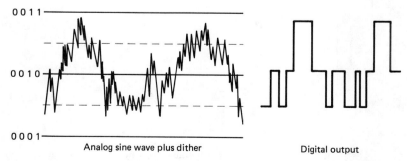

Analog sine wave plus dither   Digital output

Figure 3.6   Sine wave after a dithering signal has been added. The wave now crosses several decision regions rather than one.

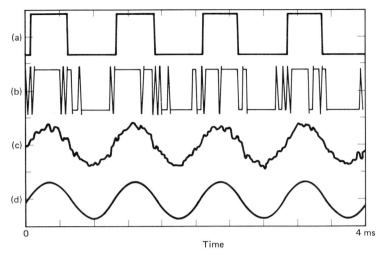

Figure 3.7 An undithered output (a), and that for a dithered signal (b). After 32 averages, the sine wave begins to appear (c), and after 960 averages, a clean sine wave is recovered (d). (Courtesy of Journal of the Audio Engineering Society.)

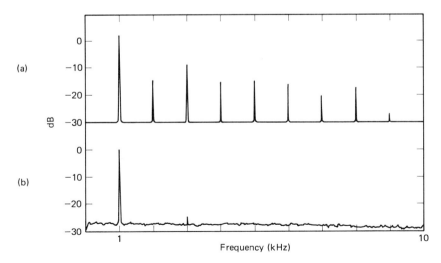

Figure 3.8 Spectrum of a 1-kHz sine wave with amplitudes of the least significant bit before dithering (a) and after (b) dithering. The undithered signal has significant artificial harmonics, while the dithered signal only shows an increase in wideband noise. (Courtesy of Journal of the Audio Engineering Society.)

well as wideband noise, that is, noise distributed over the entire spectrum. This noise is infinitely preferable to the spectrum of the upper graph because it does not affect any one frequency more than another. Listened to over a speaker, amplified wideband noise would sound like a very low level hiss rather than the more disturbing granular sound of a square wave.

Another interesting phenomenon arises when the input of a dithered A/D system is compared to its output. For an undithered system, the graph of the input versus the output looks like a staircase function. The A/D always maps a specific set of analog voltages to the same specific set of digital values. The I/O characteristic of a dithered system looks more like a continuous line since the dithering noise adds a random element to this I/O transfer function. Whereas a 5-V signal may always have been mapped to a specific bit value such as 00001111 (for an 8-bit A/D with a 10-V maximum input) in an undithered system, after dithering it may map to either the next higher (00010000) or lower (00001110) digital value. As the amount of dithering is increased to about one-third of a quantization level, the staircase smooths completely and it appears, on average, that there is a one-to-one correspondence between input and output. In effect, we are resolving signals beyond the ability of the A/D converter. So even a signal whose value is below one quantization level can still be recovered and, more important, will not contribute to the system's noise because of aliasing (Figure 3.9).

Often, noise is introduced into the signal path by an antialiasing filter or input preamplifier when it is recorded. This noise can be enough to act as

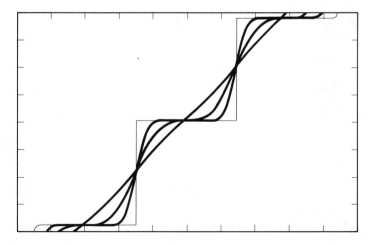

Figure 3.9 Input of a digital system plotted against its output. As dither is applied, the input/output function changes on average from a staircase to a one-to-one correspondence. (Courtesy of Journal of the Audio Engineering Society.)

dither for an incoming signal. For the sake of clarity a dither generator is sometimes included in block diagrams of digital systems.

Phase Distortion in Analog Filters: Yet Another Source of Noise

Even before a signal can pass through an A/D, it must be filtered by an antialiasing filter. Like all the other components of our digital system, this one has its oddities. Antialiasing filters, or, for that matter, all analog filters, introduce various types of distortion into the signals on which they operate. We have already discussed ripple and roll-off in analog filters, but we have not mentioned another type of distortion, that of phase. *Phase distortion* is the phenomenon whereby a filter actually delays its output in comparison to its input. The reason that phase distortion occurs is that filters are composed of a number of discrete components, one of which is the capacitor. A *capacitor* is a charge storage device, meaning that when a voltage is applied to the capacitor it holds the value of that voltage even after the input has been removed. Like a sponge, the capacitor soaks up electrical charges and remembers them. Some voltages are applied and removed too quickly for the capacitor to react to them, and so are screened out. These voltages are those of high-frequency signals, and screening them out is one of the functions of a filter. Unfortunately, the capacitor remembers the voltages of some frequencies longer than others, and this is why some are passed with a phase delay and some are not. If the input to a filter is a 3-kHz sine wave, the output is that same 3-kHz sine wave delayed by some finite amount of time, assuming that it lies in the filter's passband region. If the input to a filter consists of an entire spectrum of frequencies, all the frequencies may be delayed in time by an equal amount. This is called *linear phase shift*. Figure 3.10 depicts the time relationship between the input and output of an imaginary filter. Notice that we can express phase shifts in terms of both time and angle. A 180° phase shift indicates that the output waveform is shifted one-half of a wavelength. For a 3-kHz signal this is one-half of 1/(3000 Hz), or 0.17 ms. A 360° phase shift moves the sine wave an additional 180° and 0.17 ms, so that it appears to line up with the original input signal.

Nonlinear Phase Distortion: A More Severe Noise Source

Suppose that the phase delay of a filter were not linear. That would mean that different frequencies were delayed by different amounts of time. You can imagine what would happen if music were played through a speaker whose tweeter was 100 feet behind its woofer. The low frequencies emanating from the woofer would arrive before the high-frequency components of the tweeter. After the inputs to the speaker had ceased and the

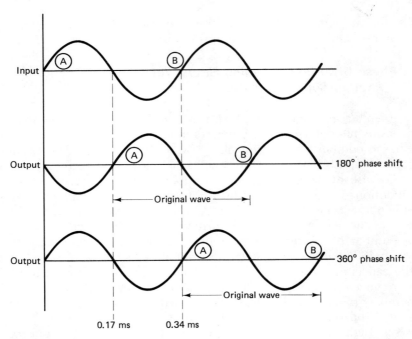

Figure 3.10   Effects of linear phase shift on a 3-kHz sine wave. Points A and B mark two reference points on the input and output waves.

sound from the woofer had faded, the sound from the tweeter would still be traveling through the air to your ear. Since sound travels at about 1000 feet per second, the high-frequency sound would be delayed (100 ft)/(1000 ft/s), or 100 milliseconds (ms). For a wave passing through an analog filter, nonlinear phase shift takes on a different meaning. A square wave, for instance, is composed of odd harmonics of its fundamental frequency. A distortion of the time relationship between harmonics will also distort the shape of the wave. This distortion may take the form of ringing, as illustrated in Figure 3.11. The filtered waveform overshoots its true amplitude as marked by the dashed lines, and then oscillates about this value. This is exactly what we were attempting to filter out with the antialiasing filter, but by negating one source of distortion, we have crated another. Also, as we attempt to construct a filter with a steeper roll-off region, less ripple, and greater attenuation in the stopband, the phase distortion increases dramatically. Distortion in the roll-off region is particularly high, and any frequencies that lie in this area may be severely distorted. So, on the one hand, there is the option of using a filter with a large roll-off region that will introduce aliasing errors due to the original signal source, and on the other hand there is the very steep filter, which introduces distortion in the form of phase noise.

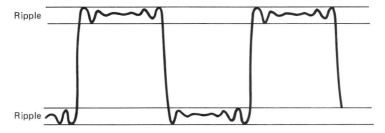

Figure 3.11 Effects of nonlinear phase shift on a square wave. This type of distortion is called ringing.

Drift in Analog Filters: Building Filters in an Imperfect World

Another challenge of designing with analog filter is that they are composed of electrical components whose properties vary with temperature, humidity, manufacturing tolerances, and time. The values of resistive components will actually change as their temperature changes. We all know that electronic equipment heats up when it is switched on. Unfortunately, this temperature rise, as well as other factors, changes the relationship between all the pieces of an analog system and introduces drift into the system's characteristics. Different batches of components, such as resistors, capacitors, and amplifiers, will vary from one production run to the next, so the components that are manufactured during one production run of an analog device may have slightly different characteristics than identical devices made during another production run. Just as no two cars off an assembly line will not be tuned in exactly the same way, so no two filters will have exactly the same characteristics. Of course, manufacturers endeavor to keep their products specifications within a certain range, and for most cases the subtle differences in performance due to the aforementioned factors are undetectable to the listener. They do, however, exist.

Distortion in the D/A Process: The Problem of Reconversion

Well, now that our antialiasing filter has distorted our phase and our A/D has added quantization noise and ringing to our once analog waveform, we have nothing to do now but to reverse this process and recover a less than intact product. What else could go wrong? Let's look now at what the digital-to-analog conversion process does in the way of distortion.

The D/A converter would seem to be a harmless device. It simply takes a digital code and converts it to the corresponding analog value. In Chapter 2 we looked at the way in which D/A converters function. Remember that they take a series of digital values as an input and convert them to a staircase output. This output is then low-pass filtered to remove the discontinuities, after which it should strongly resemble the original analog input. Although this works on paper, it is not necessarily the case in real life. Here the problem lies in the discontinuities of the D/A's output, that is, in the staircase function. Embedded in this staircase is a square wave whose frequency equals that of the sampling rate, 44.1 kHz for the case of digital audio. This causes copies of the original spectrum to be duplicated at multiples of the sampling frequency which are centered about 88.2 kHz, 132.3 kHz, and so on, ad infinitum. These additional spectra could be attenuated by the use of analog low-pass filters. Note, however, that to reduce the effects of these harmonics, a filter is needed with an extremely sharp roll-off right at 22.05 kHz. From previous discussions we know that such an analog filter will not only be costly to manufacture and complex to design, but will introduce large amounts of phase distortion into the reproduced signal. If a filter with a gentler roll-off is used, the harmonics not attenuated by this filter will alias down into the signal area, again introducing distortion. It would seem that there is no good solution to this dilemma. Enter the digital filter.

DIGITAL FILTERING: SHAPING SOUND IN THE DIGITAL DOMAIN

Digital filtering is the process whereby the properties of an analog filter are modeled mathematically so that they can be performed on the digital samples rather than the analog output. It turns out that an analog filter can be modeled by what is called a *nonrecursive algorithm*, which employs multiplication and addition on a number of digital samples. The general form of this algorithm is

$$\sum_{i=1}^{N} A_i X_i$$

In words, this means the following. First, a number of consecutive digital samples are identified. This number is determined by the type of filter that is to be modeled. These samples are then multiplied by unique values called *filter coefficients*, and these products are then summed to obtain a single output value for the digital filter. A two-coefficient filter is called a *two-pole filter* and is shown in Figure 3.12. Notice that the digital values come in from the left one at a time. The box labeled Z^{-1} is a *delay element*; it delays each binary value for one sampling period before passing it on to the next stage. After each shift, the multipliers pass their results to the summer, which then outputs a digital value. If the coefficients are chosen correctly,

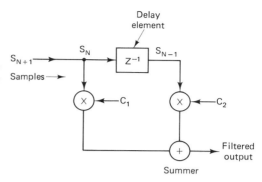

Figure 3.12 Two-coefficient filter. Binary samples enter from the left and are multiplied with C_1, then by C_2. The sample, S_N, is then passed through the delay element, after which it will be multiplied by C_2 and summed with the next sample, S_N+1, multiplied by C_1. The output of the summer is the filtered samples.

the stream of digital values coming out of the adder will appear, after they are D/A'd, as if they were filtered by an analog device. This is not apparent from either the process or the values of the digital samples, but when they are passed through an analog-to-digital converter, the filtering has been done. The benefit of a digital filter is that it introduces no phase distortion (for some types of filters). Also, since the coefficients need not change from filter to filter, the error associated with analog filters due to thermal drift and manufacturing tolerances is eliminated.

An analysis of why this multiply-and-sum technique works is not as important as the fact that it does work. As more coefficients, called *taps*, are added, the digital filter can attain impressive rolloff rates and attenuation factors. The problem of harmonics that are generated by the staircase conversion still exists, however. This was one of the issues addressed early in the evolution of the compact disc player by one of its originators, N.V. Philips of the Netherlands. To combat this problem, engineers at Philips implemented a technique they called *oversampling*, which reduces many of the complications that we have discussed.

Oversampling: Separating Sound from Noise

The engineers at Philips took an unusual approach to the digital-to-analog conversion problem. Rather than use a 16-bit digital-to-analog converter, they employ a simpler 14-bit unit. To maintain the signal-to-noise ratio and dynamic range of a 16-bit system, they use several clever tricks as well as some digital filtering techniques that make up for the lost 2 bits of resolution.

To begin, the effective sampling frequency in the D/A is increased by a factor of 4, to 176.4 kHz. This is not done by increasing the actual rate at which the both the A/D and D/A run. The sampling rate used while recording and making the compact discs is still 44.1 kHz. Rather, the stored original digital samples are sampled at the standard rate, and three sequential samples are produced whose values are all zero. If a segment of the original digital stream was 0001–0010–0101, the oversampled stream would be *0001–0000–0000–0000–0010–0000–0000–0000–0101–0000–0000–0000*. It takes just as long to get from the first sample to the last because of the increased sampling rate, but we reap some interesting benefits from oversampling.

The Noise Floor: A Bottom Limit on Sound Quality

First, there is some average noise power associated with the original audio band of 21.05 kHz. That means that the noise level from 0 kHz to half the sampling rate maintains some average value, called the *noise floor*. This noise arises from quantization error and has an average value of $q/3.46$, where q is the size of one quantization level. For a 16-bit system, this will be about 96 dB below the maximum signal amplitude. Generally, any signal below this level will be masked by the noise. By shifting from a 16-bit converter to a 14-bit converter, the S/N ratio is decreased by about 12 dB. This increases the noise floor by a factor of 15. By oversampling, this noise is distributed over a bandwidth of 88.2 kHz, which is four times greater than the original 21.05-kHz bandwidth. This diminishes the noise power in the audio band by one-fourth, increasing the signal-to-noise ratio by about 6 dB. So by spreading the noise over a wider frequency band, a net loss of only 6 dB is realized with a 14-bit D/A.

The Digital Filter: A Realization of the Oversampling Process

Next, this new data stream is passed through a digital filter. Philips employs a 96-pole filter, that is, one with 96 delay elements and 96 coefficients all feeding into one summer (Figure 3.13a). The output of this filter is the weighted sum of the previous 96 values of the higher data rate samples. Actually, the sampling rate is increased when data are passed through the filter. Each delay element in the filter chain is only one-fourth as long as the actual 44.1-kHz sampling rate. A sample presented at the filter's input is sampled only once, and the remaining three samples are data whose value is zero. This technique is called *bit stuffing*. The filter still ouputs filtered samples at the rate of 176.4 kHz, but the samples are the product of 24, rather than 96, multiplies and one summation. A diagrammatic representation of such a filter is shown in Figure 3.13b. The coefficients are 12-bit numbers, and when multiplied by the incoming 16-bit sampled values, yield a 28-bit wide product. Each sample remains in the delay element long enough to have four separate multiplies performed on it. After each multiply the products are summed and then output. Data come into the system as 16-bit-wide words at 44,100 samples per second, and leaves as a 28-bit-wide stream of samples at 176,400 samples per second. If

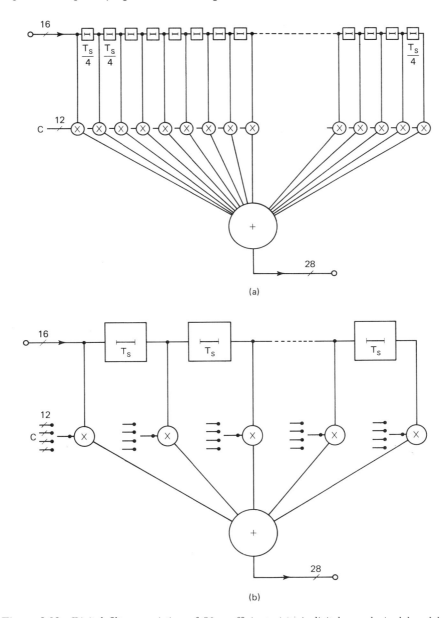

Figure 3.13 Digital filter consisting of 96 coefficients (a). A digital sample is delayed by one-fourth of a sampling period, during which it is multiplied by a 12-bit coefficient and summed with the other delayed samples. Because three out of every four samples are zeros, the filter is implemented using only 24 delay lines rather than 96 (b). (Courtesy of NAP Consumer Electronics Corp.)

these coefficients are chosen correctly, the filter transfer function will look as shown in Figure 3.14. Notice that in Figure 3.15c all the harmonics between 22.05 and 176.4 have been attenuated by about 50 dB through the process of digital filtering. The increased data rate has the added benefit of further multiplying the filtered spectrum by a $(\sin x)/x$ function, which looks like the graph of Figure 3-15d. ($\sin x)/x$ results from the 176./4-kHz square wave and is called the *Fourier transform* of that wave. This decreases the sidebands of the 176.4 kHz component by an additional 18 dB. A simple analog low-pass filter, called a *Bessel filter*, can now be used on the output side of the sample-and-hold circuit. This type of filter does not introduce phase distortion into its passband. This filter attenuates whatever harmonics remain after the digital and $(\sin x)/x$ filtering figure. Because the Bessel filter introduces some attenuation around 20 kHz, the coefficients of the digital filter are chosen so that they slightly amplify this band. The composite transfer function is flat for frequencies in the audio band.

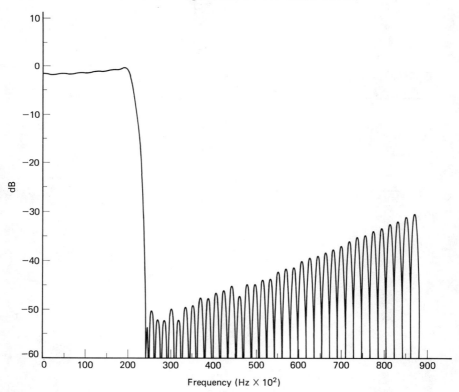

Figure 3.14   Filter transfer function of the analog low-pass filter on the output of the D/A. A slight peak between 15 kHz and 20 kHz makes up for the attenuation which is introduced by the $(\sin x)/x$ function of the sample-and-hold. (Courtesy of NAP Consumer Electronics Corp.)

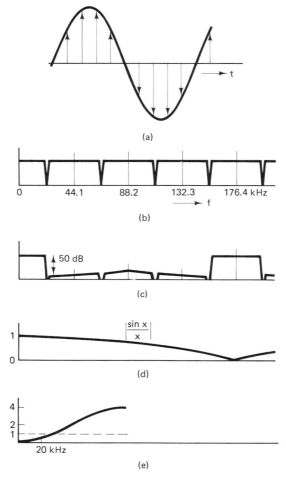

Figure 3.15 Oversampling process: sampled sine wave (a) and its spectrum (b) before oversampling. After oversampling at 176.4 kHz, the spectrum from 22.1 to 154.35 kHz has been significantly attenuated (c). The sample-and-hold circuit tends to multiply the spectrum by (c) (sin x)/x as in (d). The spectrum of noise after the noise shaper is also shown (e). This spectrum shows that there is little noise power left in the audio band, although high-frequency noise is increased out of the band. (Courtesy of NAP Consumer Electronics Corp.)

Noise Shaping: Subtracting out the Noise Floor

The product of a 12-bit-wide coefficient and a 16-bit-wide sample is a 28-bit-wide word. The only thing left to do is to convert these into narrower words. This is done by employing the noise-shaping circuit depicted in Figure 3.16. It turns out that the lower 14 bits of each word contain mostly

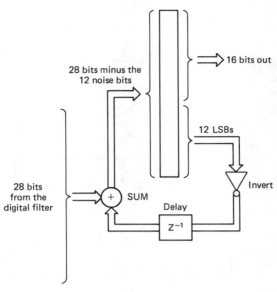

Figure 3.16 Noise-shaping circuit. The 12 least significant bits are delayed by one period, then subtracted from the next sample. This reduces the amount of noise in the audio band by 7 dB. Only the 16 most significant bits are passed on to the D/A.

noise. This should come as no surprise, since our original samples were taken with only 16 bits of accuracy. Because concurrent samples are somewhat related, the noise associated with each sample tends to introduce the same amount of error. You can imagine that since the value of an analog signal changes slowly compared to the sampling rate, the amount of noise that is introduced because of the quantization of that signal, will also change rather slowly. The noise that is present in the lower 14 bits of data is stripped off from each data word, then delayed for one period and subtracted from the next incoming word. This has the effect of subtracting out some average value of the noise and diminishing its presence in the 14 most significant bits of the output. Actually, noise in the high-frequency bands is increased, and decreased in the audio band, but since the high-frequency bands are attenuated by the analog filter, they are of little importance. The noise-shaping circuit adds an additional 7 dB of signal-to-noise ratio over a system without noise shaping.

More Benefits of Digital Filtering

The end product of all of these mathematical gyrations is a 14-bit-wide digital output which, because of the gains made by oversampling, digital filtering, and noise shaping, contains just as much useful information as did the original 16-bit samples. For even though a 14-bit system has a S/N value of only about 84 dB, the 13 dB of noise reduction gained through oversampling and noise shaping makes up for the 2 bits lost in conversion. An added benefit of this is that we can use a 14-bit D/A rather than a 16-bit D/A. Since this is a less complex device, it is easier and cheaper to build, and, more important, more accurate and less prone to error. In fact, a 14-bit D/A may cost as much as 10 times less to produce as a 16-bit device. A very gentle analog low-pass filter can be used in place of a steep one since digital filtering has reduced its burden by a large factor. This reduces the amount of phase and other types of distortion that occur inside an analog filter. Presently, digital filtering can be performed in its entirety inside one small microchip, lending an even greater appeal to its widespread use.

CONCLUSIONS

In this chapter we have seen that there are many intricate mathematical and physical quantities which must be considered when a digital system is designed. In every phase of conversion there are factors that combine to corrupt the signal and distort its appearance and content. Sampling at an incorrect rate can have disastrous results on a high-quality passage of music, as can an A/D converter with too few bits of resolution. We have noted that there are functions which can be performed on a signal during A/D conversion, such as dithering, low-pass filtering, and companding, which can extend range and quality of the signal. There are always trade-offs which are made when such functions are performed, so they must be employed in moderation and adjusted so that they impart a balance to the system. If one uses a steep low-pass filter, hoping to reduce the amount of aliasing, it will introduce phase distortion. Companding, too, sacrifices the quality of large signal amplitudes to benefit small ones. There are always trade-offs.

When digital-to-analog conversion must be performed, some tricks can be applied which seem to squeeze more signal-to-noise ratio out of a device than our intuition tells us is possible. In this case the trade-offs occur between cost and simplicity, between high-quality music and a marketable and serviceable product. High-end players will use the most reliable components and a combination of digital and analog filters which combat some of the problems we have encountered. Other budget-minded designs will use but a single analog filter at the output of their A/D. Each design has its market and balances price against volume and complexity. But every compact disc player shares a common beginning and performs some or all of the functions we have discussed.

4

MODULATION

Well, now, hopefully, you have a firm understanding of how a signal is transformed from analog form to digital and then back to analog again. In the process you have seen how an analog-to-digital converter changes audio information into a form that can be stored and manipulated and eventually reproduced. What we have not yet discussed are the types of modulation formats that are available to encode these raw digital data.

THE MANY FACES OF MODULATION

Interestingly enough, just because the output of an A/D is a 16-bit-wide binary number does not mean that it has to be stored or transmitted as such. There are a myriad of encoding schemes that designers use to change the binary information into a form more suited to storage or transmission. You might wonder why further coding is necessary before the bits obtained from the analog-to-digital converter can be put onto a disc. Isn't all the audio information already stored in this stream, ready to be put into storage? In fact, the stream of bits that are obtained in the aforementioned manner is quite unsuited to the compact disc medium. It must undergo a final conversion before it is transferable, just as the output of a microphone must be changed before it can be broadcast over the radio.

Amplitude and Frequency Modulation:
Two Familiar Schemes

You are probably familiar with the terms *amplitude modulation* (AM) and *frequency modulation* (FM). These are two popular ways of converting information, in our case music and voice, into a form suitable for transmission over the radio. These types of modulation are necessary for many reasons, the most important of which is that waves in the audio band (i.e., 0 to 20,000 Hz) will not travel very far when broadcast through an antenna. Radio waves, conversely, are of a significantly higher frequency than audio waves and can travel many tens or even thousands of miles before they are attenuated by natural phenomenon.

In *amplitude-modulated systems*, the input signal is mixed with a carrier and transmitted out over an antenna. The carrier is generally a sine wave whose frequency may vary from 535 to 1605 kHz. This carrier's amplitude is controlled by an audio signal so that the composite is a sine wave at the carrier frequency whose amplitude is dependent on the amplitude of the audio signal. In simpler terms, the original audio band is shifted up by a frequency corresponding to that of the carrier. Looking at this composite wave on a spectrum analyzer, you would see only one spike of energy at the carrier frequency (Figure 4.1). When this signal is received by your home stereo, the carrier is stripped off and the audio information is recovered.

Frequency modulation uses the same basic idea as amplitude modulation, but instead of changing the amplitude of a carrier, the audio signal modulates the carrier's frequency (Figure 4.2). Again, the effect is to shift the audio signal up to that of the carrier tone. If we examined this signal using a spectrum analyzer, we would see a spike that would continuously deviate from carrier frequency but would be centered about that carrier. The amount of deviation from the carrier frequency is proportional to the

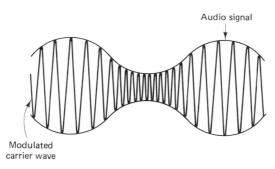

Figure 4.1 Amplitude modulation. The amplitude of a high-frequency carrier is dictated by the envelope of an audio signal.

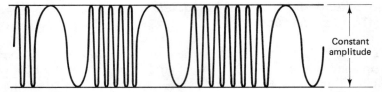

Figure 4.2 Frequency modulation. The frequency of a carrier is changed according to the changes in an audio signal.

value of the audio signal, and after the composite signal is received by a radio, this information is recovered, to leave only the original audio band.

For both AM and FM transmission, a signal of interest, sound, is converted to an intermediate medium before transmission and then reconverted to its original form after transmission. This is done to facilitate the process of transmission. Both types of modulation have their strong points, and the reasons to select either AM or FM transmission depend on many factors. AM is more susceptible to atmospheric noise, such as lightning, than is FM, but FM carries far less distance than an equally powered AM signal. The type of modulation one chooses may often depend on these and other factors.

Other Modulation Schemes

Like amplitude and frequency modulation, there are a host of encoding formats available which take an analog signal and change it into a form that is suitable for storage and transmission onto a digital medium. After the signal is transmitted or stored, it is received and read by a decoder. The decoder's job is to transfer the information sent to it by the encoder back into a facsimile of the original signal. For the systems discussed previously, the A/D converter is the encoder, and the D/A, the decoder. For an AM or FM radio system, the radio transmitter is the encoder, and the receiver, the decoder. The common telephone is a good example of such a system. The mouthpiece into which you speak transforms (encodes) your voice into electrical pulses, which are sent out over a wire and then reconverted (decoded) by the earpiece of the listener back into voice. In the digital world, sound must be encoded not into electrical pulses, but into 1's and 0's. In the following sections we examine some of the encoding schemes around which hardware can be built that performs this feat.

Pulse-Amplitude Modulation: The First Step of Digitization

Perhaps the simplest digital modulation technique is *pulse-amplitude modulation* (PAM). We encountered PAM in our discussion of sample-and-hold circuits. You will remember that a sample-and-hold converts a discrete analog signal into a series of steps. The size of these steps depends on the value of the signal at the beginning of each sampling period. If at the beginning of a sampling period, an analog wave has a value of 5.02 V, the step is assigned a value of the 5.02 V. This amplitude is maintained until the beginning of the next sampling period, when the analog wave is once again sampled and a new step is begun. The analog wave's value may, and usually will, change during the sampling period, but this change will not be caught until the next sample. The waveform produced by this scheme resembles a staircase (Figure 4.3). The problem with PAM is that there are an infinite number of amplitudes to which a step may be assigned, so they cannot be represented by a finite number of bits. This is because the analog wave can take on an infinite range of amplitudes, and it is these amplitudes that determine the step values. Since analog-to-digital converters used in digital audio are limited to 16 bits per sample, they cannot represent any more than 65,535 amplitudes, which is far less than infinity. We can encode using PAM, but there is no way to digitally record the exact values with any number of bits. So although PAM is an important intermediate step in signal conversion, it is not the final one.

Pulse-Period and Pulse-Width Modulation: Some Analog Encoding Schemes

There are other types of modulation that find use in various audio applications. Two of these are pulse-width modulation and pulse-period modulation. Although they are not used in the compact disc system, they are important to understand if one wishes to know how and why the compact disc modulation scheme functions and was chosen.

Pulse-period modulation (PPM) is a method whereby a narrow pulse is placed in a particular position in a window time (Figure 4.4), this position being determined by the value of an audio signal. These windows are analogous to sampling periods and occur sequentially.

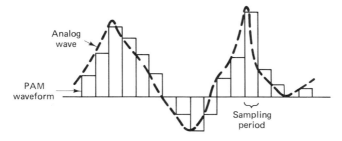

Figure 4.3 PAM waveform. The value of the analog wave at the beginning of the sampling period is held for the entire period.

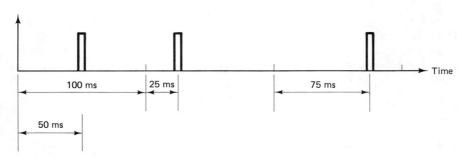

Figure 4.4 PPM pulse train. A single pulse is inserted into each window, its position corresponding to the value of the analog wave at the beginning of the sampling period. The first pulse is at one-half peak, the second pulse is at one-fourth peak, and the third pulse is at three-fourths peak.

You can think of a window as looking like the display of a voltmeter, and the pulse as a pointer that points to the voltage of an analog signal. If this analog voltage is sampled and its value is found to be large, the pointer would occur late in the window, while a small signal value would appear early in the window. Unlike PAM, PPM places a single pulse somewhere during each sampling period. The position of the pulse is directly related to the amplitude of the original analog signal when the sampling period began. The weakness of this modulation method is that as we sample faster and faster, the windows become ever smaller. The pulse which is placed in these windows has some minimum width, so as the sampling rate increases, the number of distinguishable places for the pulse to occur diminishes. Again, this limits the number of values that can be represented and encoded. If a PPM pulse has a duration of 100 ms, there are only 4400 nonoverlapping positions for it to occupy in a 44.1-kHz sampled window. As the sampling rate increases, this number of positions decreases.

Pulse-width modulation (PWM) is similar to PPM, except that the width of a pulse, rather than its position, is modulated by an input waveform. As usual, a signal is sampled and a staircase wave is produced (Figure 4.5). Each step is translated into a percentage of the maximum pulse width. This maximum width is 227 ms at a 44.1-kHz sampling rate. If the maximum input to the system is set at 10 V and a 1-V signal appears, a pulse 22.7 ms in length will be generated, corresponding to one-tenth of the maximum width. In practice, a guard band must be left between successive samples so that their beginning and ending points can be determined. The guard band is a no man's land that the pulse cannot occupy. This decreases the maximum width of the pulse to somewhat less than 227 ms.

Both pulse-width and pulse-period modulation are more suited to analog transmission schemes than they are to digital. This is because the information is stored in a position, be it width or distance, rather than in a quantized value.

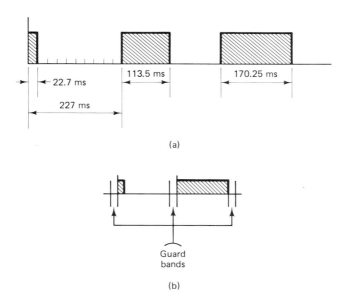

Figure 4.5 Pulse-width modulation. The degree to which a pulse fills a window in time corresponds to the amplitude of an analog input. The first pulse is at one-tenth of peak amplitude, the second is at one-half peak, and the last is at three-fourths peak (a). Also shown is the guard band between pulses which mark the beginning and ending of each window (b).

Pulse-Code Modulation: A Scheme for High-Fidelity Recording

Pulse-code modulation (PCM) is perhaps the most widely used and accepted type of high-fidelity audio encoding. PCM is the encoding scheme used by A/D converters to change analog data into digital, and since we have already discussed quantization and related subjects, PCM requires little explanation.

An analog signal is first sampled and held and the resulting PAM waveform is mapped to one of a finite collection of digital codes. One type of code can be created by mapping the smallest value to 00000000 (for an 8-bit converter) and the largest to 11111111. This presupposes that we limit the maximum voltage at the A/D's input. This is straight binary conversion.

When we considered the operation of A/D and D/A converters in previous chapters, it was assumed that they used this type of conversion scheme. There are, however, many other schemes that a PCM system might use to map an analog signal to a digital word. Two's complement and floating-point conversion are two popular such schemes.

Two's-complement conversion.   The first type of code is called *two's complement.* In this system, the most significant bit (the leftmost bit) is a sign bit. A 1 in the leftmost position indicates a negative number and a 0 indicates a positive number. 01111111 is the most positive value in two's-complement notation, and 10000000 is the most negative. Unfortunately, the negative numbers are not formed merely by adding a 1 to the sign bit of a positive. So although 00000010 is positive 2, 100000010 is not a negative 2. In fact, it is negative 126. Negative numbers are formed by inverting all the bits of the positive value of that number and then adding 00000001. To form negative 16, one would first form the positive value of 16, 00001111, then invert the bits to get 11110000, and finally add 00000001 to get the final number, 111100001. If you wish to prove to yourself that this is indeed negative 16, just add 00001111 and 11110001. The value that you will get is 00000000. Although this numbering method seems strange, it does work.

Two's complement notation is very handy because when a series of numbers are added, one need not worry that the value of the intermediate sums will cause an overflow. To explain this, let's add two 4-bit numbers. Remember first that since 1 bit is reserved for sign, the numbers that we can represent should range from −7 to +7. If 0111 and 0111 (7 + 7) are added, the result is 1110. This is −2 in two's complement. Aha, you say, that is the wrong answer. This is true, because the largest number that can be represented is 7. The sum has overflowed out past the maximum value for 4 bits. If another 0111 (7) is added in, we come up with 10101, which is again too large to represent with only 4 bits. The leftmost 1 is called an *overflow bit* because it overflows out of our range of numbers. Since there are no facilities to store this extra 1 in a 4-bit system, you would expect this to upset any further additions or subtractions. As it stands, we have added 7 + 7 + 7 to get a total of five (0101). But wait. If 1010 (−6) is added to 0101, the result is 1111, and if 1101 (−3) is then added in, the result is 1100, ignoring overflow. Adding 1010 (−6) again yields a final sum of 0110 (+6). This process is depicted in Figure 4.6, and yields the correct answer to the equation 7 + 7 + 7 − 6 − 3 − 6 = x. This is the wonder of two's complement. As long as the final answer is within the range of the number system, in our case less than 8, the intermediate values and overflows are insignificant. Even if strings of numbers were added whose intermediate sums totaled into the millions, and might, therefore, require dozens of bits to represent, the correct answer would still emerge as long as the final sum is a legitimate number in our two's-complement system (Figure 4.6).

This feature becomes very important when the binary system is used in digital filtering, for filtering requires many multiplications and sums. So although the intermediate values obtained by using such filters will often induce an overflow, the final sum is always small enough so that it does not contain any overflow. Using a two's-complement system relieves many of

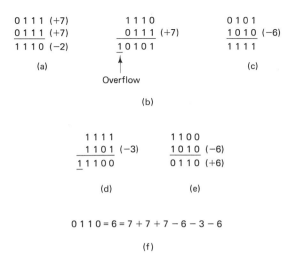

Figure 4.6 Seven and 7 are added using two's-complement arithmetic to obtain a sum of -2 (a). Seven is again added to this sum and the overflow is ignored (b). Six, then 3, are subtracted from this sum (c and d). Finally, 6 is subtracted from the sum to obtain the correct answer, 6 (e).

the problems that might be encountered while doing such operations, in particular, the problem of overflow.

Floating-point conversion.   There is a way to deal with overflow other than using the two's-complement method. Rather than say that we are sure that the final sum of series of operations will be within a known and finite range, the range of the number system can be extended so that it can represent very large numbers. This is not accomplished by increasing the number of bits that are used to encode a value, but by a method called floating-point conversion.

Floating-point converters are very useful when one is not sure of the exact range of an input signal's amplitudes. If one wished to record the sounds occurring outside a house, one might expect to hear everything from a bird's chirps to the roar of a 747 passing overhead. To accommodate this wide range of sound intensities, the range of values that the A/D converter could represent would have to be increased dramatically. A converter employing two's-complement coding, also called *fixed-point coding*, might be inappropriate because of its limited range. The maximum dynamic range of a 16-bit fixed-point converter is about 96 dB, while the roar of a jet's engines may reach 140 dB. The way that a floating-point converter overcomes this problem is by expressing its converted values in an exponential form. This is more far efficient that two's complement in terms of dynamic range since very large numbers can be expressed using only a few digits. 1^6 is the number 1,000,000 and would take 20 bits in two's-complement notation. The same number can be expressed in only 6 bits using floating point.

What the floating-point converter does is to take an input signal and convert it to an exponent and a mantissa. A typical floating-point converter might employ 15 bits. The upper 12 bits would contain the mantissa and the lower 3 bits could contain the exponent. The exponent is a kind of scaling factor. When a signal is applied to an A/D using floating-point conversion, it is automatically scaled down to a value that can be represented by the 12-bit mantissa, and the scaling factor is stored in the remaining 3 bits. During an earlier discussion about the operation of A/D converters, we assumed that the maximum input signal was of 10 V amplitude. Well suppose that we were not sure of the maximum amplitude of the signal. If a 100-V signal were applied to the A/D, the floating-point system would scale it down by an appropriate factor until it was within the range of 10 V. This scaling factor is contained in the three exponent bits. The remaining 12 bits then record the value of the scaled-down waveform just as a 16-bit converter would, only with less accuracy. Since there are 3 bits available for scaling, there are eight scaling factors from which to choose. Assume that the scaling factors are chosen as 0, 3, 6, 9, 12, 24, 48 and 96, expressed in decibels. A scaling factor of 000 (binary) indicates that the analog input was scaled by 0 dB, or a factor of 1. 001 would indicate that the input was scaled by 3 dB before it was quantized in the mantissa, while 101 would indicated a scaling factor of 12 dB. A table of these scaling factors is reproduced in Figure 4.7.

The reason that this is called a floating-point conversion is that, in effect, the converter shifts the decimal point of the incoming signal until it is within the range of a 12-bit mantissa. 3090007680.0 is far beyond what a

$$\boxed{0\,1\,0\,1\,1\,1\,0\,0\,1\,1\,0\,1\,1\,0\,1 \mid 1\,0\,0}$$

12-bit mantissa	3-bit exponent

(a)

Exponent	Scaling factor (in dB)
000	0
001	3
010	6
011	9
100	12
101	24
110	48
111	96

(b)

Figure 4.7 Bit breakdown of a typical floating-point converter (a). The exponents have been chosen arbitrarily to represent a 96-dB range of scaling factors (b).

12-bit A/D can represent. If, however, the decimal point is shifted over by five digits, then the resulting number, 3090.0, is within that range. The number 3090 would be encoded and then stored in the mantissa, while the 5-bit shift would be recorded in the exponent. When the time comes to do digital-to-analog conversion, the decimal value obtained from the 12-bit mantissa is multiplied by the shift to obtain the original number. This yields an analog value of 309000000.0. Unfortunately, the numbers to the right of the shifted decimal point cannot be recovered, since it is only the value to the left of the decimal point that is encoded.

The dynamic range of a floating-point converter is much larger than that of a fixed-point system. For the system described above, the largest representable signal is 168 dB greater than the smallest signal. For a 16-bit fixed-point system, the dynamic range is only about 96 dB. In situations where there is a great degree of variance between the intensity of the loudest and softest sounds, this increased dynamic range may be useful. The price paid for increased dynamic range is a similarly increased signal-to-noise ratio. This occurs because in order to represent a greater range of input levels with the same number of bits, we must decrease the accuracy of each digital level. In the example above, we saw that part of the original input signal was lost during D/A conversion. This leads to increased quantization errors and hence decreased S/N values. Since at least 3 bits are always taken up by the exponent, we would expect a minimum decrease in the signal-to-noise ratio of at least 18 dB.

Floating-point converters are cheaper to produce than fixed-point PCM systems with the same dynamic range. However, the S/N penalty incurred when switching to floating point is substantial enough to rule out 16-bit floating-point converters for use in digital audio applications. These converters are used extensively in large computers as well as in many digital signal-processing applications, so form an important class of PCM systems.

Data Compression: Using Fewer Bits to Represent Sound

One problem common to all types of pulse-code modulation is that they take many bits of data to represent each analog sample. A digital system recording in stereo must sample at a rate of 44.1 kHz to capture all the information contained in a 20-kHz-wide audio band. Stereo implies that we are required to record two channels of data during each sampling period, each of which is 16 bits wide. A simple multiplication yields a produce of $16 \times 2 \times 44,100$, or 1,311,200 bits per second that must somehow be processed and stored. That is quite a lot of information, and we have not even taken into account all of the extra bits that are added for the purposes of error correction. Some digital systems sample at even higher rates and may send many more than two channels of information at a time. An analog recorder that could handle our meager 1.3 million bits per second (Mbps) would require a bandwidth exceeding 2 MHz. For comparison, even the best audio recorders have only about a 22-kHz bandwidth. Compared with the original signal's bandwidth of only 20 kHz, this is a 100-fold increase in bandwidth. The bandwidth problem is not as critical in other media, such as optical discs, but there are many applications where this form of recording is impractical or too expensive. Even optical discs are limited with regard to the amount of information that they can store. A large disc in a home computer could handle only a score of seconds of digital audio information before its capacity would be reached.

There is a way to decrease the number of bits per sample without resorting to less accurate A/D converters (1's with fewer bits of output). This alternative modulation scheme is called *delta modulation* and it decreases the bandwidth required to reproduce a waveform while maintaining enough accuracy during reproduction to satisfy many applications.

Delta modulation: a simple way of encoding sound.   For every pulse of the 44.1-kHz clock, a PCM system outputs two 16-bit values which must be either transmitted or stored. Delta modulation recognizes that this is not actually necessary. Why transmit the entire value of the signal when what we actually need to know is how the signal has changed from the previous sample to the present one? If a signal's amplitude changes from 6.025 V to 6.039 V, all that need be transmitted is that change, +0.014 V, rather than 6.039. You can see that it will take far fewer bits to transmit the change than the signal's amplitude.

In the simplest type of delta modulation, the encoder transmits a single bit, either a digital 1 or 0, to indicate that the signal's amplitude is either greater or less than the previous value. The output signal is then corrected by increasing or decreasing its value by one unit. This unit, called the *step size*, is dependent on both the frequency of the input and the sampling frequency of the system. Step size is analogous to the quantization units used in PCM encoders.

Assume that we wish to track a 1-kHz sine wave with a delta modulation system. Figure 4.8 shows how the delta modulator's output straddles the sine wave. If at some point the tracking signal is greater than the input, the encoder transmits a binary 1. If the output is less than the input signal, the encoder transmits a binary 0. On the receiving side, this bit stream is decoded and the signal is reconstructed from the data transmitted. The reconverted signal resembles a staircase waveform and can be low-pass filtered to remove discontinuities.

Notice that if the input signal rises or falls too steeply, the delta modulator cannot track the signal effectively. This is because the step size and sampling rate are set parameters, and the maximum slope that the delta modulator signal can attain is the product of these two factors. In fact, if the input signal changes at a faster rate than one step per sampling period, the

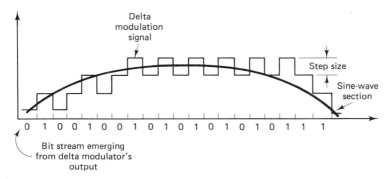

Figure 4.8 Delta modulator as it tracks the peak of a sine wave.

modulator will be unable to track the signal. This inability to track is called *overload*, because the input signal overloads the delta modulator's capability. If the step size is increased, the overload can be reduced, but a penalty is incurred. As the step size is increased, the ability to reproduce the input closely is decreased (Figure 4.9). The only way to track the signal closely without overload and with a small step size is to increase the sampling rate. This is just the thing that we were hoping to avoid when we chose delta modulation as our encoding scheme.

Let's take a minute to look at the numbers that will be needed for a delta modulator that can reproduce a 20-kHz audio signal. First, we must figure out the maximum slope of a 20-kHz sine wave. That's the derivative with respect to time of $A \sin (20,000t)$ evaluated at $t = 0$. In this equation, A is the amplitude of the signal and t is the time in seconds. This expression gives a maximum change of $20,000 \times A$ units per second. To achieve the same quality as a 16-bit PCM system, that peak value of this 20-kHz sine

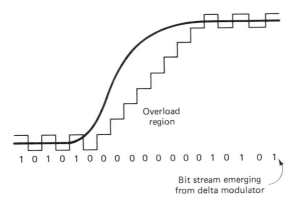

Figure 4.9 If a signal changes too quickly, the delta modulator cannot track it, and an overload condition is incurred.

wave must be 2^{16}, or 65,536, times greater than the step size. The sampling frequency multiplied by the step size must equal the maximum slope of the signal ($dS/dt = Q \times f$). Do not worry if you feel a bit lost here; the important part of all of this is the final number. After going through several mathematical gyrations, we find that to achieve the 96-dB signal-to-noise ratio of PCM, a 1300-MHz sampling frequency is required, which equates to 1 billion, 300 million bits of data per second. Remember that PCM requires only (16 bits) $\times$ (44,100 samples/second) = 705,600 bits per second per channel to reproduce the same signal. Obviously, if we want to reproduce high-quality audio signals, delta modulation is not the way to go. On the other hand, for low-quality bandlimited signals such as speech, delta modulation requires far fewer bits per second than PCM to achieve a reasonable result. Another advantage of delta modulation is that it is exceedingly easy to implement in hardware, and so may often be a cost-effective way to encode data. A delta modulator can consist of but a single silicon chip and a few capacitors and resistors whose total cost may be less than $1. Compare this to a PCM system, which often costs many times that, and you will begin to understand the allure of delta modulation.

Adaptive delta modulation: a better answer than delta modulation. But wait. Just when you were ready to throw delta modulation out the window because of its high data rate and low signal-to-noise ratio, along comes *adaptive delta modulation*. It uses the same basic idea as delta modulation, that is, to transmit the change in a signal rather than the value of each sample. The trick in adaptive delta modulation is that rather than having a set step size, the step size is continuously varied based on how well the input is being tracked.

To understand adaptive delta modulation better, let's take a look at the bit stream coming out of the delta modulator when it incurs overload. If the signal is being tracked correctly, one expects to see a series alternating ones and zeros, 0101010101010. . . . Whenever such a series of bits occurs, the adaptive delta modulator decreases the step size to some minimum value. It does this because an alternating stream means that the tracking signal is alternately above and below the value of the input signal. This condition is called *overshoot*. The modulator will continue to decrease the step size until it reaches the minimum step allowed by the system. This minimum step size is a constant for a particular system and is based on both the sampling rate and the lowest frequency that is expected to be tracked by the modulator. As soon as overload is incurred, the stream changes to either all zeros or all ones, . . . 0101011111111111 depending upon whether the overload is in the negative or positive direction, respectively. The adaptive delta modulator recognizes this and increases its step size. In this way it can track steep slopes since as the size of the step increases, the step/sampling rate product rises proportionally. In simpler terms, the larger the step size is, the faster the delta modulator can catch up with the signal. As soon as the tracking signal catches up with the input, the familiar 0101010 . . . sequence begins, and the modulator begins to decrease step size. After the delta modulator catches up with the signal, it will overshoot the signal until the step size can be decreased to a reasonably small value. The rate at which the step size is increased and decreased can also be varied depending on the parameters of the analog signal being tracked. In this way both small and large changes in the input signal can be tracked without incurring extended periods of either overload or overshoot. A popular algorithm consists of ANDing three consecutive bits of the modulators output. These three bits are usually the current output and the two preceding it. When all these bits are 1's, the output of the AND gate goes high, indicating that the modulator should increase the step size. As soon as the bits begin alternating, the AND gate's output goes low, indicating that the step size should no longer increase. The AND gate controls a capacitive circuit which either charges or discharges, depending on the value of the gate's output. The capacitive circuit, in turn, modulates the step size (Figure 4.10).

Adaptive delta modulation, also called *continuously variable slope delta modulation* (CVSD), can track signals without using the extreme data rates, and therefore bandwidth, of straight delta modulation. It is almost as simple to implement as straight delta modulation and is an interesting alternative to PCM. It is used extensively in medium-grade voice communication, and like delta modulation, can be implemented quite inexpensively with a single chip and a few peripheral components. It is, however, not as efficient a modulation technique as PCM for high-quality audio.

Both types of delta modulation, straight and CVSD, do have one great advantage over PCM transmission. This is that they are relatively insensitive to errors incurred during the transmission from encoder to decoder. Errors may occur for various reasons. Noise will be created by electrical static, glitches, and power surges, and this noise can corrupt the received signal. If an error occurs in, say, the most significant bit of a PCM code, the value of that word will either change sign or half in value, depending on the type of coding used (two's complement or straight binary). An error that causes 1111 to change or 0111 will, in two's complement, change the value from -1 to 7. If a bit is in error in a delta modulation bit stream, the signal is thrown off only by the value of a single step. So whereas an error in PCM transmission can cause changes in frequency and amplitude, and therefore introduce great distortion when the waveform is decoded, a delta modulator's error will affect the value of the decoded waveform only slightly. We look more closely at this phenomenon in Chapter 6 when we discuss error coding and correction in compact disc systems.

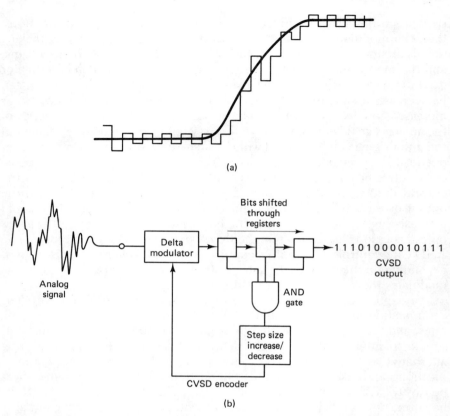

Figure 4.10 A CVSD waveform can change its step size to accommodate large or small changes in its input (a). As bits exit the delta modulator, they are ANDed together and used to change the step size for the next sampling period (b).

THE CONVERSION OF AUDIO SAMPLES
TO THE COMPACT DISC FORMAT

All of the aforementioned encoding schemes, be they PCM or others, are simply ways to change an analog input into a form that can be handled and processed by digital circuits. One should not think that these digital data are transferred directly to a medium such as optical disc for storage. As you may have guessed, there are several other operations performed on the digitally encoded sound before it is finally embedded on the surface of a compact disc. One process that must be performed before storing the encoded signal is the conversion of the parallel data into a serial format. Remember that samples exiting the A/D are 16 bits wide. Two channels, both left and right, must be produced when recording stereo signals. So for every tick of the

44.1-kHz clock, 32 bits of data must be processed. This translates into 1,411,200 bits that will be recorded every second. Even this great number of bits is less than that which is finally placed onto a CD.

The method whereby PCM data are converted into a form suited to the compact disc format is more complicated than you might think. In fact, the process of conversion is yet another type of modulation. But before we discuss exactly how the information is recorded, let's take a look at some of the factors that contributed to the format's evolution.

Transmission Channels: The Path from A/D to D/A

If the output of the A/D converter could be hooked up directly to the input of the D/A converter, we would not have to worry about how to format PCM data. Then again, there would be no need for either the A/D or D/A. But as more links are added to the chain between these two devices, considerations creep in as to just what the most efficient means of recording and transmission will be. The link between the coding and decoding sections of a digital system, that is, between the A/D and D/A, is called a *transmission channel*. And just as a telephone connection may be good or bad, so this digital channel will pass data either efficiently or inefficiently depending upon its characteristics. Just as a weak telephone link will make it difficult for the two parties on each end to communicate, so a bad transmission channel will induce errors during transfers of data over its path. Since we are contemplating the compact disc, let's see just what the channel characteristics are for this type of medium.

Basic Optics: Lasers, Discs, and Electronics

The compact disc is read by a laser that focuses on minute pits in the disc's surface. The laser reflects its light off the disc's surface and this reflected light is sensed by a set of light-sensitive pickups called *photodiodes*. The photodiodes convert the light that falls on them to a voltage which can then be interpreted by peripheral circuitry. The voltage produced by this process depends on how much light the photodiode pickup senses. The amount of information that can be stored on the disc is proportional to the amount of area on the disc that the laser can read, as well as the number of pits that can be fit on a disc and be read by the laser system. If we use a very tightly focused laser beam to read the pits, they can be made very small, and consequently, a great many pits can be placed on a disc. As the diameter of the laser spot decreases, the difficulty incurred while manufacturing the laser increases. This should come as no surprise. Tight manufacturing tolerances mean greater difficulty during the manufacturing process and hence greater cost. A laser spot diameter of about 1 millionth of a meter (1 micron) turns out to be a good compromise between information density and manufacturing considerations. A spot smaller than this is difficult to manufacture, while the savings in cost of a larger spot are negated by a loss in information density caused by the increased pit size.

The Eye Pattern and Channel Characteristics: Measures of Quality for a Transmission Channel

The surface of a compact disc can be divided into two sections consisting of pits and lands. *Pits* are the depressions in the disc, and *lands* are the areas between the pits. When a laser beam scans the surface of a disc, it is looking for the transition between pits and lands to determine the values encoded on the disc (Figure 4.11). A common misconception is that the laser gleans its information from the actual pit or land, a pit corresponding to a binary 0 and a land corresponding to a binary 1. This is not true, and it is actually the transition between pit and land that triggers the transition from 1 to 0 or 0 to 1. The ability of a laser pickup to identify a transition correctly can be measured by means of an eye pattern.

The *eye pattern* is a measure of the efficiency of a transmission channel. Suppose that we had a compact disc which consisted of alternating pits and lands of equal size and distance. When the laser scanned this disc it would see transitions spaced at regular intervals along the disc. If an oscilloscope were connected to the output of the photodiode to measure its voltage, the ensuing pattern would look something like that of Figure 4.12. This pattern does not look like the square wave that you might expect because the transition between pit and land is somewhat sloped rather than completely vertical. Also, the laser spot does not move from pit to land instantaneously, because the spot has a very small but measurable diameter. As the spot transits an edge, the amount of light that is transmitted to the photodiode increases or decreases gradually rather than abruptly (Figure 4.13). The pattern that is generated by the oscilloscope, called an *eye pattern*, is a measure of the quality of the transmission channel (Figure 4.14a). Dashes on the time axis have the same temporal spacing as the

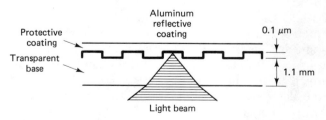

Figure 4.11   Light beam of a laser as it strikes the surface of a CD. The beam passes through the transparent base of the disc and reflects back off the aluminum coating. (Courtesy of NAP Consumer Electronics Corp.)

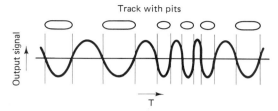

Figure 4.12 Variations in the output of the photocide appear rounded rather than as square transitions. (Courtesy of NAP Consumer Electronics Corp.)

pit-to-land transitions, and it is obvious that we can read the voltage of the photodiode at these transitions. This indicates that the transmission channel is one of good quality. This particular eye pattern results from an assumption that the laser is in perfect focus, the photodiodes are correctly aligned, and all the other pertinent parameters are at their optimum values. As these parameters become more lax, the eye pattern deteriorates until it

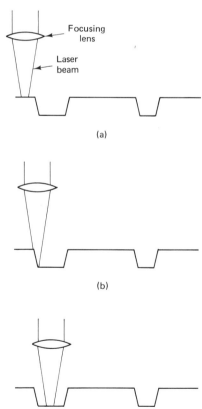

Figure 4.13 A laser beam is focused on the disc's surface by a focusing lens. The beam may be impinging exclusively on a land (a) or pit (c), or may straddle an edge as it moves from a pit to a land (b).

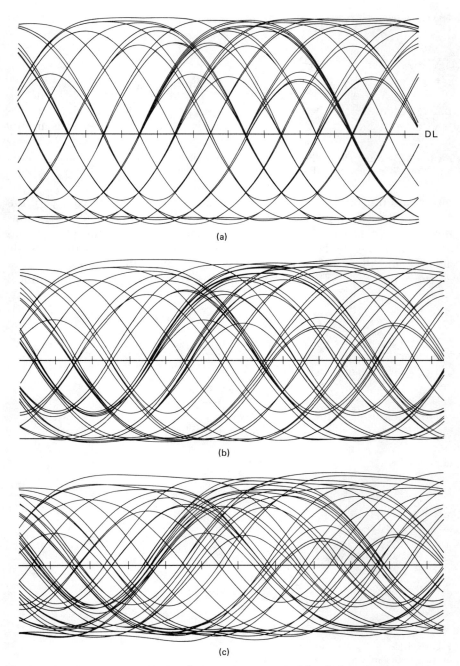

Figure 4.14 Eye pattern. At the decision times, marked by dashes, it is necessary to determine the value of the pattern. This is possible for a perfectly calibrated optical system (a), but becomes more difficult when the laser is defocused by 2 microns (b). If the disc is tilted 1.2° from the vertical, the eye high decreases and it becomes ever more difficult to determine the pattern's value at the decision points. (Courtesy of NAP Consumer Electronics Corp.)

becomes impossible to detect the transition between pits and lands (Figure 4.14c). You can think of the laser as the lens of a slide projector, and the photodetector as your eye. Although there is not a strict one-for-one correspondence in this analogy, it is useful in understanding what the eye pattern measures. If the projector's lens, like a laser beam, is out of focus, it becomes difficult to see a slide projected on its screen. If your eyes are not focused, the image is again blurred. The sharpness of the projected image is akin to an eye pattern, a good pattern equating to a sharp image and an indistinct pattern corresponding to a fuzzy image. Other things, such as the cleanliness of the projector lens and the quality of a particular slide, would also affect this system's quality, or eye pattern. If the quality of a transmission channel decreases, the maximum amplitude of its eye pattern also decreases. This is akin to losing the brightness of a projected picture in our analogy of a slide projector. The eye height is generally referred to when discussing the relative quality of transmission channels.

In a compact disc system, vibration and aging may alter the alignment of critical components, and dirt, grease, scratches, and fingerprints may make it difficult for the laser to scan a disc's surface correctly. Imperfections may also creep in during the manufacture of a disc. Pits and lands may not have perfect transitions, and the disc's surface may be wavy, causing the laser spot to come in and out of focus. It is important, therefore, to start out with the best possible eye pattern, to ensure that these problems will not result in a transition being read incorrectly, causing a loss of information.

The eye pattern is such an important parameter because it gives us a way to measure just how much information per unit area can fit onto a disc. Because the transitions from pit to land and back again are not vertical, and because of the laser spot's finite radius and the photodiode's limited sensitivity, only so many transitions can be squeezed into a limited space. The eye height gives us a feel for this limit. But what, you might ask, does this have to do with modulation? It turns out that by further modulating the signal, we can increase the eye height and the density of information on a disc.

Information Density: Packing Bits Onto a Disc

Consider first the case of an unmodulated signal. Since the change from a digital 1 to a digital 0 is indicated by the transition from a land to a pit, it follows that an alternating series of 1's and 0's will produce an alternating series of pits and lands in the disc. When a pit-to-land transition is incurred, the output of the photodiode does not change instantaneously. Its output is sloped and, in actuality, if the data rate is fast enough, the output looks more like a sine wave than a square wave. As the data rate increases, the photodiode cannot react to transitions fast enough, and the system's ability to detect a transition decreases. To appreciate what happens as the pits and lands move more quickly past the laser, try this simple experiment. Move your hand back and forth very slowly in front of your eyes. It is easy to see all the details of your palm. Now begin to move your hand more and more quickly. As you do so, it becomes difficult to see the wrinkles in your hand, and eventually, if your hand moves quickly enough, it seems as if your hand is in several places at the same time. This is the same problems that the photodiode encounters when pits and lands whiz by it at great speeds. The spacing of the transitions and the rate at which they move past the pickup, that is, the rotational speed of the disc, are both related to the decrease in eye height.

Eight-to-Fourteen Modulation: A Way to Store More Bits per Inch

There is a way to increase the eye height and the information density of a disc without resorting to a more accurate pickup system and its resultant cost and complexity. Suppose that rather than transfer an alternating stream of bits directly to pits and lands, it was first encoded so that the transitions occured less frequently. How can this be done? If 8 data bits are taken and encoded into a 14-bit stream with fewer transitions, the eye height will increase. Take as an example the data stream of 10101010. If this were transferred directly into pits and lands, it would necessitate seven consecutive transitions from pit to land, with one occurring between each digit. As we saw before, transitions become more difficult to detect as the data density of the disc is increased. These 8 bits could be mapped to the following 14 bit stream: 11100011100011. Mapping one set of bits to another simply means that when we see the 14-bit stream, we equate it with the original 8-bit stream, in almost the way that a thesaurus equates one word with another. For this particular 14-bit word, there are only four transitions instead of seven. Even if the same amount of space is used on the disc for pits and lands for this 14-bit stream as would be for the 8-bit stream, there are still fewer transitions per unit length. Assume that the minimum allowable distance between transitions is 1 millimeter (mm). The 8-bit word would require 8 mm in order to encode it onto a disc's surface, seven transitions with 1 mm between each and 2 mm for the first and last bits. The 14-bit stream could fit in the same physical space as the 8-bit stream because there are at least 3 bits between every transition rather than just 1 bit. Since there are four transitions in this 14-bit word, there is only 0.50 transition per millimeter (4 transitions per 8 mm), rather than 0.88 transition per millimeter for an 8-bit stream. The 8-bit word has 8/7 or 1.33 bits per transition, and the 14-bit stream word has 14/4 or 3.57 bits per transition, so a simple multiplication shows that both bit streams can average at least 1.17 bits per millimeter while still meeting the minimum spacing between transitions. This number is arrived at by multiplying the number of bits per transition by the number of transitions per millimeter to yield a product of bits per millimeter. The 14-bit stream will have, on average, a greater distance between transitions, which yields a greater eye height (Figure 4.15).

As mentioned earlier, mapping a value implies a one-to-one correspondence between the original value and its value after being replaced. Every time 10101010 is encountered, it is replaced by the aforementioned 14-bit word. Recall that there are 16,384 possible ways to arrange 14 bits, whereas there are only 256 ways to arrange 8 bits. When the 8-bit stream is converted, we make sure that resulting bits have transitions which occur at least 3 bits apart. This is the same as saying that there are at least four groups of three consecutive identical bits contained in the 14-bit word. This ensures that transitions from pit to land and land to pit occur less frequently than for an uncoded stream. It so happens that there are 267 of the 16,384 possible 14-bit patterns that meet this criterion. This is more than enough to encode the 256 resultant combinations of 8 bits. The values used in encoding are stored in a look-up table which is contained in a memory chip. In practice, the PCM stream is chopped up into blocks of eight, called *data bits*, and these blocks of data are then mapped to a corresponding group of 14, called *channel bits*. This is known as *eight-to-fourteen modulation* (EFM). A partial table of EFM codes is listed in Table 4.1. Since these 14 bits are encoded in the same amount of space as the original 8-bit stream, the data density does not change. However, the eye height does increase because of the additional spacing between transitions. If it is determined that the eye height for the unmodulated stream is sufficient, the spacing between pits and lands can be decreased by increasing the number of transitions per millimeter, and the eye height can then be brought back to the original value by using eight-to-fourteen modulation. This packs more data bits per millimeter onto the disc while maintaining the same eye height. In effect, we squeeze more bits onto an equally reliable channel. For the parameters

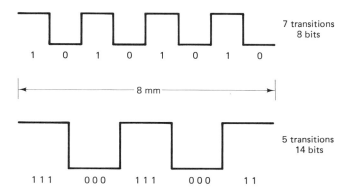

Figure 4.15 Seven transitions can be used to encode 8 bits, while five transitions can be used to encode 14 bits without violating spacing rules.

TABLE   4.1   Part of the EFM conversion table.

Decimal Equivalent	Data Bits	Channel Bits
0	00000000	01001000100000
1	00000001	10000010000000
2	00000010	10010000100000
3	00000011	10001000100000
4	00000100	00000100010000
5	00000101	00100001000000
6	00000110	00010000100000
7	00000111	00100100000000
8	00001000	01001001000000
9	00001001	10000001000000
10	00001010	10010010000000

that have been chosen for the compact disc system, EFM increases the data density by a factor of 25% over a straight PCM stream, while maintaining the same eye height.

Clock Acquisition: Synchronizing the System

It is also necessary to derive a system clock from the data stream as it is read from the disc. Devices such as the D/A converter and sample-and-hold circuit, as well as other electronic components, need to know when to perform their functions. They do this by looking at a square-wave signal called a clock. When the system is performing A/D conversion, the clock can be supplied by an electronic circuit which generates a square wave with a very stable frequency and phase. When bits are read off a disc, a clock must be derived from the data encoded on the disc. At every transition of the clock or at multiples of these transitions, the electronic components will perform functions in unison. Since timing is an important part of the accurate manipulation of data on the disc, it is important that this clock be as steady as possible. For the compact disc system, the clock is derived by looking at the time between the transitions from pits to lands. An electronic oscillator generates a clock that is near the expected frequency, and this generator is fine tuned by a feedback signal derived from the pit-to-land transitions. The oscillator measures the time between these transitions and adjusts its own output to match. More transitions translate into a more consistent feedback signal and hence a more accurate clock. Because the eye height increases as the spacing between transitions grows larger, while the feedback signal quality decreases with this interval, a trade-off occurs between the maximum eye height and the maximum clock accuracy. EFM patterns chosen for CDs are thus a compromise between the most advantageous patterns for each parameter. It turns out that transitions between 1's and 0's that are separated by between 2 and 10 bits satisfy both clock and eye height requirements, so the 14-bit patterns have transitions which, on the average, have such spacings.

Merging, Synchronization Bits, and Error Correction: More Housekeeping and Modulation

To maintain the correct number of transitions between symbols of length 14, an extra three merging bits are added to the end of each symbol. The value of these bits depends on the number of transitions at the end of the previous symbol and the beginning of the next one. These bits contain no information but are used to ensure that the length of each pit or land maintains its minimum value. If no merging bits were used, there would be a strong possibility that the minimum transition distance would be violated. A channel word such as 00011100011110 might be followed by 11100011000111. Although both are valid channel words, their junction would contain the bits 101, which violates the transition spacing. In this case, three merging bits, such as 000, could be appended to the first stream so that the transition from one stream to another met spacing requirements.

Finally, synchronization bits are added to help lock onto the beginning of each frame of information as well as *parity bits* which aid in error correction. As their name implies, the error correction bits are used to compenstate for errors that occur when bits are read off the disc's surface. If a disc is smudged or scratched, or if there were imperfections created during the manufacturing process, the pits and lands will be obscured. Electrical noise may also cause errors to be introduced into the bit stream, so some means of correcting such errors is provided. In Chapter 5 we discuss how this task is accomplished.

Merging and Interleaving Bits into a Serial Data Stream: The Mechanics of Putting Samples onto the Disc

Figure 4.16 is a pictorial representation of how bits exiting an analog-to-digital converter are modulated and interleaved on their way to becoming channel bits. Each group of 8 bits is called a *symbol*. A symbol is half of the output from a 16-bit A/D conversion. A stereo signal requires two 16-bit samples per sampling period, and thus there are four symbols per sampling period. The symbols from six sampling periods are strung together to form what is called a *frame* of information. This yields a total of 24 audio symbols per frame. One symbol containing control and display (C&D) information is added to this frame. The C&D bits contain information about the audio data, such as where the data appear on the disc and how much elapsed time a selection takes to play. Eight parity symbols used for error correction are also added to this frame, for a total of 33 data symbols. In the process of

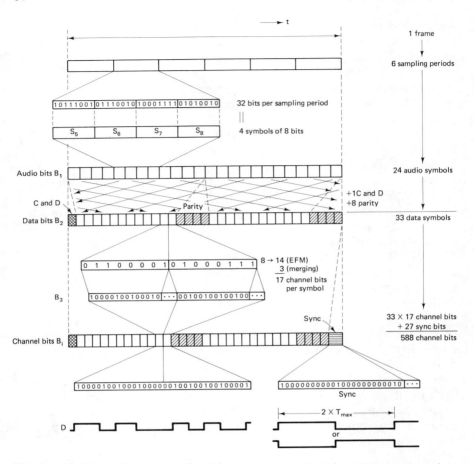

Figure 4.16 Bits as they are transferred from the output of a 16-bit A/D converter and are interleaved into channel bits on the surface of a compact disc. (Courtesy of NAP Consumer Electronics Corp.)

adding these nine extra frames, the audio symbols are shuffled to scatter the effect of possible errors. Each of the 33 symbols then undergoes eight-to-fourteen modulation (EFM), to which 3 bits per symbol are added for the purpose of merging. This gives us 17 bits per symbol multiplied by 33 symbols, for a total of 561 bits per frame. Twenty-seven synchronization bits are then added to the end of the frame to ensure that the beginning of the frame can be determined. The synchronization bits are a fixed pattern of 27 which signal the beginning of a long stream of information. Since the bits are always in the same pattern, they are easy to identify and help the compact disc player's circuitry lock on to a pattern so that it can determine where each frame begins and ends.

So what started out as 192 bits of audio information exiting the A/D ends up as no less than 588 channel bits. These bits are then translated into pits and lands on the compact disc's surface which are ultimately read and reconverted back into an audio signal. Because the PCM samples are encoded with so much care, almost every error that occurs when the disc is either manufactured or read can be detected or corrected by the decoding circuitry. This is one of the many advantages of the compact disc system and is a tribute to its conceivers.

5

ERROR CODING, DETECTION, AND CORRECTION

You may have heard that compact discs are indestructible. People say that you can drop them, scratch them, get greasy fingerprints all over them, and they will still sound good. Although this is not completely true, it is true that CDs can tolerate abuse which would send LPs into fits of skipping and popping. The reason for the compact disc's resiliency is that unlike other storage methods, that of the compact disc takes into account the inevitability of damage, and corrects for it.

STORING INFORMATION ON A COMPACT DISC

One unique feature of the CD is the way that it stores audio information. For not only must an analog signal be digitized, but it must also be converted from parallel to serial form, then further encoded before being stored on the surface of a compact disc. To begin, remember that when digital samples come out of an analog-to-digital converter, they are in parallel form. That means that all 16 bits of the digital word come out at the same time. Unfortunately, the only way to store these words is in serial form, meaning that the bits must be available one at a time. This is because the bits must be encoded one at a time as pits and lands on the disc's surface. Also, there will inevitably be errors when the samples are read, decoded, and converted back into an analog form by the disc player. There must be some facility for detecting, correcting, and handling these errors when they occur. Errors may creep in in a number of places, such as when the disc is read by a laser pickup, and can be attributed to such things as machine error or damage to the disc. To decrease the number of errors that occur and correct as many errors as possible, digital samples are not transferred to a storage medium, such as the optical disc, directly. Rather, the PCM samples are further encoded to ensure that the signal reproduced is as error free as possible. In Chapter 4 we saw how EFM extends the data density of the compact disc medium. You will remember that along with synchronization bits and control and display information, digits were added to allow error correction and detection to be performed by the decoding logic. In this chapter we discuss just how and why those digits are added.

DETECTING AND CORRECTING ERRORS

Errors are an inevitable part of everyday life. We are forever mismatching socks, picking out the wrong-color shirts for Father's Day, and putting too much salt on our food. We are also accustomed to seeing errors of a different kind, such as when a grocery clerk adds up our bill incorrectly or the bank muffs a monthly statement. The former types of mistakes are part of our nature, while the latter can be attributed to both human and mechanical errors. The "why" behind these errors is as important as the ways in which they can be corrected, for often the two subjects are closely related. If you fear that a list of important numbers may be misinterpreted, you may choose to spell them out rather than to list them numerically. It is, after all, easier to mistake the number "5" for "6" than a "five" for a "six." Another way to ensure the validity of the numbers is to make two identical lists of them and check the lists against each other for accuracy. Finally, you can choose to add all the numbers on the list together to form a checksum, much like totaling a column of numbers and using that sum to check the correctness of the list at a later time. These are all simple forms of error correction.

As an example, suppose that you wished to record three numbers, perhaps the combination to a safe. Let's say that they were 38, 22, and 17. You might write the numbers down on a pad and stow them away, but if the numbers became smudged, there would be no way of recovering them. Alternatively, you might choose to add some type of error correction to the list. By adding three more numbers to the list, each of which was the sum of the two digits in each combination number, you could ensure that the list could not be misread. The 38 would yield $3 + 8 = 11$, the 22 would yield $2 + 2 = 4$, and the 17 would produce $1 + 7 = 8$. A new string could be then formed, namely 38 22 17 11 4 8 (Figure 5.1). The final three numbers, called *checksums*, were derived from the previous sentence. If the "3" in 38

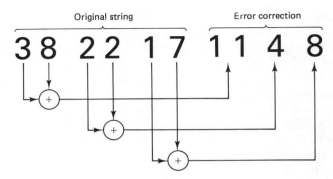

Figure 5.1 A sequence of numbers, 38-22-17, is combined to form a new sequence consisting of data and error correction. (Courtesy of NAP Consumer Electronics Corp.)

became smudged so that it could not be read, its value could be extrapolated by subtracting the second digit, 8, from the first number's checksum, 11, to get the 3 back. This is a form of error correction, and can be used to recover any single digit in the sequence. Because the number was smudged, you knew where the error occurred and could correct it. If you were not certain of the validity of an entry, such as the 22, you could check it against its checksum and determine if it was correct. If someone changed the string to 38 22 23 11 4 8, the change could be detected, since the third checksum, 8, would not match the third entry, 23. Notice, though, that you could not correct the problem, since two digits were changed. We see that our coding scheme has a shortcoming. This simple type of coding allows the correction of only one digit per entry. It is also possible to change an entry without voiding its checksum. The first entry, 38, could be changed to 74 without altering its checksum. This particular algorithm allows the detection of only certain types of errors and the correction of up to three nonconsecutive errors. By combining the numbers in more creative ways, even more errors could be detected and corrected. The new string of numbers could be recombined to form new checksums, which would allow correction and detection of even more errors. The price that is paid for this increased reliability is a multiplication of the amount of information that is needed in order to encode the original data. At some point, the probability that an error cannot be corrected by a certain code does not warrant any more additions to the checksums. This point is determined by many factors, some of which we examine in the following pages.

The idea of adding information to a string of data in order to detect and correct errors is one of the most important concepts in understanding the way in which information is encoded on the compact disc. Unfortunately, the actual method by which information is encoded is quite complex, and its discussion is better suited to a university environment than to this book. For those of you with a less than keen interest in mathematics, let me state this. The bits that come out of the A/D converter are further encoded before they are laid down onto a CD. This coding, called *cross-interleaved Reed–Solomon coding*, performs much the same function as the checksums that we have discussed. This code is used to detect and correct errors.

BLOCK CODING: A BASIC METHOD FOR CORRECTING ERRORS

When a vinyl record is damaged by dust or scratches there is virtually nothing that a record player can do but track the groove and pass on the clicks and pops that are generated by such damage. If the speed of the record player varies or the record itself is warped, these irregularities will degrade the quality of sound. There is virtually nothing that can be done, short of taking better care of the records, that can change this. In a compact disc system, errors can be detected, corrected, or concealed before the sound reaches your ear. This is done by adding error-correcting bits whose values are derived from the original PCM samples that exited the A/D converter.

The most predominant code used in digital communications is the *block code*. Block codes take streams of information and divide them up into groups. The error-correcting bits are then determined by the characteristics of that group. One type of block code might take a digital stream and group every 12 bits into a block. These bits would then be coded by the addition of parity check bits. To determine the value of these check bits, we would first arrange the data into a matrix as follows:

$$
\begin{matrix}
X_{11} & X_{12} & X_{12} & X_{14} \\
X_{21} & X_{22} & X_{23} & X_{24} \\
X_{31} & X_{32} & X_{33} & X_{34}
\end{matrix}
$$

The X's represent bits. X_{11} is the first bit, X_{14} the fourth, X_{21} the fifth, and so on. The parity bits are then generated by adding up the values of each row and column and choosing the parity bit such that the number of 1's in each row and column is always even. This is called *even-parity generation*. If the original digital stream consisted of 111001010001, the initial matrix would look like this one:

$$
\begin{matrix}
1 & 1 & 1 & 0 \\
0 & 1 & 0 & 1 \\
0 & 0 & 0 & 1
\end{matrix}
$$

Since there are three 1's in the first row, the parity bit would be another 1. This brings the total number of 1's in the first row to an even number, four. If this is done for the remaining rows and columns, our matrix ends up looking like this:

$$
\begin{array}{cccc|c}
1 & 1 & 1 & 0 & 1 \\
0 & 1 & 0 & 1 & 0 \\
0 & 0 & 0 & 1 & 1 \\
\hline
1 & 0 & 1 & 0 & 0
\end{array}
$$

Notice that the parity bits for each row and column are tagged on to the end of that row or column. The parity bit in the lower right-hand corner is chosen such that the total number of 1's in the block is even. Saying that the number of 1's is even is the same as saying that the least significant bit of their sum is equal to zero. This makes the calculation of parity bits an easy matter for digital logic to handle. In fact, although many bits may have to be added together, only a 2-bit adder is required to keep track of parity. For even though a 1 and 1 add to 10 in binary system, we need only worry about the least significant bit, the 0.

Correcting Errors Using Block Codes

Suppose that when this block is encoded and then decoded, an error occurs in the second position of the first row, X_{12}, so that rather than a 1, it flips to a 0. When the parity bits are checked, we will find that those for both row 1 and column 2 are incorrect. The intersection of these two pointers marks the bit where the error occurred. We could then reflip that bit from a 0 back to a 1, thereby correcting the error (Figure 5.2a). A problem occurs when several bits change due to errors in the transmission of bits. If bits X_{11}, X_{12}, and X_{21} change during transmission, it will be possible to detect that an error has occurred, but it will be impossible to locate or correct it. This is because the parity bits for both rows 1 and 2 are still correct even though errors occurred in both of these rows. Only column 1 and row 4 show parity errors, indicating that the error is in X_{42}, a parity bit (Figure 5.2b). Obviously, this type of coding has its limitations. A measure of this limitation is the *Hamming distance*.

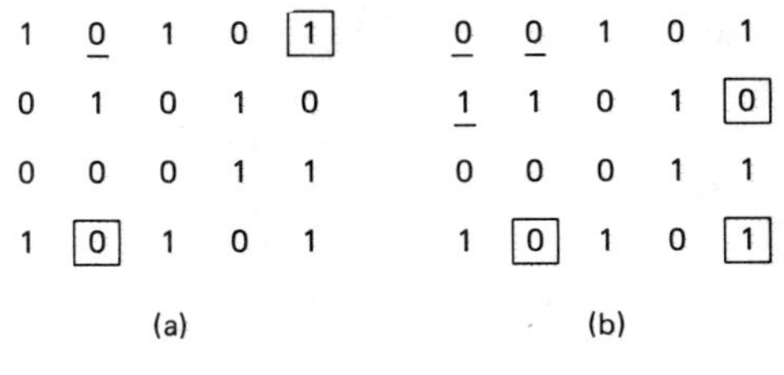

Figure 5.2 If a single error occurs in a data bit of a block code, the intersection of the parity bits will point it out (a). If three errors occur, the parity bits will not be able to point out the location of the errors (b).

Hamming Distance: One Measure of a Block Code's Ability

In the previous example, 8 parity bits were used to correct 12 data bits for a total of 20 bits in the encoded word. This is referred to as a *(20, 12) code*. In general, a code consisting of *n* bits which encode *k* bits of data is called a *(n, k) code*. The number of parity bits, designated by an *r*, is equal to *n* − *k*. For the previous example, *k* is equal to 12 data bits, *r* is the 8 parity bits, and *n* is 20 total bits. An important parameter of a block code is called its *Hamming distance*, the number of differing digits between two code words. For the code above, the minimum Hamming distance between code words is 4. If one bit in the original block changes, the parity check bits for that bit's row and column must change to maintain an even parity. Also, the bottom right-hand corner bit must change to keep the total number of ones in the block at an even count. These changes total 4 bits, hence the Hamming distance of four. To correct *t* number of errors in the block, the Hamming distance *d* must satisfy the equation t ≤ (d − 1)/2. This relationship, derived from coding theorems and calculations, tells us that our (20, 12) code can correct up to two errors. That is why when 3 bits were changed in the previous example, it could detect, but not correct, the error. When an error is indicated by this type of code, it can be corrected by selecting the code word that is closest to the received word. Again, "closest" means the code word that has the fewest different digits. The values of the two numbers are unimportant. Although 1000 is a binary 8 and 0111 is a binary 7, their Hamming distance is four. The least significant digit of binary 8 is 0, and that of binary 7 is a 1. These are not the same, so they increase the Hamming distance between these two numbers. In fact, every digit of binary 7 and 8 is different, which is why their Hamming distance is four. A binary zero, 0000, is closer in Hamming distance to 8 than is 7. That is because it differs by only one digit, the most significant, whereas 7 differs by four digits (Figure 5.3). When Hamming distance is used to correct errors, the code word with the least Hamming distance between it and the received word is taken as the correct one and treated as if it were the original. Suppose that we knew that only three code words were to be transmitted: 0000, 0011, and 1100. If a 1101 were received, it would be checked against the three known code words. Since 1100 has a Hamming distance of one from the received word and the other code words have a distance of three, 1100 is the corrected value. This comparison can be accomplished with a

1 0 0 0 (8)   1 0 0 0 (8)
0 1 1 1 (7)   0 0 0 0 (0)

(a)   (b)

Figure 5.3 Every bit of binary 8 and binary 7 differ, so their Hamming distance is four (a). Only one digit of binary 8 and binary 0 differ, so their Hamming distance is one (b).

fairly unsophisticated electronic circuit. Because there are a limited number of code words for any given code, they can be stored in a table in electronic memory and compared to each word that is in error. This is something like comparing a misspelled word to those in a dictionary to determine which has the closest spelling. If, however, there are enough errors in the original data to change its value by more than the Hamming distance, a problem will occur. Since the equation $t \leq (d - 1)/2$ cannot be satisfied, we will not be able to choose the correct code word unambiguously. When we try to correct three errors with a (20, 12) code, the equation becomes $3 \leq (4 - 1)/2$, or $3 \leq 1.5$. This is obviously incorrect.

Graphically, you can think of each code word as being encircled by a boundary whose radius is the Hamming distance. The center of the circle is the correct code word, while any code words that fall within the Hamming radius are assumed to be derivations of the center word. If an error occurs that moves the value of the code word out beyond the boundary, it cannot be corrected. In the previous example, a 1010 has a Hamming distance of 2 from each of the code words, so how can it be corrected? Sometimes an error may be so great as to move the original code word's value inside the boundary of another code word. When this occurs, the error will be detected but corrected incorrectly. This occurs because when the incorrect code word is checked against the list of correct words, it will be mapped into the nearest one, which in this case is not the correct one. Again, if in the previous system, a 0000 was transmitted but a 0011 was received, no error would be detected, so the mistaken word would go uncorrected.

From these examples it can be deducted that these simple parity-checking schemes are to be inadequate for use in a real, high-fidelity system. More elaborate schemes abound, one of which is using not one but two coding algorithms to encode data and correct errors.

Redundant Coding: Adding More Error Correction for Better Fidelity

Sometimes we may wish to use a code not to correct errors, but rather simply to point them out so that another decoding scheme can be used to correct them. The logic behind this is that it is much easier and faster to detect an error than to correct it. Remember in the previous example that a 3-bit error could be detected, but not corrected, in a system with a Hamming distance of four. If it can be determined in a few steps that there are no errors in a particular code word, the error-correcting step can be circumvented. If, however, the code indicates that an error has occurred, the word can be corrected without being unnecessarily delayed before it is output. The error-detecting part of a two-step decoding process marks symbols that contain errors as erasures, meaning that their values are unreliable. If the error-correcting section of the decoder does not see any erasures, it need not attempt error correction. If it sees erasures, error correction takes place.

TYPES AND CAUSES OF ERRORS

Before we go any further, a discussion of the types of errors that occur in the compact disc system is in order. There are basically two types of errors, burst and random. *Random errors* are those that are uncorrelated from bit to bit. That means that an error in one bit of a stream does not mean that there will be errors in the other bits of the stream. A *burst error*, conversely, will change the value of a chain of consecutive bits. CDs are susceptible to both types of errors. Some of the causes of burst errors include defects that occur to the disc during manufacturing and damage incurred during the disc's use and handling. Random errors may arise from variations in the rotational speed of the disc as well as electrical errors during the reading process. In general, random errors are easier to correct than burst errors. This is because a burst error may wipe out a large number of symbols, including the error-correcting bits, whereas random errors, as their name implies, will destroy random bits which are dispersed over a number of symbols or frames (Figure 5.4). As we saw before, the number of consecutive bits that a block code can correct depends on the number of parity bits that it uses. So if our goal is to add the least number of parity bits to the data, it makes sense to hope for random rather than burst errors. Unfortunately, scratches, smudges, and fingerprints on the surface of a compact disc manifest themselves in the form of burst errors. You can imagine how many bits a grease smudge may wipe out when you consider the fact that there are about 37,000 bits per linear inch packed onto a single track of a compact disc. A smudge only 1 mm long could mask about 1600 consecutive bits. To combat this, data on the disc go through a process called interleaving before they are encoded as pits and lands.

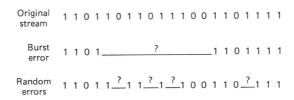

Figure 5.4 A data stream may be affected by burst errors, which wipe out a number of consecutive bits, or random errors, which wipe out random bits.

Interleaving: Shuffling Bits to Combat Burst Errors

Interleaving is a process whereby the original sequence of bits is rearranged into a new sequence before it is transferred to the medium of a compact disc. This dispersal serves an important purpose. Suppose that the average burst error spans a distance of 12 bits. The greatest number of consecutive bits that is likely to be blotted out by a burst error equals this number, 12. Let's also say that the error-correcting block code can correct up to two errors per symbol. If a burst error occurs in a frame of six symbols, each of which contains 8 bits, chances are that this error will totally wipe out at least one full symbol (Figure 5.5a). This is because the symbol length is less than the average length of the burst error. In the best case, the burst error would affect the last 2 bits of one symbol, then all of the next symbol's bits, and the first 2 bits of the following symbol. The first and last symbols could be recovered using its error-correction bits, but the middle symbol would contain too many errors to be saved. If the bits from each symbol are taken sequentialy, a new frame can be made out of them, as in Figure 5.5b. This will improve by a dramatic amount the likelihood of correcting a long burst error. For now when a burst error occurs it will wipe out at most 2 bits from the original symbols. Although every symbols will require some error correction, every symbol can be corrected, unlike the uninterleaved stream (Figure 5.5c). Because this code can correct these 2 bits, the burst error's effect is minimalized. After the correction has been made, the symbols undergo a deinterleaving process and are restored to their original order.

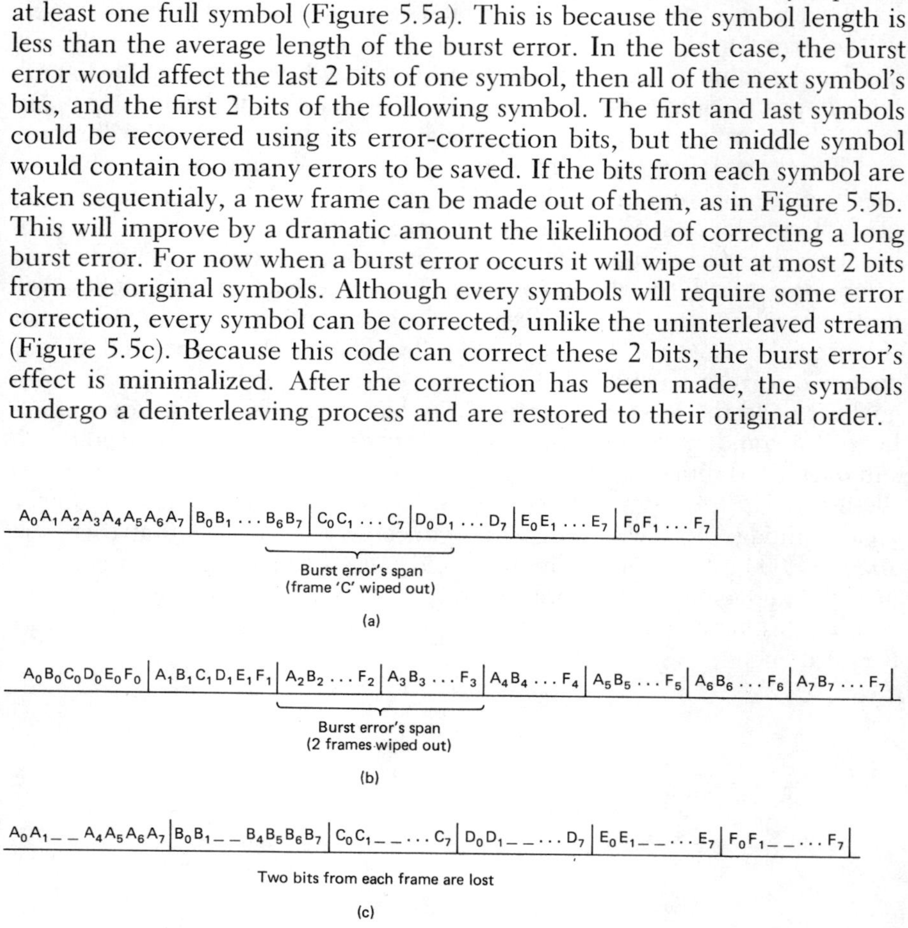

$A_0 A_1 A_2 A_3 A_4 A_5 A_6 A_7 \mid B_0 B_1 \ldots B_6 B_7 \mid C_0 C_1 \ldots C_7 \mid D_0 D_1 \ldots D_7 \mid E_0 E_1 \ldots E_7 \mid F_0 F_1 \ldots F_7 \mid$

Burst error's span
(frame 'C' wiped out)

(a)

$A_0 B_0 C_0 D_0 E_0 F_0 \mid A_1 B_1 C_1 D_1 E_1 F_1 \mid A_2 B_2 \ldots F_2 \mid A_3 B_3 \ldots F_3 \mid A_4 B_4 \ldots F_4 \mid A_5 B_5 \ldots F_5 \mid A_6 B_6 \ldots F_6 \mid A_7 B_7 \ldots F_7 \mid$

Burst error's span
(2 frames wiped out)

(b)

$A_0 A_1 \_\_ A_4 A_5 A_6 A_7 \mid B_0 B_1 \_\_ B_4 B_5 B_6 B_7 \mid C_0 C_1 \_\_ \ldots C_7 \mid D_0 D_1 \_\_ \ldots D_7 \mid E_0 E_1 \_\_ \ldots E_7 \mid F_0 F_1 \_\_ \ldots F_7 \mid$

Two bits from each frame are lost

(c)

Figure 5.5 A noninterleaved stream of data will lose a full frame to the average burst error if the error correction code cannot compensate (a). An interleaved stream loses just as many bits to the burst error (b). When the stream is deinterleaved, every frame is affected, but all the errors can be corrected (c).

You should see that interleaving is a very powerful process when used in conjunction with error correction. The drawback of this elaborate system is that it increases the complexity of the compact disc system in both the recording and playback areas. Because a burst error may affect many symbols rather than just one, the amount of error correction per symbol will increase. We saw this in the previous example. Interleaving and deinterleaving also take both time and hardware to be accomplished. The benefits of these processes are an increase in the integrity of the data which are transferred to and read from the compact disc, and, ultimately, a better-sounding playback.

REED–SOLOMON CODES: THE ERROR CODING USED FOR COMPACT DISCS

There are many algorithms for encoding data and determining how to form parity bits. The previous block code which was discussed employed a most general and simple system to form its code words. Each type of code has its strong points. Some may be better suited to correcting random errors; some may correct burst errors more efficiently. For reasons that are beyond the scope of this book, it turns out that the Reed–Solomon codes are a class of error-correcting codes which are very well suited to the types of errors that occur in compact disc systems. The Reed–Solomon codes are of the linear variety, meaning that when two code words are added, their sum is also a code word. This is important because the compact disc format uses not one but two Reed–Solomon codes which are interleaved together to form a final, third code word. The first encoding of the data is used so that erasures can be detected in the decoding process. You will remember that an erasure is simply a symbol that is tagged as containing an error and requires error correction. The second Reed–Solomon code does the actual error correction, if necessary. The products of these two codes are cross-interleaved to form the final code word.

A CIRC Encoder: Implementing the Reed–Solomon Coding

The actual method whereby the Reed–Solomon codes are combined and decoded are fairly complex. Upon encoding, the two block codes are cross interleaved. Spatially, you can think of the two blocks as being placed next to each other so that they form a three-dimensional block. A diagram of the encoding process is shown in Figure 5.6. A number of samples, represented by the letters L for left channel and R for right channel, are separated into symbols of 8 bits per word. The even-numbered words are delayed by two frames (a) and then all the symbols are interleaved (b). These interleaved symbols are then passed to the first encoder, C_2, which

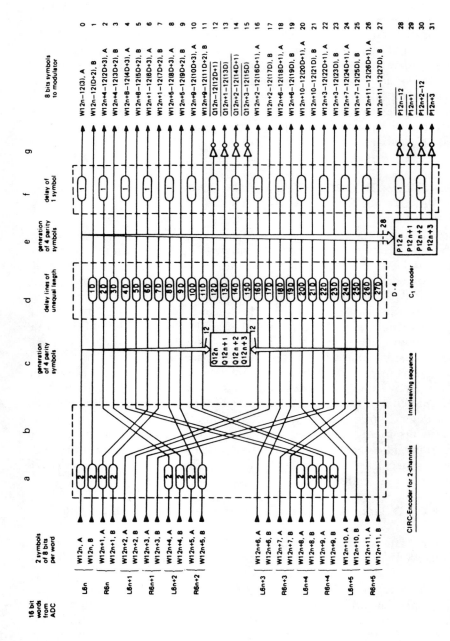

Figure 5.6 CIRC encoder showing the interleaving and multiplexing stages of a two-stage system. [Courtesy of Pioneer Electronics (USA) Inc.]

generates four symbols worth of parity bits and then inserts these 24 parity bits along with the 24 data symbols (c). These 28 symbols, now containing some error correction, are delayed by varying amounts of time so that they are spread out over 108 frames (d). When the symbols reach the second encoder, C_1, more parity symbols are generated and inserted (e); then the even-numbered symbols are delayed once more and the parity symbols are inverted (f). This output is modulated by EFM and used to determine the placing of pits and lands on the disc's surface. The actual delays and the method by which this encoding takes place are fairly intricate and from our standpoint are not as important as how they aid error correction and detection when the information is decoded. Since the entire encoding process can be carried out by a single digital integrated circuit, the process is invisible as far as the average user is concerned.

Decoding the Compact Disc Using CIRC

During decoding, the 32 symbols of a frame are deinterleaved and then passed to the first decoder, which decodes the incoming signals in accordance with the rules of the Reed–Solomon code. If there are no errors, these bits are passed to a bank of delay lines, which further deinterleaves the symbols so that they are returned to the order in which they were before passing through the encoding section's delay elements. If, however, there are errors in some of the symbols, all the symbols are marked as erasures before they are sent to the next decoder. Since each symbol is delayed by a different amount of time, the erasures are spread out over several code words, thus decreasing the number of errors per code word in the second decoder. Decoder 2 is designed such that it can correct up to four errors. If there are more than four errors in the incoming code word, the decoder passes on the decoded symbols and marks them as erasures (Figure 5.7). By using this cross-interleaved Reed–Solomon code, (CIRC) a burst error of about 4000 bits can be completely corrected. This equates to a smudge or mark on the disc surface of roughly 2.5 mm in length, about a $\frac{1}{10}$ of an inch (Table 5.1).

ERROR CONCEALMENT: HIDING ERRORS THAT CANNOT BE CORRECTED

When errors occur that are detected but cannot be corrected by the CIRC, there are several methods by which they may be concealed. When a frame of symbols exits the decoding section marked as erasures, it can be assumed that these values are unreliable and should not be converted to an analog signal. What, then, should the audio output of the compact disc player be during the sampling period which otherwise would have been occupied by

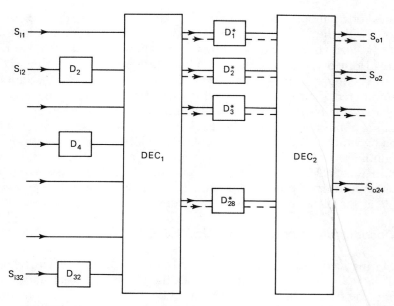

Figure 5.7 Decoder for use with CIRC. Frames are fed into the first decoder after the appropriate delays. They are then decoded and erasures are marked. More delays follow, after which the frames in error are corrected by decoder 2. The emerging frames may be marked as erasures if the errors were too severe to correct. (Courtesy of NAP Consumer Electronics Corp.)

TABLE 5.1 Specifications of CIRC

Aspect	Specification
Maximum *completely* correctable burst length	≈ 4000 data bits (i.e., ≈ 2.5 mm track length on the disc)
Maximum interpolatable burst length in the *worst* case	$\approx 12{,}300$ data bits (i.e., ≈ 7.7 mm track length)
Sample interpolation rate	One sample every 10 hours at BER $= 10^{-4}$; 1000 samples per minute at BER $= 10^{-3}$
Undetected error samples (clicks)	Less than one every 750 hours at BER $= 10^{-3}$; negligible at BER $\leq 10^{-4}$
Code rate	$\frac{3}{4}$
Structure of decoder	One special LSI chip plus one random-access memory (RAM) for 2048 words of 8 bits
Usefulness for future developments	Decoding circuit can also be used for a four-channel version (quadraphonic reproduction)

Source: NAP Consumer Electronics Corp.

those samples? Obviously, the actual analog value of the sample cannot be computed since its digital value cannot be trusted as accurate. There are several ways to handle this. The most common method is to average the previous sample and the sample after the one in error and assign that average value to the interval of uncertainty. In short, we guess that the sample which was lost lay directly between the one before and after it. This has the net effect of increasing the noise and distortion in the audio output for a very short interval, on the order of 0.02 second. If a string of erasures is indicated, as might be the case during a very long error burst, this method of linear interpolation will not be useful because there will not be any good samples with which to interpolate. Also, it is likely that by the time enough samples were accumulated to make a reasonable guess as to the value of the others, a long period would have elapsed during which the disc player had no output. In this case the signal must be *muted*, or turned off. Muting does not consist merely of turning the player's output off; rather, the amplitude of the output is turned down slowly relative to the time for one sampling period. The reason for this is that if the player's output were turned off and on very quickly, a square wave would appear. This artificially creates high-frequency components since a square wave consists of odd harmonics of a fundamental frequency. Turning off the music is a rather drastic way of correcting an error, so there a third alternative is available. The output of the disc player can be held constant until a good sample is decoded and ready for output. Unfortunately, if the amplitude of the sample being held is drastically different from the next good sample, a high-frequency spike will occur at the moment the new sample is output. Again, distortion will be introduced into the music. The way in which a signal is corrected, be it muting, interpolation, or error correction, is one of the most important aspects of a compact disc player's design. Most manufacturers use a combination of these practices. Interpolation is preferable to muting or holding, and so is implemented after it is determined that an error cannot be corrected. Only if interpolation becomes impossible will muting or holding occur.

CONCLUSIONS

In this chapter we have explored many aspects of error detection and correction as they apply to the compact audio disc. It is error correction that makes the compact disc medium so radically different from those that have come before it. Block coding provides a convenient method of detecting and correcting certain types of errors that are common to the digital world. Interleaving is a way to reduce the most harmful burst errors while adding little complexity to the system. Erasure handling provides a last chance to fool the listener into believing that the digital samples originally recorded were the same ones presented to the D/A converter and output as sound.

These types of measures—coding, interleaving, and erasure handling—apply to a broad range of communications technologies. One should not think that all of these methods were invented solely to bring the audiophile a clearer image of recorded sound. In fact, most of these methods have been known, used, and appreciated for decades. It is the disc player's owner who reaps the benefit of this modern technology by having available a system which, only a few years ago, would have been out of the financial reach of almost every one of us. Although the electronic circuits that perform these algorithms are physically complex, they are often consolidated into but a single chip or a set of chips that can be wired together to form a complete disc decoding system. Without error correction, the compact disc would be inferior in every aspect to both records and tapes, while the inclusion of such coding propels this medium far beyond the traditional limitations.

6

THE COMPACT DISC PLAYER: CONSTRUCTION AND FEATURES

Well, the time has come for us to break away from the theory of operation of compact disc players and examine some of the features that you will encounter when you operate and listen to a CD player. There are perhaps as many features available on disc players as there are players themselves. Their front panels abound with switches and buttons, displays and remote controls (Figure 6.1). As if this does not make choosing a player difficult enough, the insides of these machines often contain as many innovative and confusing features as their exteriors. How does one choose between double or quadruple oversampling, dual or single digital-to-analog converters, multiple power supplies, and digital or analog filters? What can you look for in manufacturers' spec sheets that might reveal the strengths and weaknesses of a particular player? What should you look for when reading independent tests of equipment in audio magazines? Perhaps most important, what should one listen for when auditioning various compact disc players? These are probably the questions that you wished to answer when you started reading this book. Now with the knowledge that you have gained of how CD players function, you can begin to gain some insight into the answers to these questions.

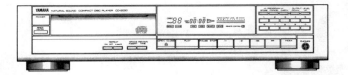

Figure 6.1   Front panel of a typical disc player. (Courtesy of Yamaha Electronics Corporation, USA.)

FRONT-PANEL FEATURES

The first thing that you will be confronted with when buying a compact disc player is its front panel. This would thus seem like a good place to start our examination.

Almost every manufacturer has a slightly different notion of what its buyers want in the way of front-panel features, and consequently, there are many and varied features available to the audiophile. We will discuss the most basic features available on players, and then look at some of the various add-on's that manufacturers incorporate into their designs. Bear in mind that there are many implementations of these basic functions. So although every player must provide certain basics in order to allow you to handle the disc, these functions may not operate in exactly the same way on every machine. In the following pages you will find an explanation of how a generic compact disc player functions. Not all players will be like this one, but most will follow this general outline.

The Power Switch

Obviously, before you can operate a disc player, you must turn it on. Most machines have a pushbutton marked either POWER or ON. Push it and you are in business. At this point one of two things will happen. If the player already has a disc in it, it will scan the disc and may begin to play the first selection. If there is no disc inside, it may prompt you with a message such as DISC, indicating that it is empty. These actions may take a few seconds to occur because the player must first check to see if it already contains a disc, and if so, it will scan the disc for information before it begins to play. The better players will also run a set of diagnostic tests on their internal circuitry to make certain that all of the electronics are working correctly.

Display

The front panel will have some type of lighted display on its face. The display contains information about such things as the track number, elapsed time into a track, the status of the player, as well as a host of other things. In case you are not familiar with the term *track*, it refers a particular song or selection on the disc. When you first power-up your machine, the display will come to life. If there is no disc inside the carriage, the display will show a message such as DISC to indicate that it is empty. It is also likely that whenever you press one of the front-panel buttons, its function name will appear on the display. Depressing the OPEN/CLOSE button may cause either OPEN or CLOSE to appear. If the disc is not seated correctly in the drawer or the machine experiences some type of malfunction, ERR, short for "error," may flash. Alternatively, there may be a separate error light for this. Pushing the PLAY button will cause PLAY to appear momentarily, and then the track number of the section being played will be substituted. As each successive track is played, its number will be displayed. There will also be a button marked TIME or DISPLAY, which, when activated, will switch the display to an alternative mode. If this button is pushed while a disc is in play, the display will show the elapsed time of each selection rather than its track number. The time will be shown in minutes and seconds and will start over at the end of each selection. If you press DISPLAY while the disc is not in either the play or pause mode, the total playing time of the disc will be displayed. Although a compact disc can hold up to 75 minutes of music, the total time that you see will probably be considerably less, perhaps 45 minutes for the average disc. After spending almost twice as much for a disc than for an average-priced LP, this feature can be a rather disheartening one. When the disc has been played to completion, a message such as END will probably flash onto the display, indicating that it is time to load in another CD.

Open and Close Buttons

There will also be a button on the front panel marked OPEN/CLOSE. As you may have guessed, depressing this will slide the disc drawer to the open position so that you can remove or install a disc. Most drawers have some type of sensor built into their mechanism to prevent the door from jamming. If, when the OPEN button is depressed, an obstruction prevents the drawer from opening fully, this sensing system will prevent the drive mechanism that opens the door from burning itself out. The drawer may close itself or simply stop motion until the obstruction is removed from its path. Once a disc is dropped into the drawer, you simply depress OPEN/CLOSE again and the drawer will slide into the play position. If the disc is not seated correctly in the drawer, it may not close, may reopen, or may even close without playing the disc. Depending on the player, you may also have the option of simply tapping the front of the drawer to slide it shut. In this case, the same type of device that sensed an obstruction will sense your touch and close the drawer. After the drawer slides shut you may hear a few faint noises as the disc is grasped by the spindle and the laser pickup reads preliminary information off the tracks. Your player is now set to begin operation and play a disc. If you are auditioning a fairly high-end piece of audio gear, you may not be confronted with a drawer at all. Some units have swing-out doors, much like those found on tape decks. When this type of door is opened up it swings out and the disc is inserted vertically into it. You will probably be able to see both the spindle, which holds the disc in place, and the disc itself through the door, as most such doors have transparent sections. The only problem with the swing-out door appears when one attempts to extract the disc. It is sometimes difficult to remove a disc without touching the playing surface and getting fingerprints and dirt onto it. Depending on the design of the player and your dexterity, you may or may not have this problem.

Playing a Disc

The only thing left to do after loading the disc is to hit the PLAY button. Once this is done, the laser pickup will move into position and your compact disc player will do the job for which it was designed, to reproduce music. If the disc drawer was open when you hit PLAY, there is a good chance that the drawer closed itself and the player began operation on its own. Unless you have preprogrammed some selections beforehand, the player will access the first track on the disc and play each selection sequentially.

The Pause and Stop Controls

The PAUSE and STOP controls may or may not be integrated into the same button, depending on the configuration of the particular player. The PAUSE button is used to stop a selection while it is being played. When it is depressed, it stops the selection without resetting the laser pickup to the first track. It is much like the cue or pause control on a record player or tape deck. Pause comes in handy when you want to stop the player momentarily to answer a telephone or doorbell without resetting the player. To resume play, simply depress the PLAY button once. The music should start at exactly the same point at which it left off. Some models may require that PAUSE, rather than PLAY, be hit again for the music to resume. There is no "thump" sometimes associated with replacing a tone arm onto a moving record when the disc starts up again. If the pause and stop controls are integrated into the same button, pressing pause twice will stop the selection from being played and place the pickup in position at the first selection. Pushing PLAY then starts the disc from its beginning. If these controls are separate, STOP need be pressed only once to reset the player. Pressing the OPEN/CLOSE button will have the same effect as depressing STOP, with the added feature of having the disc tray slide out so that you can change the disc.

The Skipping Controls

When you wish to hear a particular song on a record album, you simply lift the tone arm and position it over the correct groove, unless, of course, the song is on the other side of the album. Fortunately, you need never flip a compact disc to hear any selection. There is, however, an analogous method when moving from track to track. It is called *skipping*, and the buttons that control this function are normally labeled either "+" and "−" or ">" and "<." The "+" or ">" buttons control forward skipping, and the "−" or "<" control reverse skipping. Pressing the forward skip button will move the laser pickup to the beginning of the next track. If the disc is being played while you depress this switch, the machine will cease to play the current selection, then move to the beginning of the next selection and begin to play it. If either the pause or stop mode are invoked before the skip button is pressed, the pickup will move to the next selection and wait for play to be pressed before playing that track. The reverse skip button, "−" or "<," will cause a skip to the nearest beginning track. If, for instance, the machine is playing a selection, pressing "<" will cause it to return to the beginning of that selection and resume play. Notice that you will not skip to the beginning of the previous selection, but rather, to the beginning of the one already in play. If you hit "<" again before play is resumed, you will skip the machine to the beginning of the previous track. The same is true when in the pause mode. In this way it is possible to use the skip function to move between selections while the disc is playing without experiencing a wait between songs.

The Index Function

There is yet another way in which to skip to a particular place on this disc. The INDEX button has a function that is seldom used by those who do not listen to classical music. This is because discs containing such music often have special markers called indexes which mark movements within the recording. These indexes are not part of the audio information, but allow the classical music listener to access the beginning of each movement without resorting to the scan function (discussed later). Pressing INDEX switches you into the indexing mode, and the "+" and "−" buttons then move not from track to track, but from index point to index point. Pressing INDEX once again returns the machine to its normal mode of operation. To access the third movement on the second track of a disc, one might press "+" once to move to the beginning of the second track, then press INDEX to switch to the indexing mode. A light would probably light to indicate that INDEX had been activated. Pressing "+" two times would then ready the machine to play the third movement of the second track. Rather than displaying just the track number, it is likely that the display would show both the track and index number. Pressing INDEX once would return the machine to its normal mode. Note that some manufacturers may have distinct keys which perform the same functions as "+" and "−," but which are reserved for the indexing function.

Scanning the Disc

Tape decks have fast forward and reverse buttons which allow you to move quickly to particular points on a tape. Unlike the compact disc system, the only way to judge how far a tape has played is either to check the tape visually or to examine the foot counter. The CD player offers a more eloquent method of moving to particular points on a selection. The forward and reverse scan controls of the CD player are just that solution. The forward scan control is usually labeled ">>" and the reverse scan is designated by "<<." Like the fast forward and reverse controls of a tape deck, they allow you to move through a selection faster than the normal playing rate. Unlike the tape controls, they also allow you to hear the music as it is scanned, and the front-panel display of the player indicates, in minutes and seconds, just how how much time has elapsed in the selection. You might expect that like playing a 33F rpm recorded at 45 rpm, the music would increase not only in speed, but also in pitch during a fast scan. This is not so. The music during a scan will maintain the same pitch as during regular play, but the volume of the music will be lessened so as not to be disturbing to the ear. Thus you can listen for the exact place in a song or movement and then release the scan button and return to listening at the normal speed and musical intensity. If the scan button is held down for longer than a few seconds, the scanning rate will be increased and the music will move by even faster. If the button is released and then depressed again, the normal scan rate will be resumed. This feature serves two functions. The first is that it allows you to fast forward close to a point in the selection in which you are interested using the fast scan, and then slow scan to an exact point in time. The second function is to allow both the fast and slow scans to be controlled by only two, rather than four buttons. Some manufacturers choose to use four buttons rather than two, labeling the slow scan buttons "<<" and ">>" and the fast scan buttons "<<<" and ">>>." Listening to a player scan through a song backwards is rather unusual experience, but it is quite impressive when one thinks of the impossibility of doing this with a record player or conventional tape recorder.

Programming Selections

On almost all types of record players and tape recorders, you must listen to songs in the order in which they were recorded unless you wish to manually move the machine from selection to selection. The compact disc player is not so limited. Virtually every disc player on the market gives you the option of programming the order in which tracks on the disc will be played. If there is a song on your favorite disc that you happen to hate, you can simply program it out of the playing cycle. Or if there are songs or movements that you prefer to hear consecutively, you have the option of changing the order of play so that they appear together. The programming function is accomplished in different ways on various players, and so we look at two of the most common methods that manufacturers have implemented for controlling this function. The first consists merely of a button on the front panel marked PROGRAM. To use it, the machine must first be in the stop mode; that is, the disc cannot be in play mode. When PROGRAM is depressed, the display will probably change to indicate that the machine is ready to accept the first track of the program. A typical display will show "P1." If the "+" button is now pressed, the display might show "1 P1." Pressing "+" again would advance the display to "2 P1." Simply continue to press "+" until you reach the track that you want to play first. To store that choice into memory, you will probably need to press the PROGRAM button again. If the display showed "5 P1" when this button was pressed, track five would be the first selection stored in memory. After PROGRAM is pressed, "P2" will appear, indicating that the machine is ready to accept another selection. Using the "+," "−," and PROGRAM keys, one would continue to select tracks until they were satisfied with the contents of the machine's memory. The INDEX key could also be utilized to select a particular movement within a track in the same way that the "+" and "−" keys are used. To finalize the program sequence, press PROGRAM once more. When the PLAY button is next depressed, the machine will play each programmed track in the order in which it was programmed. The skip, scan, pause, and other functions will still work as usual, but they will operate only upon the tracks in memory. If, for instance, you were to program in tracks 1, 3, 4, 7, and 11, and then wished to skip to track 5, you would be unable to. The option for adding selections to the program sequence is, however, available on most machines. By activating the PROGRAM key while the machine is in the stop mode, you will have the option of changing your previously programmed tracks. Be aware that opening up the disc drawer will probably erase the programmed-in values. This is because it is assumed that when you open the drawer, you do so to replace the disc with a new one, so the old programmed values would not be valid. This can be a frustrating feature when the OPEN/CLOSE button is inadvertently hit after a disc has been programmed. The other method by which tracks can be programmed into the player is via a keypad on the machine's front panel. The keypad will resemble that of a Touch-Tone telephone's, although the number of keys may vary from as few as 10 to as many as 20 or more. The keys will be labeled with numbers and are used to select the number of the track you desire to play. So rather than using the "+" and "−" keys to choose tracks, you program directly in the track's number via the keypad. To program track 19 on keypad with only nine numbered keys, you would press PROGRAM, then "1," and "9," and then PROGRAM once again. If the keypad were numbered to 20, the key "19" could be substituted instead of "1" and "9." There may also be a CLEAR key which allows you to clear out all the values stored in the programming memory, as well as other keys which allow the user to check or alter the status of the programmed tracks. Finally, there may be a key whose function is to enter a selection into memory after it has been selected using the keypad or "+" and "−" buttons. This key would make it unnecessary to touch PROGRAM in order to enter a selection. There are a plethora of programming schemes used by manufacturers, certainly too many to discuss fully in the limited space of a book. Most machines are quite adequately and logically labeled, and knowing the basics of programming will allow you to deduce the method by which a particular manufacturer chooses to allow the user to program a machine.

The Repeat Function

Yet another feature of the compact disc player is the repeat function. Touching the button marked REPEAT will cause the machine, upon completion of the last track, to replay all the selections automatically. So rather than the player stopping after the last track of a disc is played, it will reset itself and begin to play from the first track. This is true even if you have chosen to preprogram your selections via the PROGRAM key. In this case, only the programmed tracks would repeat, rather than the entire disc. Many players also have the ability to repeat a single track, or at least allow you to program in a single track and then repeat the program. Both these accomplish the same end. The repeat function usually has a lighted indicator to signal that this function has been activated. Pressing REPEAT when this indicator is on will cause the repeat function to be deactivated and the indicator to turn off.

Shuffle Play

One feature that is becoming increasingly popular among disc player is the SHUFFLE control. As we have seen, it is possible either to program the order in which tracks are played or to let the machine play the tracks in the order in which they were laid down onto the disc. The former method introduces some amount of novelty when listening to the same recording over and over again. A disc may seem almost new in content when different songs appear in varied order. The SHUFFLE key adds even greater novelty by giving the machine the power to decide the order of play. Pressing the SHUFFLE key does just what one might deduce from its name—it shuffles the order in which the tracks will appear. This shuffle is done by random selection, so playing the same disc over several times will produce various patterns of play. If you do not wish to take the time to program in your selections, the SHUFFLE button is an easy alternative. With the advent of multiple-disc players, which can access a number of discs at one time, the shuffle function can turn your machine into an electronic disc jockey.

Front-Panel Outputs

Depending on the design of a particular compact disc player, it may or may not include an output for headphones on the front panel. The reason for this is that headphone outputs require additional circuitry and complicate the design of the entire player. Also, some manufacturers feel that a headphone amplification circuit that is not good enough to keep pace with the quality of digital sound is not worth including. So rather than using a simple but inferior circuit, they choose not to include one at all. Because many receivers and amplifiers that are used with disc players already contain a headphone amplification circuit, the omission of one on the player is not a huge issue.

If a player does have a headphone jack, all that needs to be done to utilize it is to plug the male headphone jack into the machine's receptacle. There will probably be some type of control, either a knob or a slide switch, which controls the output level of the headphone circuit. This control will function just as the volume control of an amplifier does. It will, however, have no effect on the output level of the player's main outputs, which reside on its rear panel.

REAR-PANEL FEATURES

The Main Outputs

Our discussion of the headphone output leads us, logically, to the rear panel of the machine, the area where the disc player's main outputs reside. The main outputs are those of the right and left channels. They carry the same type of information as that of the outputs of a phonograph player or tape deck. They should be connected to the left and right channel inputs of a receiver or amplifier. Be certain not to reverse the left and right channels when this connection is made. Although it would in no way injure either the disc player or the amplifier, it would degrade the sound quality of many stereo setups. Included with the compact disc player will be a specifications sheet which lists the output voltage of the player. Check to make certain that these voltages are within the limits of whatever amplification device to which they are connected. Most players have outputs that range from a low of 0.5 V to a high of 3.0 V. This is just fine for most modern amplifiers. The output voltage level may be adjustable via a potentiometer on the rear of the unit. Turning this screwlike device with a screwdriver will cause the output voltage to vary between its maximum and minimum values, depending on the direction in which it is turned. Alternatively, this control may reside on the player's front panel. In either case, the output level of the player can be matched to that of the other components in the system by adjusting this control. This is beneficial when switching from one component to another, such as from a disc player to a tape deck. If the output voltages of these two devices were different, one would appear louder than the other when listened to at the same volume setting. If both outputs are the same, the output level will remain constant between components. For most players, these will be the only connections that are brought out to the rear panel. Some high-end players do, however, have additional output on their rear panels (Figure 6.2).

Digital Outputs

Some of the newer players have provisions that allow the digital stream of decoded information to be monitored at the rear panel. This PCM data stream is the same one that is decoded after being read by the laser mechanism, demodulated, demultiplexed, and decoded using error-correcting algorithms. It is the serial form of the outputs of the analog-to-digital converters which were the first step in encoding the music into bits. There are a variety of uses for this information, such as digitally altering the signal before it is converted back to analog form, and we look in detail at some of these uses in a later chapter. Unless you have some types of device that accepts digital data, you will not need to connect this output to anything.

Another digital output is that of the subcode information. This is that part of the digitally encoded data which resides on the compact disc and pertains to track number, elapsed time, indexes, and other nonmusical data. Although this subcode data has its uses, it is not of great concern to the average CD buyer. Again, we take a closer look at the uses of subcode in a

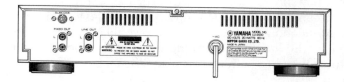

Figure 6.2 Rear panel of a typical disc player. (Courtesy of Yamaha Electronics Corporation, USA.)

later chapter. Like the digital outputs, you need not connect this to anything in order to use the player.

This covers everything that you can plan to find on the outside of the average compact disc player. The features that we have discussed, except for a noted few, are standard fare for even the lowest-priced representatives of this class of audio reproduction devices. As you might expect, there are a gaggle of bells and whistles available to augment these most basic of features, some of which we examine next.

REMOTE CONTROL

Remote controls for disc players—in fact, for almost every type of audio and visual appliance—are ever increasing in number and popularity. A typical remote control fits in the palm of your hand and may duplicate all the functions available on the main control panel of the machine it controls (Figure 6.3). This is quite a feat when you consider that the remote unit normally contains about five times less area that a front panel of main controls. More than anything, the remote control is a convenience, but once you begin to use one, it transforms itself into a necessity. If you understand and can use the functions that reside on the disc player itself, you should have no trouble with the remote. START and STOP, PLAY, PAUSE as

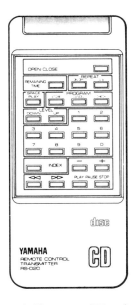

Figure 6.3 Typical remote control. (Courtesy of Yamaha Electronics Corporation, USA.)

well as "+," "−," and all the other functions will work the same way on the remote control as they do normally. Interestingly enough, many players include OPEN/CLOSE on their remote controllers. This is rather odd when you consider that using OPEN/CLOSE is usually either preceded or followed by the replacement of a disc, which necessitates your being at the player. At any rate, the remote controls are all quite handy, and usually function up to 15 or 25 feet from the unit as long as they are pointed within 20 or so degrees of the player's direction. A remote control becomes an even greater necessity when bought in conjunction with a multidisc player.

MULTIDISC PLAYERS

Most of us probably remember a time when record changers were the standard for vinyl disc listening. Who can say that somewhere in the darkest recesses of their basement, garage, or attic, one of these monsters does not lurk. They were handy because they allowed you to stack a number of LPs on the spindle, press the PLAY button, and forget about changing a record for a few hours. The problem with most of these devices was that they usually produced less than acceptable sound quality when judged through more than a $20 pair of loudspeakers. They belong to a time gone by.

Enter the compact disc changer. This device can hold multiple discs and can access and play any selection on any disc with the push of a button. One multidisc player can actually hold up to 240 discs at one time. Try that with anything from a record changer to a jukebox. This class of players has all the functions of normal players, plus a few that are unique to themselves. Let's examine those features now.

The first thing you might wonder about multidisc players is how they store and access several discs at once. Most accomplish this by the use of a disc tray into which can be slid from 5 to 10 discs at a time. The disc tray, complete with CDs, then slides into an opening in much the way that the disc drawer of a conventional player does. The discs are separated by a small distance and are mechanically removed from the tray by an arm in the player and then clamped onto a spindle. The disc selected is then read in the conventional matter by a laser pickup. Most manufacturers sell additional disc holders to augment the one that comes with the unit, so that you could conceivably store all of your discs in these holders and merely switch between them rather that changing individual discs in the holder. There is an EJECT button which performs the same function as the OPEN button of a single-disc player, ejecting the cartridge when you wish to alter or replace its contents. There is also an additional button which allow you to choose which disc you wish to play, and an addition to the front-panel display to indicate which disc in the stack has been selected. Another type of multidisc player does not use a removable cartridge to store its discs. Rather, one unit holds the discs while the control functions are contained in a separate chassis. This type of arrangement usually allows for more discs to be stored and accessed without necessitating a cartridge change. One machine allows up to 60 discs to be loaded into its disc-carrying chassis, and provides expansion chassis that could allow you to store and access up to 240 discs. As you might expect, this type of storage capacity does not come cheaply. Presently, multidisc players cost considerably more than a single-disc player with similar features. This is because of the added complexity not only of the electronics necessary to control such a device, but also the added problems involved in moving the discs in and out of the holding tray so that they can be clamped by the single spindle. The price of these multiplay machines is decreasing rapidly because of the ever-decreasing costs of parts and an increasing market for them.

EXPANDING THE DISC PLAYER'S VERSATILITY

This covers most of the features that will be found on the average disc player, as well as some that may be included on only the most sophisticated of players. The number of functions that a player can perform is virtually unlimited because of the digital nature of the players themselves. If you are at all familiar with computers, you know that such functions as elapsed time and track number display are trivial to implement with modern electronics and programming techniques. Indeed, players that provide digital outputs could conceivably be connected to a home computer, which could display further information about the digitized music. One manufacturer has proposed an interface to home computers which would allow its unit to be controlled by the computer. This type of interface would greatly expand the scope of compact disc player controls. Imagine a multidisc machine that could be programmed by a home computer. A virtually unlimited number of songs could be preprogrammed for parties or general listening. The computer could remember various sequences of tracks that could be played depending on your mood or the type of music you wished to hear. But enough speculation. Suffice it to say that the scope of disc player controls is ever growing and providing new and more convenient features for you, the listener.

WHAT TO LOOK FOR INSIDE THE CHASSIS

No matter how many buttons and switches are on the outside, one must always keep in mind that they merely control what goes on inside the CD player. This seems obvious, but the quality of a disc player should never be judged on its front-panel alone. There are too many differences in the design factors which go into a machine that are not evident from its looks. A black anodized front panel with a slick control layout does not always indicate that a machine is of high-quality construction. To judge a player properly, you must delve into its innards and explore the technology that drives it.

Oversampling: Better S/N Values

Perhaps the most widely publicized specification of the compact disc features is whether it uses single, double, or quadruple oversampling. Some people may deduce incorrectly that a machine which uses double oversampling has twice the bandwidth of a nonoversampling machine, and that a quadruple oversampling scheme will yield four times the bandwidth. From the discussion of this technique in Chapter 3, you should already know that this is incorrect. Oversampling increases only the signal-to-noise ratio of a player, not the bandwidth. The maximum bandwidth that the best disc player can hope to produce is a theoretical 22.05 kHz, and even that bandwidth can never actually be attained. Any frequencies above that 22.05 kHz cutoff point arise from aliasing and are never desirable.

The evolution of oversampling has come in stages. The first machines that were introduced onto the market had a 44.1-kHz sampling clock. They also employed a single 14-bit digital-to-analog converter, and their signal-to-noise ratios were what one might expect from such a machine, in the range 85 to 95 dB. Compared to the average or even above-average phonograph or tape deck, this was exceptional. When the second generation of machines hit the market, many of them had kept the same 44.1-kHz clock, but many had gone to double or quadruple oversampling as a way to improve the S/N value. Some manufacturers deemed this unnecessary, since they were already attaining such impressive S/N values with their present sampling clocks and there were still a host of improvements to be made in other areas of disc player design. Those manufacturers who did introduce models employing oversampling had the added advantage of not only decreasing their noise figures, but of using digital rather than analog filtering. Signal-to-noise ratios for oversampling machines may range from 90 dB to over 105 dB. As you know, the S/N value depends on more than just what type of sampling scheme is used, so one finds that a manufacturer with a 44.1 kHz clock may out perform another with a 176.4 kHz clock, depending on the design of the respective system. If all other parameters are the same, however, the oversampling method will produce a greater S/N value than that of the standard sampling rate.

Digital Versus Analog Filtering: The Issue of Phase Shift

As long as we are on the subject of oversampling, we might as well look into the question of digital versus analog output filters. In actuality, there is no real question, since everyone uses an analog low-pass filter on the output of their machine. Not all, however, put a digital filter before this stage. Digital filtering and oversampling are synonymous. Although the two functions can be performed separately in laboratory-quality machines specifically designed for such a purpose, digital filtering is never seen without oversampling in commercial CD players. In fact, they are the same process. As you will remember, oversampling decreases the noise level in a signal, also called the noise floor, and decreases the amplitude of harmonics above the Nyquist frequency (22.05 kHz). This allow an analog filter with a very gentle roll-off to clean up harmonics of higher frequencies without introducing phase shift into the audio frequencies. If digital filtering is not employed, an analog low-pass filter must be used. There are several disadvantages to this. If the filter has a very sharp cutoff region, harmonics above the audio band will be negated, but only at the expense of introducing phase distortion into that same region. If a filter with gentle roll-off is used, harmful harmonics will creep into the audio band, causing both harmonic and intermodulation distortion. Since digitally filtered and oversampled systems also benefit from higher S/N values, the allure of digital filtering becomes even greater. Again, a machine with a good analog output filter can attain some impressive distortion figures, but it cannot compete with a similarly well-designed oversampling and digitally filtered system.

Dual or Single D/As: Two D/As Are Better than One

There is yet another permutation of the seemingly endless combination of features found inside compact disc players. A machine may have a single digital-to-analog converter that works double time for both right and left channels, or it may have two D/A converters, one dedicated to each channel. As you know, although data are read off a compact disc in a single stream, they are ultimately demultiplexed into both a left and a right channel, after which they are converted back to stereo sound. A single D/A converter is capable of performing this function for both channels because the D/A can do its conversion at a very fast rate, much higher than 88.2 kHz, the combined data rate of both channels. If a single D/A is used, digital information, after being decoded and error corrected, is passed sequentially to the converter. Both channels cannot be reconverted back to analog form at the same time, and so there is some time lag between the two channels. The sound emanating from one speaker will be slightly delayed compared to that from the other. Also, a quadruple oversampled system would need to use a single D/A capable of doing 352,000 conversions per second, not to mention the sophisticated multiplexing circuit that would be needed. At such speeds, A/D converter prices rise considerably, and it is sometimes less expensive to use two slow D/As than a single ultrafast unit.

When dual D/As are used, time lag, also called *phase shift*, can be completely eliminated. Using two D/As, the right and left channels can be converted simultaneously back to an analog signal and then output to an amplifier at the same time. There is no need to switch D/A's output from one preamp section to another, nor is there a need for a single D/A to work any faster than the 44.1-kHz sampling rate dictates.

There is a great controversy as to whether phase change is audible to the listener. Certainly, a great enough phase change will be audible, but the slight change introduced by CD players falls into an area of uncertainty. Some say that the change does affect the quality of listening; others say that a small change cannot be heard. Ultimately, it is up to you, the listener, to decide if this feature is important. The problem with trying to decide whether or not dual D/As make an audible difference is that there are so many subtle differences between players that are caused by other components that narrowing down the cause to dual D/As as opposed to a single D/A is next to impossible. Often, this difference can only be seen on an oscilloscope, and so the question again arises as to whether this makes an audible difference.

Besides negating phase changes, dual D/As have another selling point. It is possible when switching a single D/A between two channels that small amounts of noise may be introduced into the system by the act of switching. Again, this may be a very small amount of noise, or none at all, but depending on the design of a disc player, this can be detrimental to the overall sound of the system.

Digital-to-Analog Converters: How Many Bits are Enough?

If you happen to have decided between all the aforementioned features, you are still not out of the woods. Now you must ask yourself whether you need a 14- or a 16-bit D/A converter. In previous chapters we discussed oversampling and digital filtering as they applied to a 14-bit converter, and how such tricks could actually make up for 12 dB worth of signal-to-noise ratio which were lost when a 14-bit converter was used. But now, partially because of the popularity of compact disc players, the price and availability of 16-bit converters has made them an attractive option to their 14-bit counterparts.

You may wonder why a 16-bit converter is needed if a 14-bit device can be made to mimic its actions. Again, extra accuracy is the answer. A 16-bit D/A does not need oversampling to attain the full S/N capability of the compact disc standard. If, however, oversampling is used, a 16-bit converter can attain even more staggering levels of musical clarity. The same trick that allows a 14-bit converter to increase the signal-to-noise figure by 15 dB also works for the 16-bit converter, and since its maximum S/N value is already so great, the extra boost is receives from oversampling and digital filtering makes it virtually untouchable as far as S/N goes. Indeed, there are probably few audio amplifiers that can claim as high a signal-to-noise figure as that of a 16-bit digitally filtered disc player, so the question arises as to whether this benefit makes it past the amplifier to your ears. Like most other fine points of audio, this is a question that individual listeners must decide for themselves. The benefit is quite obvious on a laboratory measurement instrument such as a spectrum analyzer, but whether this carries over to your amplifier, speakers, and ears is another matter.

Another advantage of the 16-bit machines is an expansion of dynamic range. You may recall that a 14-bit converter throws away the 2 least significant bits of the original 16-bit word when it performs its function. In effect, all the information in those 2 bits is lost, as is some of the finer detail of the digitized music. Some of the information contained in those 2 bits is noise, and again, some might argue that it is all noise, but in point of fact there is some information to be gleaned from those bits. If oversampling is used along with a better D/A, some of this information can be salvaged, so the quality of the music reproduced will be heightened and the dynamic range will be expanded. If you listen to very loud passages of music such as rock, you may not notice this extra measure of clarity. If, conversely, your delight is soft passages of classical music, you might very well benefit from the added detail.

The same arguments hold true for the new generation of disc players which have 18-bit D/A converters. These use digital filtering and noise subtraction techniques on full 16-bit samples to produce 18 bits of accuracy, seemingly more information than is stored in the 16-bit samples. These machines are truly beginning to use digital filtering methods to their full advantage, but whether or not these gains will be audible to the average listener is still an unanswered question.

Multi- and Single-Spot Lasers: Which Is Better?

There are two types of laser tracking systems, the single- and multispot systems. The single-spot system is discussed elsewhere in this book. A single laser beam is used to both read the pits and lands from the compact disc and to provide control signals to maintain tracking and focus (Figure 6.4). If the beam deviates from the center of a track, the amount of reflected light will change, and this change can be registered and used to realign the optical tracking mechanism. Similarly, an out-of-focus condition will be detected by specially designed components, and the focus of the beam can then be corrected. Players may use a single laser beam to perform all these functions, or they may split the laser beam into three separate beams by using a prism. The three-beam method uses the center beam to read the pits and lands, while the two other beams scan in front of and behind the main beam. These two peripheral beams are used to provide focusing and tracking information. Since these beams extend in front of and behind the main beam, any misalignment of the laser will cause a large change in their

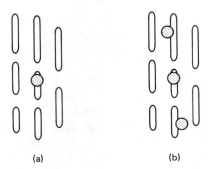

(a)   (b)

Figure 6.4 A single-spot laser both reads the disc information and is used to correct for tracking and focusing (a). A three-spot laser's center beam is used to read information, while the two outside beams are used to control tracking and focusing (b).

alignment, larger than would be noted in a single-beam arrangement. For this reason, a multibeam pickup can react more quickly to small changes in the pickup's geometry and so track a disc more effectively. Both multi- and single-beam players abound, and manufacturers of both claim that their method is the most advanced. As with most design philosophies, a badly implemented multibeam system may not out perform a well-designed single-beam setup.

Isolated Circuitry: Combating Electrical Noise

Another thing to consider when you are planning to invest several hundred dollars in a compact disc player is whether or not it uses multiple power supplies to supply current to its circuitry, and whether or not the circuitry is electrically isolated.

The circuitry inside a CD player can be divided into two major parts, the analog side and the digital side. The digital parts of a machine are those parts which read the disc, handle digital data, and process and error correct the data. The analog components are those that amplify the D/A'd signal and output it to either a preamplifier or a headphone amplification circuit. There is an extremely good reason why these two types of circuits should be kept as separate as possible, one that has its basis in electromagnetic wave theory. One device, the digital-to-analog converter, bridges these two gaps, since it embodies aspects of both types of circuitry.

Parasitic Noise. If you were to look inside almost any electronic device, you would see various components, such as microchips, capacitors, resistors, and many other strange-looking and strange-sounding devices. These devices are usually mounted on a fiberglass board called a *circuit board*. The inputs and outputs of the devices are electrically connected by small strips of copper which are etched into the circuit board when it is manufactured. In this way the individual components do not have to be wired together by hand since all the connections are present when the board is manufactured. The components need only be placed in their correct positions and fastened onto the board in order to function. The connecting strips of copper, called *traces*, may sometimes extend for several inches, and in doing so will act as small antennas which radiate and pick up all types of noise (Figure 6.5). Obviously, the main function of the traces is to interconnect various components on the circuit card. But just as a vacuum cleaner may cause interference on a television or radio even though it is running in another room or house, traces will emit and receive electrical noise, and in doing so will reduce the overall signal-to-noise ratio of the system. Digital circuits are especially prone to this antenna effect. The signals that travel on the digital traces may contain signals of a very high data rate. The serial stream that issues from a laser pickup runs at over 1 million bits per second. Since the data stream is digital, it has the appearance of a square wave. This square wave has an amazingly high bandwidth and will produce harmonics of an even higher frequency than itself. This type of high-frequency energy radiates much more than the relatively low frequency audio signals that travel along the analog traces.

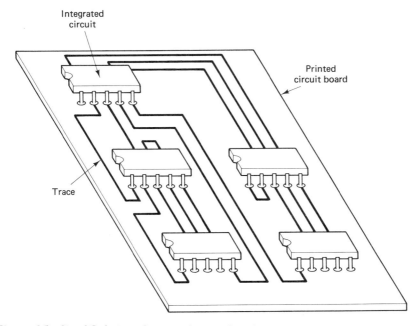

Figure 6.5 Simplified view of a printed circuit board. Traces that run parallel to each other can leak noise, as can long or looped traces.

What is worse is that these noise signals will leak into the power supply which provides electricity to every component on the circuit board. When this happens, every component on the board will be affected by this noise rather than just the devices with antennalike traces. This is very bad news for the analog circuits since their main job is to amplify signals, and they will amplify noise just as well as an audio signal. The digital circuits will be similarly affected, and the electrical noise that is transmitted to each device may cause errors in tracking, data buffering, timing, and error correction. In short, every circuit in the disc player can be adversely affected by spurious noise.

To combat this problem, some manufacturers have taken steps that have long been employed by other electronic designers. They have isolated their digital and analog circuits and added multiple power supplies to each isolated unit. Isolating a circuit means that it is physically separated from the circuits around it. In the case of digital audio, isolation entails either moving all the digital circuits to one area on the circuit card or providing separate circuit cards for both digital and analog sections. Care must also be taken when the circuit card traces are laid out to ensure that they are kept to a minimum distance. This practice by itself will cut down on some noise paths, but if both sections were to use the same power supplies, noise could still travel from one section to another. It is for this reason that several power supplies may be incorporated into one disc player, one for the digital section and one for the analog. The digital section is often broken down even further into its component sections, each of which is isolated and given its own power supplies. It is possible to find CD players that use five separate power supplies for different sections of their circuitry.

Even with all of these precautions, one must still eventually connect all the isolated systems together so that they can pass information between them. If this is done by conventional means, with wires or traces, some of the benefits of isolation are lost. For the same noise that propagated between sections can propagate along these interconnections. There is a way to isolate fully all the sections, and this is by the use of optoisolators.

Optoisolators.   As their name implies, optoisolators use a form of light, rather than wire, to interconnect two sections of circuitry. If a conventional wire is used as a connector, it will also function as a loop antenna. This will both transmit and pick up noise. The optoisolator breaks this connection. One side of the isolator is connected to the input side, the other to the output. Electrical pulses are converted into light by one side of the pickup, and then reconverted back into electricity on the other side (Figure 6.6). Since there is no physical connection between the transmitter and the receiver inside the optoisolator, the antenna loop is broken and noise will not be as easily transmitted between the two sections. Still, noise which was present that was not due to an antenna effect will be transmitted,

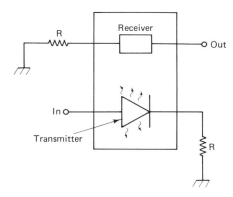

Figure 6.6 Optoisolator. The transmitter is stimulated by the input and transmits light to the receiver, which converts it back to electrical impulses. The entire process is carried out inside a single chip.

although interaction between the various power supplies will be eliminated (Figure 6.7).

As you can see, there is more to constructing a disc player than merely tossing components together. Correct electrical design and layout are an integral part of a good-sounding machine. Like some of the other points that we have examined, electrical isolation provides one means to defeat the effects of noise in a system, and can substantially improve the S/N value of a system over that of an unisolated counterpart.

ERROR CORRECTION

In Chapter 5 we discussed various error-correction schemes and, in particular, the CIRC standard for compact discs. From that discussion you should remember that although the cross-interleaved Reed–Solomon code is capable of correcting a large number of the types of errors common to CDs, not every manufacturer takes full advantage of this capability. Some manufacturers will merely mute a sample with errors, others will hold the value of the previous sample, and still others will use linear interpolation to average out the error. Most use a combination of these methods, depending on the severity and length of a detected error or errors.

Errors will always occur during the playing of a CD, so it is very important that you are aware of the type of error correction that your player uses. Unfortunately, there is no standard by which CD players are judged for their error-correcting capability, so there are no specifications that can be used when comparing machines. Be aware that a machine with mediocre error correction may introduce strange effects into the music it reproduces.

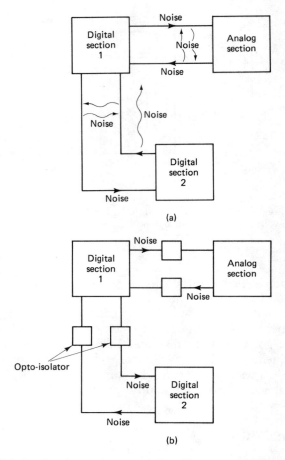

Figure 6.7 If digital and analog sections are separated but not isolated, noise will travel along the signal path and between leads (a). Inserting optoisolators reduces the amount of parasitic noise between sections (b).

In a later section we discuss just how you can perform your own error-correction test. At least one manufacturer has included, along with the typical specifications of signal-to-noise ratio, frequency response, and the like, a spec on how large an imperfection can be corrected by their player. This is the first step in realizing a standard by which error-correction schemes can be judged.

PLAYER CONSTRUCTION

It may sound strange, but the cabinet that houses the complex circuitry and technology inside compact disc players can have just as much to do with the quality of sound as the components themselves. The newest players out on the market have attacked this area with both advertising hype and actions. The product of these efforts have a parallel in the world of analog audio reproduction, in particular, the turntable.

Is there anyone who has not experienced that dreadful moment when they bump a turntable while it is playing and send a stylus screeching across the record's vinyl? How about slamming a door or stamping on a floor and having the stylus skip or bounce? If you own an average turntable, chances are that you have done one of these things. It is possible to affect the path of the tonearm because the turntable platter is not completely isolated from its surroundings. Vibrations can be transmitted which cause a stylus to mistrack the record groove. The same is true, to a lesser extent, of the compact disc player. The laser pickup, just like a tonearm, is sensitive to vibrations and can be affected by its environment. A book falling on a table on which the player rests may cause the CD to skip, and although the disc itself will not be damaged, the quality of sound will be. Vibrations, be they from an intense drum beat or a slamming door, can cause errors and mistracking just as a dirty disc or misaligned laser can. Even a spinning disc can be made unsteady by a careless brush against the player's chassis. Disc players have drawn a lesson from turntables and have begun to isolate their machines acoustically from the outside world. One way this is accomplished is by adding special insulating feet to the bottom of the player. These feet are usually large solid rubber cups that absorb mild shocks. They may also have some type of air suspension, much like shock absorbers, and so will lend an even greater measure of protection to the player.

Another isolating point is the disc drawer and laser transport. These assemblies can be isolated from the rest of the casing with rubber bushings so that any vibrations that make it past the insulating feet can be further damped. These assemblies may also be made of stiff materials which resist flexing and vibration. In fact, the outer casing of the player is complex in its own right and may be designed such that it too resists vibrations that are induced by the sound which it itself produces. Some manufacturers claim that conventional chassis will flex under certain conditions and may vibrate in sympathy with certain frequencies of sound. Like a tuning fork, these chassis can be more sensitive to some frequencies than others, especially low frequencies. Special chassis designs can reduce these sympathetic vibrations and therefore decrease disc errors.

All these points of fine tuning can and do reduce disc errors and may indeed tip the scales between two players matched electronically but not mechanically. Like error correction, there is no unit of comparison that facilitates direct comparison of two chassis or isolating mechanisms. So, as is often the case, the buyer must take the manufacturer's word that a particular feature functions as it is described. To be sure, isolating a player from outside vibration is a good idea. Tapping a badly isolated player usually causes it to skip, while a well-isolated machine will resist such jolts. Every unit will skip if it is sufficiently disturbed, but considering the delicate nature of most audio equipment, this is to be expected. So it is the degree of isolation that should be taken into account when comparing disc players on this basis.

CONCLUSIONS

Well, that is about it for the differences between players. Summed up, there cannot be more than a few dozen comparable features, and perhaps a few dozen more incomparable ones. Your head is probably spinning trying to decide whether you need a quadruple oversampled, digitally filtered machine with dual 18-bit D/A converters, optoisolators, multiple power supplies, and a supercomputer to handle error correction. In this section we have discussed why one disc player may cost $100, and another one, $1000. We have delved beyond flashy exteriors into the realm of electronics and digital theory. You can see that there may be much more inside a machine than is indicated by its front panel. There may also be much less. It is sometimes difficult to tell whether some of the features that we have discussed here are actually implemented or even implemented correctly inside a machine. A knowledgeable salesperson can go far in filling you in on some of these points. Most manufacturers who take the time to engineer a good compact disc player will also advertise their endeavors. It is up to you, the buyer, to sort out truth from hype and decide which features you need or can afford. Of course, what all the aforementioned practices are geared toward is improving the sound of a player. And these improvements are often echoed by the manufacturers' specifications or tests performed by competent audio magazines. If you do not wish to sort through all the design features incorporated in a player, it may behoove you to check the specifications for an indication of a machine's quality. In Chapter 7 we learn how to read and interpret these specification, as well as how to use a product report to our advantage.

7

MANUFACTURERS' SPECIFICATIONS AND PRODUCT REVIEWS

What separates one disc player from another? Sure, you can look at their front panels and compare brand A to brand B. But front panels do not tell about the most important aspect of a player—how it sounds. And that really is one of the major allures of the compact disc—its amazing sound. Some will say that all CD players sound alike. Without question, these people are incorrect. Every disc player adds its own color to the music that it reproduces. This fact should not come as a shock to anyone who has ever auditioned a pair of loudspeakers, a receiver, a phonograph player, or any type of audio equipment. They all shape the electrical impulses that pass through them on their way to becoming sound. Even the wires from a receiver to a loudspeaker can change the quality of music. And these differences are not audible only to the most discerning listeners. Almost anyone can hear one or all of them, and the same holds true for disc players. One type of machine may accent bass, another treble or midrange. Some may impart a more realistic stereo image than others, and some may simply have a subtle yet audible quality which defies verbal description. These differences arise from the internal architecture of players, which, as one might expect, varies from manufacturer to manufacturer. Some of these qualities are revealed not only by listening to a player, but by testing how well its components work together.

In previous chapters we have looked at both the theory and implementation involved in the digitization and reproduction of sound. As we saw in

Chapter 6, there are many variations in the implementation of the compact disc standard. Not every so-called "improvement" in hardware yields a proportionate improvement in sound quality. One way to form opinions about different players, and indeed, one of the few ways to perform comparisons, is to compare those qualities that can be tested on the lab bench with unbiased test equipment. In this chapter we take a look at what manufacturers' specifications describe and how to compare them, as well as how to read and interpret a compact disc player product review.

As you may know, manufacturers employ a somewhat standard set of tests which are performed on every type of audio gear. Of course, every manufacturer wishes to show their equipment in the best possible light, so their specifications must be carefully scrutinized to determine both their validity and meaning. This is certainly not to say that manufacturers falsify their tests, but the manner in which a test is performed can have a substantial impact on the figures it returns. Product reviews, which are carried out by a number of magazines, can be quite helpful when sorting through the myriad of standards—which, unlike their name, can be anything but uniform.

SPECIFICATIONS: WHAT DO THEY MEAN?

The first item that you are likely to encounter when reading a product review is a list of the manufacturer's specifications. This, then, seems like a logical place to start our examination. There are many types of measurements that are made to determine the limitations and strengths of various machines. Some, such as total harmonic distortion, are made for almost every type of audio equipment. Other measurements, such as the one for wow and flutter, are restricted to such devices as tape recorders and turntables (Table 7.1). Compact disc player manufacturers use both of the aforementioned standards, as well as a few that are unique to the digital

TABLE   7.1   Typical Specifications of a Compact Disc Player and Turntable

	Compact Disc	12-inch LP
Frequency range	20 Hz–20 kHz	30 Hz–20 kHz
Dynamic range	> 90 dB	< 55 dB (1 kHz)
S/N ratio	> 90 dB	~ 60 dB
Channel separation	> 90 dB	25–35 dB
Harmonic distortion	< 0.01%	0.2%
Wow and flutter	0	0.03%
Playing time	60 min	20 min/side

Source: NAP Consumer Electronics Corp.

world. One of the most often quoted of these specifications is total harmonic distortion, and this is the first that we examine.

Total Harmonic Distortion: A Moderate Source

Having read and understood the preceding chapters, you should be able to figure out for yourself the meaning of *total harmonic distortion* (THD). We know what harmonics are: They are the overtones associated with fundamental frequencies which give a musical instrument its particular sound and character. These harmonics are located at multiples of the fundamental frequency, and their amplitudes relative to this fundamental frequency should be maintained when they are recorded or reproduced. If a note with a fundamental frequency of 1 kHz has a harmonic at 2 kHz, which is 10 dB below the fundamental, and another harmonic at 3 kHz, which is attenuated by 15 dB relative to the fundamental, these ratios should be maintained when the note is reproduced. If, due to the design of a recording device, the harmonics' amplitudes are changed to 12 and 16 dB, respectively, the note will be distorted and will not sound the same as when it was originally played. This is one form of harmonic distortion (Figure 7.1).

An alternative form of harmonic distortion is incurred when harmonics are added to a single, pure tone. Again, because of the design of amplification and reproduction circuits, harmonics that did not exist in the original music may be created and therefore change the quality of sound for the worse. As an example, consider a 1-kHz tone without harmonics which is first recorded, then reproduced by an audio device such as a tape deck. The electronics of the tape recorder can add harmonics to this tone even though they did not exist in the original source. Obviously, these harmonics are not added by design, but rather by the design's limitations. Harmonics

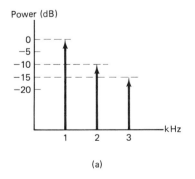
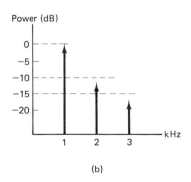

Figure 7.1 Harmonic distortion. If the ratio of a fundamental tone to its harmonics is as depicted in (a), these ratios should be maintained when the signal is reproduced. If these ratios are not maintained, distortion is introduced (b).

may arise at 3 kHz, 5 kHz, 7 kHz, and so on. If this is the case, the original sine wave will start to take on the attributes of a square wave, which, as you know, is composed of odd harmonics of its fundamental frequency (Figure 7.2). The amplitude of these harmonics relative to that of the original tone is the measure of the harmonic distortion at 1 kHz. Various types of such distortion will occur at differing frequencies. Because of the imperfect nature of all electronic devices, there will be a variation in this distortion which is dependent on the frequency at which it is measured. This is to say that the distortion at 1 kHz may differ from that at 15 kHz. Since it is impractical to quote distortion figures at every possible frequency, manufacturers normally measure and report on harmonic distortion over a range of frequencies. This figure is the total harmonic distortion (THD).

Harmonic distortion is measured with the help of a disc that has encoded on it pure tones without added harmonics. The disc is played on a disc player and the power of this fundamental tone is compared to the combined power of all the harmonics. The resulting figure is the total harmonic distortion at the fundamental frequency. This procedure is carried out at a number of frequencies so that the total harmonic distortion over a stated frequency band can be ascertained. A typical specification might read: 0.05% THD from 20 to 20,000 Hz. This means that nowhere in the stated frequency band (20 Hz to 20 kHz) would harmonics be created whose total power exceeded 0.05% of the fundamental's. It also means that the original harmonics of this tone which were present when the music was recorded will not be distorted by more than this figure. Although this spec may seem rather easy to understand and interpret, the nature of the compact disc player introduces some twists that must be considered when looking at this specification. In particular, the test tones will sometimes interact with the sampling frequency so that each modulates the other.

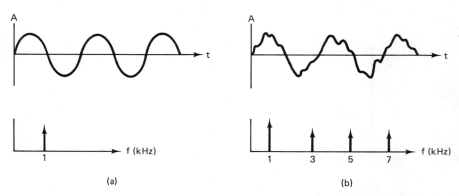

Figure 7.2 Harmonic distortion. A 1-kHz tone before it is recorded, showing its clean spectrum (a). After recording, the odd harmonics will distort the shape of the sine wave (b).

These artificial components appear to be harmonic distortion when in fact they are not. This can lead to deceptively high figures for THD at frequencies above 10 kHz.

Intermodulation Distortion: A Severe Source

There is another type of distortion which is potentially much more destructive than harmonic distortion. It is called *intermodulation distortion* (IM). IM distortion occurs when an audio device attempts to reproduce two different tones at the same moment in time. If, for instance, an amplifier tries to reproduce both a 2-kHz tone and a 700-Hz tone at the same time, these tones, along with by-products, may actually be output. The by-products arise from the same phenomenon that makes frequency modulation possible. You may recall that in an FM encoder, two frequencies are mixed to produce a composite waveform. Later, this composite is split apart to recover the original audio information. This process occurs inadvertently in other types of audio equipment. In the aforementioned example, a 2.7-kHz component will arise from the 2 kHz + 700 Hz term, while another 1.3-kHz component will arise from the 2 kHz − 700 Hz term. These extra components appear because the two fundamental tones, 2 kHz and 700 Hz, may try to modulate each other in much the same way as an FM carrier is modulated by its baseband frequency (Figure 7.3). The important aspect of

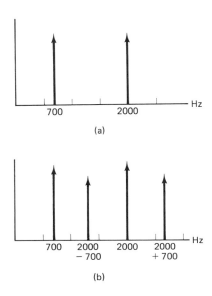

Figure 7.3 Intermodulation distortion. Initially, two tones have no interaction (a). After they have been recorded and reproduced, the two tones mix to form new frequency components (b).

all of this is not how intermodulation distortion occurs, but rather that its products are not harmonically related to either of the original tones. 2.7 kHz and 1.3 kHz are unrelated harmonically to either 2 kHz or 700 Hz. This is very bad, since they will not be masked by any of the true harmonics of 2 kHz and 700 Hz. So whereas harmonic distortion creates or alters harmonics, intermodulation distortion actually introduces new tones into the original music. These tones will be considerably more annoying than harmonic distortion, which is why the IM distortion figure is so important. In fact, intermodulation distortion is much like the distortion produced due to aliasing. Remember that tones which alias down from above $F_s/2$, the Nyquist frequency, are not related harmonically to the tones in the audio band, and so, like those produced by intermodulation distortion, are not masked by related harmonics. These two phenomena can be difficult to separate from each other, so one cannot be certain if what is mistaken for intermodulation distortion actually arises from aliasing, or vice versa. In either case, the effects are unwanted, so a good machine will have low numbers for this specification.

Like the total harmonic distortion specification, intermodulation distortion is usually quoted for a specified frequency band, and the maximum amount of distortion in this band will be given. IM distortion is measured by playing a test disc which has two tones recorded on it, neither of which has any harmonic interaction. Any intermodulation distortion would then appear as the sum and difference of these two tones. If the two tones were known to have been recorded at 10 and 12 kHz, the power of these two tones would be compared to the power of the resulting 2-kHz component which appears because of intermodulation distortion. The 22-kHz component is ignored because it is above the cutoff frequency of the analog low-pass filter. The ratio of the power of the two original tones to the power of the intermodulation component is expressed in decibels as the IM distortion figure.

Frequency Response: Bounds of the Musical Highs and Lows

After all the discussions we have had about Nyquist frequency, sampling rate, aliasing, and oversampling, the frequency response of a compact disc player should certainly have been embedded into your memory. During conversion from analog to digital, the audio signal is band limited. This means that there are certain upper and lower limits to the frequencies that are recorded on the compact disc. Theoretically, these limits are 0 Hz, referred to as dc, and 22.5 kHz. Because the human ear can not hear this full range of sound, and because of the irregularities encountered at the extreme limits of this range, frequency response is usually quoted from 2 to 20 Hz at the lower limit, up to 20,000 Hz at the upper limit.

By frequency response, we mean the band of frequencies that can be faithfully reproduced with a minimum of attenuation. Along with the frequency response comes a number expressed in decibels which has to do with variations in amplitude of the frequencies in the stated band. Think back for a moment to Chapter 2, where we discussed the meaning of ripple. To refresh your memory, ripple is the variation in gain in the passband of a filter. The figures that are stated as part of the frequency response are the maximum amount of ripple expressed in units of decibels. Suppose that a manufacturer claimed a frequency response of 5 to 20,000 Hz ± 0.3 dB. This tells you that between 5 Hz and 20 kHz, the disc player will not alter the true amplitude of any frequency component by more than 0.3 dB. A 2-kHz sine wave whose maximum value is 4.5 V would, at most, be altered by 0.158 V. Outside these upper and lower frequency limits, the amplitude of the signal will be attenuated more significantly. By itself, this number actually tells you very little about the actual frequency response. That statement seems surprising, but consider this. All that you learn from reading the frequency response is what the maximum corruption will be. You are not told if some frequencies are more distorted than others. You also are not told about what occurs beyond 20 kHz and below 20 Hz, and for many audiophiles, these are important areas. Indeed, the low note of a pipe organ can be but a few hertz, and a crashing cymbal can have important harmonics above 20 kHz. You will get a better idea of the overall frequency response of a system by looking at a graph of its frequency response. In this manner, you can physically see where the peaks and valleys are, and judge the extreme high- and low-frequency response for yourself. In fact, virtually all compact disc players have quite excellent frequency responses. In fact, it is unusual to see even a low-priced player whose frequency response will not match that of a high-quality amplifier.

Dynamic Range: A Measure of the Loudest and Softest Sounds

We touched on the term *dynamic range* when we encountered A/D conversion. Dynamic range is the ratio of the smallest detectable signal to the largest reproducible one. As you may remember, dynamic range is, for the most part, dependent on the number of bits in the original analog-to-digital conversion. This theoretical maximum is around 110 dB, but in practice this limit means very little. Noise often seeps into the signal path of a compact disc player, and this, along with other design considerations, can lower the dynamic range by a considerable amount. Although a decrease in dynamic range will not affect loud sounds, it may actually mask quiet ones. The dynamic range figure is, then, a measure of just how well the disc player can reproduce both loud and soft passages of music. Dynamic range is measured in relation to the lowest possible audible sound of a particular test instrument. For human beings this is the threshold of hearing of the human ear. The dynamic ranges of several sounds have been listed in Table 7.2. As you can see, the dynamic range that is required to reproduce a space launch is far beyond that of any conventional audio system. This is, no doubt, a good thing.

If you think back to the process of A/D conversion, you will remember that any signal above the maximum input signal is converted to a full-scale number consisting of all binary 1's. For the rocket launch, any sounds beyond the dynamic range of the CD player are all mapped to the same full-scale binary value. They will sound the same because they are represented by the same number. A similar thing happens for signals below the level of audibility, except that these are mapped to the lowest binary value, all 0's. These sounds are forever lost to the digitization process.

Note that with a big enough amplifier and stout enough speakers, the claxon of a jack hammer can be reproduced by a CD player with dynamic range to spare. Typical dynamic range figures vary from about 90 dB to over 100 dB. Compared to the average record player's dynamic range of less than 60 dB, this is quite an impressive figure, and is higher than that of many audio amplifiers. Unlike distortion figures, the larger dynamic range numbers are the better ones.

TABLE 7.2 Sound Intensity in Decibles of Various Events

dB	Sound Source
175	Space rocket
160	Wind tunnel
140	Jet plane taking off
130	Machine gun
120	Propeller plane taking off
100	Subway train
90	Rivet hammer (20 m distance)
80	Vacuum cleaner
70	Crowded street
60	Conversation (1 m)
50	Quiet restaurant
40	Residential area at midnight
30	Movie theater without audience
20	Whispering (2 m)
10	Breathing
0	Lowest audible level (0.0002 μbar)

Source: Pioneer Electronics (USA) Inc.

Stereo Separation: Keeping the Left
and Right Channels Apart

Stereo separation is one of the least discussed specifications of most audio equipment. It is defined as the separation between channels, measured in decibels. In fact, it is a measure of how much the right and left channels of a stereo system interact, that is, how much of the right channel's signal seeps into the left's, and vice versa. Since the object of stereo reproduction is to separate right and left channels, you may imagine that this figure is quite important. Separation has a lot to do with a listener's ability to place particular instrument in space. If a band is recorded with an electric guitar playing to the right of the stage, a saxophone playing to the left, and a singer in the middle, when they are reproduced they should maintain their spatial positions. If left and right channels are mixed, the instruments to the left and right will seem to move toward the center of the listening area, in between the speakers. This is detrimental to the illusion of stereo. The stereo separation figure measures this leakage in decibels. Higher figures point to the fact that little leakage occurs, while smaller figures are less desirable. Like some of the other specifications, separation is also dependent on the frequency at which it is measured. A graph of stereo separation is rarely provided by a manufacturer, so the quoted figure is usually established for a 1-kHz reference signal. This signal is played exclusively on one channel, and then the opposing channel is monitored for any sign of the 1-kHz wave. The differences in amplitude between these two signals is converted to decibels, and this figure is quoted. Figures from 70 dB to over 100 dB are the norm for compact disc players, while most fall in the 85 dB range.

Wow and Flutter: Measuring the Unmeasurable

The terms *wow* and *flutter* are almost meaningless for compact disc players. They refer to measurements which are standards for turntables and tape decks, but because of the way disc players are designed, rarely occur. Wow refers to the amount of low-frequency oscillation that occurs physically in the rotational speed of a record or tape. As you may know, a standard LP revolves at 33F rpm. The turntable is driven by a motor whose speed may be closely monitored and held steady, but will always vary somewhat. If the speed of the platter changes slowly, this is called wow. Wow introduces slow variations in the pitch of a reproduced signal. Flutter is similar to wow, but occurs at a higher frequency. This will cause faster variations in the platter's speed and hence faster changes in pitch. The rotational speed of a compact disc may change while it is playing, so you might expect that the rate at which samples are passed to the D/A converter would vary. This does not occur because samples are buffered before they are passed on to the D/A. This buffer is an electronic memory into which the data from the disc must pass. A number of samples will fill up this memory before it begins to output them to the D/A. In this way, a reserve of samples are always available. If the disc revolves too slowly, the buffer begins to empty. As soon as this emptying is sensed, the disc motor speeds up. If the disc spins too quickly, the buffer will start to fill up, and the disc can be slowed to the proper speed. While these fluctuations occur, samples can be drawn from the buffer at a constant speed so that it appears to the listener as if there are no fluctuations at all. In fact, since the time at which the buffer outputs data to the D/A is controlled by a very accurate clock, wow and flutter, which are present at the buffer's input, are not present at the output. For this reason most manufacturers state that wow and flutter are below measurable limits, as they are. A proposed test standard would require that a steady tone be encoded on a test disc, and variations in this tone when it is replayed would measure the wow and flutter of the disc player (Figure 7.4).

Line-Level Differences: The Final Output of a Player

Although stereo channels may be recorded at one level onto a disc, they may be replayed at differing levels. A particular player may emphasize the right channel over the left, or vice versa. This difference can be measured by playing a disc containing two tones of equal amplitude on each channel, and then measuring the difference in these amplitudes when they exit the player. This difference can be compensated using the balance control of an amplifier.

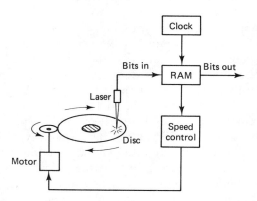

Figure 7.4 Because bits that are read from the discs are buffered, they can be clocked out of the RAM at a constant rate while the rotational speed of the disc is adjusted.

More Specifications

For the most part, this covers all the specifications that are likely to be thrown at you during the course of a disc player review. Although manufacturers may vary their methods of testing, they do state the conditions of every test, and most adhere to a set of standards by which each can be compared to the next. If you are not totally confused by this myriad of numbers, there are even more ways for you to befuddle yourself. A good disc player review will not only quote the manufacturers' numbers, but will also perform several of their own tests, which may reflect important aspects of the CD player's design. If you have made it past the first set of specifications and are still not satisfied with them as a basis for comparison, the magazine review is your next step. The following pages should tie together the terms you have already learned and identify some other laboratory-based tests which can further increase your insight into a player's performance.

THE PRODUCT REVIEW: HOW TO INTERPRET AN EXPERT'S OPINION

You may ask why it is necessary to read a product report when virtually all of a player's specifications are provided by the manufacturer. The answer to this question is simple, for many reviews go far beyond the electrical specifications of a player. They list its features and describe how well they work, measure the usual specifications with greater detail, and provide an insight into how accurately the player reproduces sound. Since many reviews are written by people whose livelihoods result from such work, they often point out the importance of certain features and describe both the shortcomings and strengths of particular machines. Armed with your knowledge of digital theory and practice, you should be able to obtain a wealth of knowledge from a well-written review.

Most sections of the typical review are rather straightforward. By now, you should know what the basic features of a typical disc player consist of. A product review will list these, as well as any unusual or particularly useful features that a player employs. You will also be given an idea of how easily the controls are to identify and operate, as well as how quickly they work. The disc drawer of a particular player will operate either quickly or slowly, and a remote control, if it has one, may only operate a few feet distant from the player. These are the types of information that you will not get from a manufacturer's spec sheet. Various reviewers will go into differing levels of detail about these functions. Some may always test some basic feature, such as the time it takes for the disc to begin to play once the PLAY button has been depressed. These types of figures are useful, for although they do not necessarily reflect on the quality of the player, they do reflect on its ease of use.

Once you are past the externals of the CD player, you will be plunged into a section of the review filled with graphs, numbers, and fairly technical observations. The better reviews will go past the traditional measurements and provide you with a few of their own which can be very helpful.

Logarithmic Plots: A Different Kind of Graph

In the beginning of this chapter we covered harmonic distortion, intermodulation distortion, frequency response, and stereo separation. A product reviewer will measure these values and compare them to those of the manufacturer. In most cases, these numbers will match rather closely. A good review will also present a number of graphs of these and other measurements, some of which may be less than straightforward in their content. To begin, you will notice that a graph of anything that varies with frequency will be plotted on a logarithmic scale rather than a linear one. Figure 7.5 is a logarithmic plot of the frequency response of some generic device. Notice that the frequency divisions do not progress in a linear manner; that is, they are not evenly spaced. In fact, as the frequency increases, the spacings are pushed more closely together. What actually happens is that the logarithm of each frequency is plotted linearly on the lower axis. Certain frequencies are then labeled so that the reader has a reference by which to judge that axis. The first frequency plotted is 10 Hz. The logarithm of this is 1. The log of 20 Hz is 1.3, but the log of 30 Hz is only 1.47. As you can see, the spacing between the logarithms of these frequen-

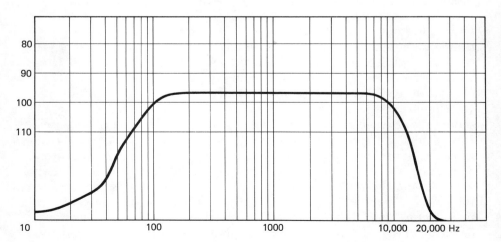

Figure 7.5 Log periodic graph of frequency response. Note that the graph's divisions increment logarithmically rather than on a linear scale.

cies is not linear—hence the irregular spacing of lines of the graph. The first nine lines represent 10 Hz, 20 Hz, 30 Hz, . . . , 90 Hz, 100 Hz. The next nine lines increase in multiples of 100 Hz, and the following nine increase in multiples of 1000 Hz. This gives the logarithmic graph its characteristic period, and in fact it is often called a *log periodic graph.*

The reason for using a logarithmic plot is that there are more variations in figures such as THD and IM distortion in the lower-frequency ranges than in the higher. The change in harmonic distortion from 20 to 200 Hz may be several decibels, while there will be virtually no measurable change from 19,000 to 19,180 Hz, which has the same 180-Hz span. So that all the significant low-frequency variations can be visually depicted without using a 20-ft foldout graph, the higher frequencies are compressed and the lower ones expanded. Aside from this difference in frequency spacing, logarithmic graphs are interpreted in the same manner as others.

Interpreting Graphs: How to Read Them

The ability to read a graph correctly is all based on the premise that you know what to look for. For the most part, graphs of ratios such as signal to noise and harmonic distortion should all have one thing in common. That common thread is smoothness. Whenever you glance at a plot, you should look not only for optimum numbers, such as the point of highest signal-to-noise ratio, but also at how smoothly the graph progresses as it transits from low to high frequencies.

Frequency Response.   When you examine a graph of the frequency response of a player, you should look not only at the cutoff regions but also at how much ripple there is in the intermediate frequencies. A lot of ripple indicates that the amplitudes of adjacent frequencies are not being reproduced accurately. Contrarily, a smooth, flat line indicates that the audio spectrum has been reproduced intact. Too many people look only at the low-end cutoff and high frequency, thinking that an acceptable frequency response is dictated solely by these parameters. A rippled graph means that the player is performing the function not only of a sound reproducer, but also a graphic equalizer. That is, it selectively attenuates or amplifies certain frequencies. Although not stated as such, ripple in the frequency band is as much a form of distortion as is a source of noise or any other type of distortion.

Stereo Separation.   The graph of stereo separation has only one twist to it. That is that the separation from the right channel to the left may not be the same as from the left channel to the right (Figure 7.6). This indicates that signals from the right stereo channel may leak into the left-hand channel by a different amount than the left-channel signals leak into the

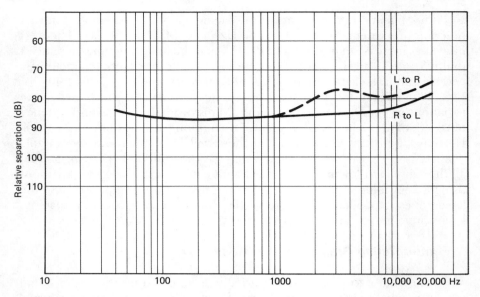

Figure 7.6   Plot of stereo separation. Separation may differ from left to right channels.

right. This has the effect of collapsing one stereo channel toward the listening center more than the other. In most cases, this difference is virtually inaudible. Note that for most players, stereo separation decreases as the frequency increases. This is due to the fact that high-frequency signals are more prone to radiation and leakage than low-frequency ones.

Total Harmonic Distortion.   The graph of THD is probably the trickiest of all the plots that you are likely to encounter in the course of a product review. Because of this, some reviews will not include a THD graph as part of their column. The reason for this is that above 10 kHz, plots of total harmonic distortion are relatively meaningless because of the interaction between the sampling frequency and the high-frequency signals embedded upon the compact disc.

Square-Wave Reproduction.   Finally, you will no doubt be presented with a reproduction of how the disc player produces a square wave. By this time you should know that a square wave is one of the more difficult waveforms to reproduce, and that there is often quite a bit of overshoot associated with the transitions from one level to the next. This overshoot, or ringing, is a function of many variables, including the sampling frequency, whether or not oversampling is present, and the steepness of the analog output filters. In most cases, a digitally filtered signal with a gentle analog filter will have a superior square-wave response to a player that does not employ oversampling but rather, uses a sharp low-pass filter to smooth its output signal. Here you should look for a square wave that is as ripple free as possible, with sharp transition regions and flat tops and bottoms (Figure 7.7). A perfect square wave can never be reproduced by any compact disc player, but there are some very close approximations by high-quality machines.

Phase Shift.   The final type of pictorial information embedded in a product review is that which pertains to the amount of phase shift which a player introduces between the left and right channels. Phase shift is mostly a function of how the output of the D/A converter is multiplexed. Its effects can be likened to those introduced by placing the woofer and tweeter of a loudspeaker at different distances from a listener. The graph of phase shift is made by photographing the output of an oscilloscope which is connected to the audio output of the CD player. An oscilloscope is an instrument that plots voltage against the time axis, in effect displaying snapshots of the input signal. To measure phase shift, the reviewer obtains a test disc with a recorded sine wave and plays this disc while monitoring both the left and

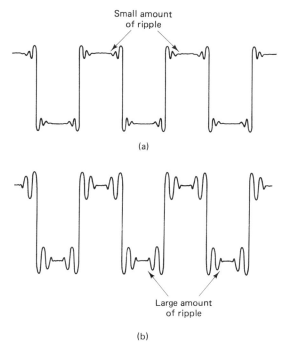

Figure 7.7   A high-quality reproduction of a square wave shows little ringing (a). Phase and other forms of distortion will increase the amount of ringing to an unacceptable level (b).

right output channels. The oscilloscope displays both these outputs on the same time axis, so any discrepancies between the phase of the two waves is easily visible. The period of a sine wave is the time it takes for it to complete one full cycle. If we consider the apex of a wave as its starting point, we need only compare the relative positions of the two waves to determine if they are in or out of phase. The time between these two maximums is recorded in microseconds and is the phase shift in these units. One can also express phase shift in terms of degrees. This is done by noting that the number of degrees in one full cycle of a sine wave is 360. You need only calculate what fraction of a period the two sine waves differ by then multiply this number by 360, to obtain the shift. Another method whereby phase shift may be displayed is the so-called Lissajous pattern. To obtain this pattern, the horizontal axis of the oscilloscope is swept by one channel and the vertical axis by the other. If the two sine waves are in phase, the resulting image will be a line that cuts across the screen at a 45° angle. If the components are out of phase, the Lissajous pattern will change from a line to a very tight oval, and may deviate from the optimum 45° angle (Figure 7.8). A long as the phase shift of the player is stated, there is no reason to display a graph of it. Also, there is a raging debate in audiophile circles as to whether phase shift has an actual effect on the quality of sound, so measurements of this parameter are of dubious value.

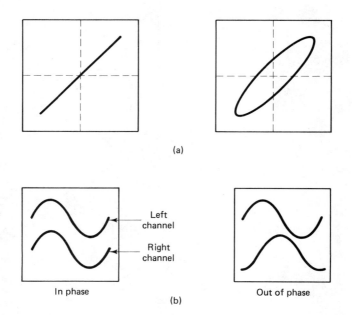

(a)

In phase   (b)   Out of phase

Figure 7.8 Lissajous pattern (a) and dual-trace plot (b) of phase shift between the left and right channels of a CD player.

Error Correction: The Unquoted Specification

The one item that is almost universally not reported by manufacturers is how well their equipment tracks through errors. There will invariably be errors in the data stream as it is tracked by the laser pickup and passed through all of the electronics between it and the D/A converter. Unfortunately, manufacturers never seem to report how sensitive their machines are to imperfections in the disc's surface, such as scratches, smudges, or manufacturing defects in the pits and lands. Luckily, many magazine reviews will perform some type of test on this aspect of CD players. They may use a test disc which is manufactured with specific types of defects built into it to perform this evaluation. The disc will have imperfections that simulate smudges and scratches of varying lengths, as well as errors in the information encoded on the disc's surface. The test disc is played in the targeted CD player and the ability of that player to track through these imperfections is noted. If the player mutes the sound or uses some type of linear interpolation to fill in errors, the reviewer will note these occurrences and report them. Sometimes the review will list the maximum diameter of an imperfection that can be tracked by the player. This is the biggest spot, such as a spot of dirt, that can appear on the disc's surface without causing an unrecoverable error. Unfortunately, not many reviews quote this spot size, so it is difficult to compare players on this basis. Often a review that uses this test will list the results for the best player they have reviewed, to provide a benchmark for purposes of comparison.

Added Information: Some Bonuses of the Review

Besides numerical information, the product report will clue you in to the manner in which the disc player under review was constructed, and what, if any, innovations the manufacturer has included into the design. In Chapter 6 we saw that there are a sea of design considerations that go into the construction of any piece of electronic equipment. A good product review will clarify how these considerations combine in the final product. You will be informed as to whether a single- or tribeam laser pickup is used, what type of filtering is present, as well as how many and what type of D/A converters are used. In short, many of the inner workings of the player which are often not publicized by the manufacturer will be revealed by the reviewer. Some of these revelations may not affect your impression of the particular player but will be more for interest and completeness. Often, the reviewer's impression of the sound emanating from the disc player will fall into this category. Every ear perceives sound a little differently, and so what one person classified as an audible defect may be pleasant to another. For this reason, your own ears are the best way to judge the sound of a CD player, not the impressions of another. But because our ears cannot always pick up subtleties, which become apparent only after listening to a number of players or listening to a single machine for an extended period, the product review is an important tool. The reviewer has the time and facilities to do tests that the average buyer would neither think of or have the means to perform. In this respect the product review is a helpful and informative yardstick. Combined with your knowledge of the workings of disc players, the manufacturer's specifications and product review information can yield as much information about a machine as you need or want to know.

8

HOW TO CHOOSE
A COMPACT
DISC PLAYER

If you have made it to this chapter, you should be a veritable compact disc guru. You can now wow your friends with talk of quadruple oversampling, phase response of analog filters, and the trade-offs between dynamic range and quantization noise. There will come that time, however, at a dinner party or casual gathering, when some digital neophyte will ask you how actually to choose a disc player from among the multitude. No doubt you yourself have wondered what the bottom line is on these high-tech wonders. For when all the bits are counted, what is important is not how the player does what it does, but how it sounds while it is doing it. How, in a phrase, should you pick a CD player? The average stereo store carries a gaggle of brands and models, many of which have more features and state-of-the-art electrical designs than you know what to do with. In this chapter we explore some of the things to look for in the showroom and learn about a few tests that you can do to check out what appears to be your perfect choice. We look at how to test out error correction schemes to see if they are up to snuff. We also learn a few things to check in the way of convenience features that you may find particularly useful. Finally, you learn to match a CD player to your present and future stereo needs, and to buy a player that works with your system and musical tastes.

YOUR FIRST IMPRESSIONS

When you walk up to that wall of CD players in your local audio store, you will probably be confronted with a mass of black anodized faces, all of which, at first glance, look like the slickest things ever to hit a stereo rack. If you are like most people, you will have a good idea of what you want to spend, and a vaguer idea of what you will end up spending. Usually, the latter will be greater than the former. You can run the gamut of prices when shopping for a CD player, for there are models that range in price from under $100 to well over $7500. Undoubtedly, there is a CD model that meets your listening needs and price restraints. The best way to approach buying a player is to identify a few models in your price range, compare them, and then look at some both above and below that range. When you have done this, you are ready for some hard-line comparisons.

BRING ALONG A DISC

A good thing to have when listening to various players is a disc containing music with which you are familiar. There is no better way to judge a piece of audio equipment than by listening to how a favorite tune, one that you know thoroughly, sounds on it. In this way you can listen for details that you might miss if you let a salesman wow you with a demonstration disc featuring a jet airplane zooming by at Mach 2 or a racquet ball bouncing off echoing walls. If you are not enchanted with the idea of buying a disc before you purchase a player, you may be able to rent one at a video rental store or check one out of a local library. These two sources are becoming ever more plentiful. An even better idea is to borrow a disc from a friend. That way you will be able to listen to it on his or her player and get an idea of what to listen for.

IMPORTANT FEATURES

Convenience Features

Armed with a test disc, you should be able to march right up to a player having a good idea of what all its buttons and knobs control. The first thing that you will want to do is to fiddle with these buttons so that you can form an impression of how well they work. To begin, try pressing the OPEN/CLOSE button to see how fast the drawer extends and retracts. Believe me when I say that a slowly operating drawer can be a real source of annoyance after a few hours of use. This is especially true if you switch discs often. If the player has a swing-out door rather than a retractable one, see how easily you can insert and extract a disc without getting fingerprints all over its surface. This can be a difficult process with some drawer configurations. Now pop a disc into the drawer and note how quickly it cues up and is ready to play. Most players take a few seconds to do this. Again, a quick time here is a great convenience. Once the disc is cued, try switching between tracks and again, observe how long it takes for the laser pickup to move into place. You can play the disc even if the player is not hooked up to a speaker system so that you can check out the forward and reverse scan features. Get an idea of how quickly they scan by watching the digital elapsed time display on the face of the player. When the player is connected to a speaker system, the slow scan should be slow enough to allow you to identify particular spots in the music, while the fast scan should be brisker without totally obscuring the musical content of the disc. If the player that you are examining is programmable, as most are, you will be well advised to check on how easily tracks can be programmed into the machine. Some players require but a few keystrokes to program in selections, while others use more obscure and difficult methods to achieve the same results. In particular, some disc players have a separate keypad that is used to program in selections. This keypad has numbers on it which can be used to select particular tracks on the disc directly. This method of programming in a disc is somewhat faster than those units which use their "+" and "−" keys to select and program in tracks.

Remote Controls

Another very popular feature is the remote control unit. With this, you will be able to manipulate many of the compact disc player's features without being near the machine. The first thing to note here is how many of the player's front-panel functions are controllable by the remote unit. In most cases almost all will be, but be sure that the ones that you are most interested in using are there. In particular, the buttons that start and stop play, as well as the PAUSE and SCAN buttons, are the most essential. These are the ones that you will use most often, such as when you wish to skip past a song or pause to answer the telephone or door. You will also want to point the remote away from the player and see just how far off axis it can face before the remote no longer affects the player's controls (Figure 8.1). Some remotes require that you point the unit directly at the player or cant it in a particular direction when they are used from a distance. Others are better designed and work when pointed in the general vicinity of the player. You can test the range of a remote unit by moving it away from the player and noting when it begins to lose effectiveness. Make certain that this distance is less than the distance from where your stereo resides to where you plan to listen to it from.

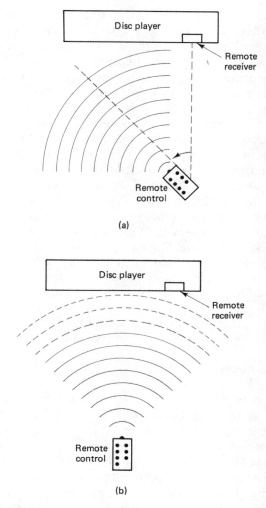

Figure 8.1 The remote control for a disc player may not function correctly if it is pointed too far off axis (a) or is out of range (b).

Headphone Outputs

If the model you are interested in has a headphone output and you have access to a pair of headphones, plug them in. Change the volume control on the headphone output to make sure that it can produce listening levels that match your preferences. It is unlikely that the output will not go low enough, but some may not be satisfied with the output at the upper volume levels. The headphone circuit of some players often seems to be more of an afterthought than an integral part of their design, so the quality of sound at this output may not equal that at the line-level outputs. This is not unexpected, for the average disc player is designed not as an amplifier, but as a source. For some, this will be a consideration. Remember that headphones do not produce the same listening effect as regular speakers and their frequency response may be significantly less than that of a good pair of floor standing speakers. So if the headphone outputs of a disc player do not sound as good as through a pair of loudspeakers, it may be the fault of the headphones, not the CD player. It is also very easy to overdrive the headphone output circuit if the volume is turned up too high. This causes distortion to occur and can damage the headphones, headphone amplification circuit in the player, and your ears.

AUDITIONING A PLAYER: WHAT TO LOOK AND LISTEN FOR

By this point in your evaluation you should have been accosted by a stereo salesperson. Now is the time to ask him or her about how the player is constructed. You can find out what type of oversampling, if any, is used, as well as inquire about some of the many features that we discussed previously. The real test is, of course, in the listening.

Listening to a Player: They Do Not All Sound the Same

Compact disc players do not all sound the same. Unfortunately, there are no hard rules for rating on player's sound better than another. In fact, only your ears can guide you in this area. For although CD players do shape the sound that they reproduce just as does any other audio device, it is difficult to say which audible effects are desirable and which are not. Some players may emphasize a particular frequency band over another. One machine may produce excellent bass but seem lacking in the midrange or treble. Another may reproduce all equally well, but emphasize some more than others. The trick is to identify those points that are pleasing to your ears as well as those that give a good overall audio experience. If you can, listen to the disc that you brought with you. If there are drums in a particular piece, listen for both the high-frequency cymbal crash and the low-frequency thud of a bass drum. You may well hear musical subtleties that you have never heard before on vinyl or tape. You may pick out nuances that one player accentuates over another. There may also be some quality to a particular player which cannot be expressed verbally. Terms such as "warmth," "harshness," "smooth," "rough," "sharp," and "clean" are often used to describe sound, but who is to say what the difference is between a harsh-sounding machine and a rough-sounding one?

You should also note how well you can pick out the images of particular instruments, that is, how well you can place them in space. Players with extended dynamic range and stereo separation will show their benefits in this area. Also listen to very soft passages and note how the background noise varies from one player to another. This is an indication of the signal-to-noise ratio, and players with digital filters and 18-bit A/D converters will shine in this area. Try not to bias yourself toward one player because it uses more advanced technology than another. Rather, let your ears be your judge. Even if you do not normally listen to classical music, you will find that this is an excellent medium for comparison. Many classical discs are recorded fully digitally from the initial recording through to mastering, so they realize the total benefit of the digital process. Their plethora of instruments and sounds also provides numerous points of comparison for both ultrahigh and low frequencies, as well as midrange.

Amplifiers and Speakers: They Shape the Sound, Too

While you are listening, remain aware that the speakers you are listening to as well as the amplifier that drives them have a profound effect on the sound that you experience. For this reason you should listen to different players over the same amplifier and speakers. Listening to two players over different systems is a total waste of time, since it is never certain which component causes the difference in sound. This point is particularly true when you compare a low-priced player to a high-priced one. Often, the high-priced player will be hooked up to a better system than the inexpensive one. Of course the high-priced player will sound better in this situation because you listen to it over a better amplifier and speakers. Always compare disc players over the same amplification chain.

How to Rate Error Correction: Tests That You Can Do

Once you have compared a few players you will probably narrow down a couple as your favorites. If the difference in their sounds are negligible or both sound good in different ways, you may want another avenue of comparison to explore. One such avenue is that of error correction. Although you will not find any specifications on machines' respective error-correcting capabilities, there are a few quick tests that you can perform which will reflect these capabilities and shortcomings.

The best way to test a player's error correction is to introduce errors and then observe how well they are masked or corrected. One way to do this is by putting a fingerprint on a disc before it is placed in the disc drawer. You can do this by grasping the disc by its clear bottom surface and pressing your finger onto it. If a player can track through this, it has passed its first test. If the player cannot track through a fingerprint, it will either mute it or continuously play the last good stretch of music that was correctly detected. The latter effect sounds like a cross between a skipping record and a rap music song. Needless to say, this is not a good sign. It means that every time a disc is soiled by fingerprints or dust, it will have to be cleaned. This is both a tiresome and a potentially destructive process.

If the player passes this test, there is yet another that you may perform. Before you go to test a player, cut some pieces of electrical tape into very thing strips; about d⅛ of an inch is a good width. If you have a half-inch roll of tape, cut across its width with a scissors and place the strips on a small square of waxed paper. When you want to test a player, take a strip from the paper and place it on the disc so that it radiates from the center outward. Press the tape onto the disc's surface using the waxed paper so as not to get any dirt onto the disc. Be sure that the tape is radiating outward from the disc and is not sideways. If you like, you may use a thin grease pencil in lieu of tape to make the same type of radial mark. Now play the disc. If the player tracks through this, put another strip of tape or grease pencil mark 180° opposite the first one, again making sure that it radiates out from the center of the disc like the spokes of a bicycle's wheel. Continue doing this until the player mistracks. The strips of tape cause burst errors to occur when the disc's surface is scanned. As the number of tape strips are increased, so are the number of errors per unit time. The more strips that you can place on the disc, the better is the player's error-correction scheme. When you reach the maximum number of strips for one player, you can remove one strip and place the same disc in another player. If the second player will not track this disc, you can deduce that the first player's error-correction scheme was more effective than the second's. If the second player does track it, add strips until it mistracks. You can continue this process until you are satisfied that you have isolated the best player or have worn out the salesman's patience. Be sure to make the tape strips as thin as possible. If you cut them too wide, they will knock out an inordinate number of bits, and no player will be able to track through them. When playing this error-enhanced disc, listen not only for mistracking, but also for how well the player covers up uncorrectable errors. Some players will begin to gently mute the sound before others, and you can hear this when the disc is playing. Others will not handle the errors as well, and this, too, will be apparent. Also, remember that a disc is played from the inside track to the outside track, so place the tape or grease makrs on the inner circle of the disc rather than on the outer edge (Figure 8.2).

Chassis Isolation: How Shock Resistant Is the Player?

Chances are that you may not want to go to all the trouble of sticking strips of tape onto a disc. If so, there is another point that you can check. Since the laser pickup and disc transport system are both ultimately

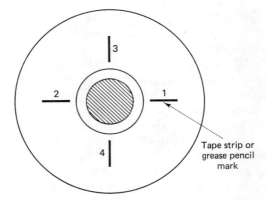

Figure 8.2 Testing error correction. Place tape strips or grease pencil marks in a radial pattern. If the first mark does not cause an error, continue making marks until a mistrack occurs.

connected to the player's chassis, any shock transmitted to the chassis can affect their performance. If a shock is severe enough, it can cause the player to mistrack. Also, vibrations that are introduced by feedback from loud-speakers can cause the laser pickup to mistrack and introduce errors into the data stream. A simple way to test this is gently to tap the surface on which the disc player rests while it plays a disc. If a gentle tap causes mistracking, the transport and tracking mechanism are probably not very well isolated from outside vibrations. If it does not mistrack, tap the player's chassis directly and listen for any irregularities. As with all electronic gear, a compact disc player is a delicate instrument, so be sure to tap, not hit or shake, the player while it is in operation. Some players isolate their chassis from external shock with insulating feet, so these may not damp shocks that are applied directly to the chassis. This does not mean that they are not well isolated; it merely means that they are more susceptible to direct shocks, which occur far more infrequently than those transmitted through the feet. If this is the case, tapping the surface that the player rests on will give a better indication of its isolation than will touching the machine's chassis.

MULTIDISC PLAYERS

As the price of compact disc players have come down, the once high-priced multidisc players have become competitive in price with their single-disc counterparts. These *disc changers*, as they are called, have some allures of their own that can warrant their increased price over a single-disc player.

The benefit of a disc changer is that you need not switch discs in and out of a tray every time you wish to listen to a new disc. It would seem logical to say that an important feature of a multidisc player is the number of discs that it can hold at one time. Just about all such machines have cartridges which hold from 6 to 50 discs. These cartridges are removable, so it is possible to buy a number of cartridges and fill them with discs, switching these rather than individual discs. This has the benefit of exposing your discs to human contact only once, when they are loaded. The disadvantage is that since extra cartridges cost $15 or more apiece, they indirectly add to the already high cost of the compact discs which they house. And since no cartridge provides a handy method of keeping track of which discs are in which cartridges, the burden is on you to maintain such a record. You must also remember which disc occupies which slot in the cartridge, for discs are referenced by their position, not their name. Selection of a particular track is also more time consuming than with a single-disc player since you must choose from more possibilities. Similarly, skipping between discs takes longer because they must be removed from the disc tray when they are selected and replaced before another disc can be played.

Having brought these points to your attention, let me also enlighten you as to the benefits of disc changers. As I said, a disc is exposed to dust and dirt only once, when it is loaded into a cartridge. Inevitably, this will prolong the life of a disc and reduce the amount of error correction that a disc player must use since there will be fewer errors on a clean disc than on a dirty one. There are also a number of interesting ways that you might group discs in cartridges. You may choose to put all the discs of one composer or artist together and form disc packs of their works. You might group particular types of music together, or put together various types of music to add variety to your listening. It is also far more convenient and quick to load a number of discs together than to change between discs continuously. This feature is particularly useful if you are the type of person who does not listen to an entire album at a time, but rather, listens to a few songs from one album, then switches to another, and so on. In this respect, the added access time of the multidisc player is actually less than that of a single-disc machine, which requires you to get up and swap discs in and out of it. Most disc changers also have a shuffle play option which will randomly switch between selections on various discs. This can provide you with hours of digitally reproduced music without ever having to touch the player.

Disc Capacity: How Many Can it Hold?

That covers the pros and cons of single- versus multidisc players, so now how about exploring the differences between individual disc changers? As you would expect, there as many differences among disc changers as there are among regular machines. The first thing to look for is how many discs a cartridge holds. The average number seems to be around six discs, with a low of two discs and a high of an impressive 50. The latter player will cost an estimated $4000, raising the average price per disc to around $93. If your budget is not quite on a par with that price, you can still find a multidisc player which holds a good number of discs. Since the entire point of such machines is convenience, it would seem that more disc space is better than less. You may also want to compare the availability of extra cartridges and their respective prices to the number of discs they hold. Cartridges seem to load into a disc changer about as easily as video tapes load into their players. One interesting feature of some disc changers is that they also include a disc cartridge which holds only one disc. This effectively allows a multidisc machine to function just like a single-disc player. A single-disc cartridge is handy when you want to keep some discs out of cartridges, such as those you seldom play and do not want to take the time to load into a magazine when you do wish to play them.

Access Time and Programmability: Two Convenience Features

The time that the laser pickup takes to switch from disc to disc is a variable quantity and is usually much greater for a disc changer than for a single-disc player. It also varies greatly between models. If you are interested in using the shuffle play option, look for a player with a fast seek time, since it will provide you with more music and less dead space between songs. You should also check how many selections can be programmed at once, how many steps are required to input each selection, and whether or not the player can store the program steps after it is powered down. This last point is an important one. Suppose that your player holds six discs, each with 10 tracks per disc. Your player may have a 30-selection memory, and if you take the time to choose between 60 or so songs and thousands of possible program variations, you do not want all your work wiped out the minute you turn off the machine's power. Some players will hold your programs in a memory that does not erase when the machine is powered down, so you can recall a particular program or even keep separate programs for various disc packs. Similarly, if a player can hold 10 or more discs but its programming memory only allows you to program five or 10 tracks, some of the flexibility of the player is sacrificed. On the other hand, if a player does not have a nonerasing memory, you will seldom find yourself programming a large number of tracks, and the benefit of an extremely large program memory is diminished.

Electronics: State of the Art or Old Hat?

Another area to consider is whether the manufacturer has sacrificed the player's sound performance for multidisc operation. In some cases, incorporating state-of-the-art features such as quadruple oversampling or dual D/A converters has been sacrificed to bring down the price of a disc changer. As you might expect, the cost of designing and constructing a disc changer is far greater than that of a single-disc player. It is mechanically and electronically more complex, and manufacturers sometimes make concessions so that their multidisc players can compete with lower-priced single-disc players. It seems a shame that such a versatile machine would use anything less than the best electronics and digital techniques, but in some cases, to make a player more financially attractive, it may be lacking in terms of sound reproduction capabilities. Too many disc changers still employ first-generation architecture, and some manufacturers have not changed their disc changers in several model years, choosing instead to update the better-selling single-disc machines. Happily, there are several disc changers that do benefit from digital filtering and other niceties, and as compact discs grow in popularity, there will be an ever-increasing selection of such machines available in lower and lower price ranges. Overall, a well-designed multidisc machine is both a pleasure and a convenience to own. It is for you to weigh its benefits against its drawbacks and decide whether such a convenience is worth an extra investment.

WHICH FEATURES DO YOU NEED IN A HOME PLAYER?

You may well wonder how many of the numerous features available on compact disc players are really necessary for your needs. If you have an unlimited budget, you may just choose for the best-sounding, most heavily feature-laden machine on the market. If you are more concerned about getting the most for your dollar, perhaps you should first think about how many of the bells and whistles are really necessary.

Matching a Player to Your System

To begin, ask yourself about the type of stereo system into which you plan to integrate your player. If your present components, such as the receiver, tuner, amplifier, turntable, or tape deck, do not have remote controls, you may not miss one on your CD player. On the other hand, if you buy a multidisc player, its versatility may warrant including a remote. Also, if you plan to upgrade your stereo system in the future, you may enjoy the remote feature. The remote control for many players is a separate item that need not be purchased initially, so if you find that you want a remote control after using the player for a while, you can always pick up the remote at a later date. One drawback of remote-controlled stereo is that every component requires its own control unit. At last count, an acquaintance of mine had six remote units strewn about his coffee table, one each for the VCR, receiver, CD player, tape deck, turntable, and television. You may wish to look into components that are supplied by the same manufacturer and can all operate from a single, multifunction, remote control. You should also be aware that some remote control features are not very useful, so comparing such units on the basis of the total number of their features is not always a valid method. One can only wonder of what value is remote control of the opening and closing of a disc drawer, since to change a disc, you must invariably get up and go do it.

Programmability: How Much Is Enough?

If you are wondering how many selections a machine should have the ability to program, ask yourself how many you think you will want to program into it. A 30-track programming capability sounds nice, but do you think that you will actually program that many tracks, especially when the average CD has only about 10 or 12 songs on it? Personally, I have never programmed in more than eight or nine tracks. After that, it seems more logical to program in which tracks to skip rather than to play. To my knowledge, no player offers this ability. If you are looking at a multidisc machine, you could conceivably program the music for an entire party if the player has a big enough memory, if you want to go to that trouble. In any case, remember that more is not necessarily better if the extra capability is not used.

Special Features: More Noise-Reduction Circuitry

Some players incorporate features that we have not yet discussed. They may have special compression or expansion circuits that can be switched in and out of the audio path. These circuits perform similar functions to the Dolby and DBX encoding and decoding circuits that are often used with tape decks and turntables. The benefits of these added circuits vary with the type of listening that is done. Like any sound-processing circuit, these will alter the sound of the player. Whether this is good or bad depends on your tastes, so you, the listener, must judge the benefits of such add-on's against their cost.

Aesthetics: Please Your Eyes as Well as Your Ears

This next point may sound strange, but you should be as happy with your player's looks as with its sound. If you have a stereo with components whose faces all have black anodized finishes, a black player may win out over a silver one of equal quality. Many manufacturers produce the same models with different-finished faceplates for just this reason, so inquire into this when purchasing your player.

Ergonomics: The Human Touch

An item related to the way a player looks is how its controls are marked and laid out. If the front panel looks like an instrument panel at mission control, it will be very confusing to operate. You will want big buttons for controls you use often, such as PLAY and the scanning buttons, whereas the programming buttons, which are less seldom used, can be smaller. If the controls are very tightly packed, you will find yourself hitting one button when you actually want to invoke another. Similarly, if the markings for the controls are not clear in meaning or are too small to read, you will have trouble determining which button controls which function. These are points that seem minor at first, but they can prove a nuisance as time passes by.

Disc Player Performance: Will You Hear the Difference?

When comparing the specfications of players, you should temper your judgment with the knowledge that the other components of your stereo system may not equal those of your new disc player. If a particular player specs out with 100 dB of stereo separation and your amplifier has only 90 dB of separation, you will hear only 90 dB of separation. That extra 10 dB will be lost when the audio signal from the CD player passes through amplification circuits of the receiver. The weakest link in the chain from your disc player to your speakers will invariably determine the ultimate specifications of the system as a whole. Also, do not agonize over whether to choose a player with 110 dB of dynamic range versus one with 100 dB of range if your receiver is underpowered, because you will not hear the difference. On the other hand, if you have a very fine set of components or plan to upgrade in the future, that extra 10 dB of dynamic range may be important to you. As is often the case, after a certain threshold, small gains in things such as dynamic range, signal-to-noise ratio, and the like, come with ever-increasing price tags, so remember that you do not wish to pay for gains which you will never hear. Some specifications, such as total harmonic distortion and intermodulation distortion, are additive, meaning that they add to their counterparts in other portions of the system. These effects will not be masked by the weaker components, but will increase them For such specifications you may hear some difference between players even if the system they play through has specifications which are inferior to both players.

There is another problem associated with compact discs that you should know of. The dynamic range, and hence the output levels of many players, are greater than those of the average stereo or tape deck. When a disc player is connected to a receiver or amplifier, it will often call upon that device to put out more power than can safely be produced. This is especially true if you are playing a selection with both loud and soft passages. You may increase the volume during the soft passages, and when a loud passage comes along it will overdrive the amplifier into clipping its output signal. Besides distorting the sound emanating from the speaker, this energy can permanently damage your speaker's midrange and tweeter. If the output level of the disc player is greater than that of your other components, you will not be able to turn the volume control of your amplifier as high as you do for the other input sources. For this reason you should look for a disc player with an adjustable output level, or one that matches the line level of your other audio inputs.

This brings us to yet another point of contention—that the frequency response of your speakers could severely limit the appreciation of any CD player. Just because a player has a rated bandwidth of 20 kHz does not mean that you will hear all of its sound through cheap speakers. As you may well imagine, speakers that are rated with less than 20 kHz of usable bandwidth will act to bandpass filter the disc player's output, and you may end up with only slightly better sound than that from a good-quality tape deck or turntable. The CD player does have benefits besides bandwidth, such as the durability of the discs, so for your particular system some specifications and features may carry a greater weight than others. If your stereo system's specifications are considerably less impressive than those of a low-end disc player, you might concentrate on choosing a player based on its features rather than its sound. Conversely, if you have a very high quality system, you will be better off spending your money on a disc player with a better sound and will possibly sacrifice some convenience features to achieve this aim. With the abundant selection of players on the market, it is possible to find a good-quality player with enough options to fit both requirements, but remember that the sound you hear is only as good as the worst component that it passes through on its way to your ears.

PORTABLE DISC PLAYERS

In the history of the audio industry, there have emerged portable reel-to-reel tape players, portable eight-track tape players, portable cassette decks, turntables, receivers, and complete stereo systems that can be carried around like a suitcase. It is even possible to buy an FM radio the size of a credit card that slips into your wallet. After all these innovations, the portable compact disc player should come as no surprise. The "compact" part of the compact disc's name implies that it is made to be transported, and so it can be. Portable disc players are not only convenient but have some advantages that can make them more attractive than either single- or multidisc players. They also have drawbacks to which neither of the other types of machines is subject.

Their Advantages

Let's begin with the advantages of owning a portable disc player. The first is that you can take it anywhere. Portable players are small and light enough to accompany you everywhere that a portable radio would. They are also useful in places where you would not consider using a portable radio. For example, your car is usually equipped with its own mobile stereo. If you have considered buying a separate car disc player, reconsider using a portable player as a source. Many popular car stereos have auxiliary inputs just like those of a home stereo. A disc player's output can drive your car stereo amplifier and presto—you have instant digital sound. Portable CD players can often operate off a 12-V power supply, the same voltage that your car provides. This is no coincidence. If you take the time to look around your car's dash, you will probably find a place to mount a portable player using Velcro or a snap-on or suction mount. This has the added advantage of allowing the disc player to be removed when you leave the car so as not to attract the attention of stereo thieves. Once you arrive at your destination, you can remove your player, and with a set of headphones, can enjoy compact disc music wherever you go. Portable players are provided with a shoulder strap or belt loop so that you need not occupy your hands with them. They also have the ability to act as an input to a home stereo system, so that you need buy only one player for home, car, and personal use. The output of the CD player plugs into the auxiliary input of a home receiver or amplifier and works just as well as units specifically designed for the home. They also take up less physical space than a home unit and can be toted around the house and used with more than one stereo if you have more than one. Portable units can also be taken to friends' houses, so that they too can enjoy digitally recorded music. You can obtain a converter that plugs into a wall outlet which will convert household current into a form that the disc player can use for power. Or you can use rechargable batteries or regular dry cells. In short, the portable CD player can fill the shoes of a number of other types of players by providing versatility which neither home nor car players can match.

Their Disadvantages

Lest you come to believe that the portable player is the only sane choice for a prospective buyer, let us examine the negative side of portable units. Their first disadvantage is also one of their great advantages. They are small. Less volume implies greater portability, but it also decreases the number of features that a player can offer. Consider the busy front panel of many full-sized players. They are already crammed with buttons and knobs, some of which can be difficult to see and operate. These controls provide either convenience features or features that are essential to the operation of the unit. Since the digital display area of most home units is as large as the entire front panel of portables, these smaller units cannot offer as many features as can their larger cousins. The operations that you may control from their front panels must include play, stop, forward, and reverse skip. Beyond that, some players will provide a repeat function and some programmability. The display will show the usual track number or elapsed time into a track. These are the most used and most needed functions, and indeed, are the only ones found on some home units. The buttons and display are, however, many times smaller than those of a home unit, and some buttons will do double duty to control several functions. Although you may be able to program portable units, you will not find this as simple to perform as with home players. The markings for functions will be proportionately smaller and will be more difficult to read and interpret. Basically, the portable player is rather spartan compared to a full-blown home unit. If you are driving in a car, the small size of the controls may make it impractical to use many of its functions while the car is in motion. And because these players require that their disc covers be opened and closed manually, it can be difficult to change discs while the car is moving. If you plan to use the player in your home as well, you may miss the features that such a small machine cannot or does not provide. On the other hand, the most often used controls are those that play and stop the CD. Since most of your listening will involve just that—listening—you may not care about the extra few seconds which are required to locate and operate controls. And as you become more familiar with a unit, you will find that the controls will fall naturally at your fingertips. For these reasons, the more spartan portable player can be as handy a unit as one designed for the home.

The size limitation of such players imposes a limit to the amount of electronics that can be packed into its chassis. Only so many microchips can fit into a tiny space, to say nothing of the disc drive assembly, laser pickup, and power supply. Some of the electrical design consideration that we examined in Chapter 6 cannot be implemented in such a confined area. Luckily, advances in the miniaturization of both electronic and mechanical components have eased this space crunch. A process called very large scale integration (VLSI) allows microchip manufacturers to combine many chips into a single one which consumes less power, is smaller, and is less prone to noise transmission than the ones it replaces. The manufacturers of portable players have been quick to identify these chips as prime candidates for their products, and some manufacturers produce their own custom chips for inclusion in their machines. Even with these advances, there are limitations. Multiple power supplies are difficult to implement, as are separate circuit boards for analog and digital components. In fact, the player's components are sometimes stacked on top of each other. How these will affect the output of the player depends on a number of factors, and so, as with home players, a listening test is the only one of real value.

Manufacturers have done a fine job of overcoming these problems, and whether you plan to listen to a portable player through your home or car stereo or just a pair of headphones, you will, no doubt, be pleased with its sound.

The Dangers of Portability

Portability also brings its own uniqueness to CD player care—for anything that can be picked up can be dropped. A severe jolt to a CD player will do several things. At the least, it will cause a playing disc to skip or mistrack. At worst, the laser assembly will be thrown out of alignment, causing serious errors in tracking when the unit is again operated. The CD player is a more temperamental device than the average portable stereo or tape deck, so special care must be taken not to damage its inner parts. You will find that portable players are more rugged than home units, so a shock that might damage a sedentary machine will not hurt a mobile one. Unfortunately, a portable player will receive greater and more severe shocks than a home unit, so even its increased shock resistance is not always enough to protect its mechanisms from damage.

Because it is often exposed to the elements, a portable compact disc player can ingest dirt, dust, and water, three of its least favorite dishes. These elements can destroy the inner electronics, mechanical devices such as a motor or pickup arm, and even damage a disc that is spinning inside the player. If you plan to frequent the beach, be aware that salt water will quickly corrode just about any metal surface, and combined with sun, sand, and suntan lotion, can diminish the life of both your disc player and discs. Realizing this, many manufacturers have taken special care to seal as many components as possible from the outside, but they are still not made to be rolled in the sand or left to bake under a summer's sun.

Finally, unless you plan to purchase a very long extension cord, you will need a power supply for your player. This will be a separate unit, sometimes larger and heavier than the player itself. You can opt for either regular batteries or rechargables. Alkaline batteries will provide about five hours of playing time, while rechargables will yield less, normally three to four hours. This is about as much as a portable tape player can provide, and should last through 5 to 10 CDs' worth of playing time. When you use the player at home or in the car, you will be able to plug an adapter into either a wall outlet or a cigarette lighter, and power the unit without running down its batteries.

What Should You Look for in a Portable Player?

If you have weighed the pros and cons of portable disc player ownership and have decided to go ahead and buy one, you will want to know what to look for in a machine. What has been said before about home CD players holds for the portables. Listen to them, get a feel for how they sound and function, and make your decision. In each of these categories, there are a few extra points that you may want to consider.

First, you can choose between a stand-alone portable player and one that is integrated into a complete mobile stereo, including speakers, tape deck, radio, and amplifier. This type of system is a bit more cumbersome, but is better suited for all-around use since it is part of a self-contained stereo. If your tastes run toward such "boom boxes," this is your ticket. You will be certain to have the best-sounding (and most expensive) "box" around.

While you are examining different players, check to see how shock resistant they are while they are playing. Walk around with a player, give it a gentle bump, and see if it mistracks or not. This is an important point—more so than with home units. Note that few manufacturers recommend that you run or jog with their players since these actions introduce severe shocks from which few players will recover.

You may also wish to check how tightly the seams seal on the player's case and how well the disc door appears to shut out the elements. If the seams look like they will not seal out dirt and dust, you will need to take special care of the player when it is taken out of doors. Also note how the buttons mount on the front panel. Any dirt here can cause buttons to discontinue their operation or admit dirt into the player's interior. While on the subject of dirt, you may wish to check how well the player tracks a dirty disc, since it will encounter more of these on the road than in your living room. If every speck of dust sends the machine into a mistracking fit, you will have to practice scrupulous cleanliness when handling and storing your discs. Even if the unit appears to seal well, there is still the possibility of introducing dirt into the mechanism when a disc is loaded. For this reason, loading and unloading should be accomplished easily and should not require you to touch anything but the edges of a disc. If you must pull the disc out by its playing surface, you will dirty the disc as well as the inner mechanisms.

Portables will run on batteries when they are used in the field. You will want a battery case that is small and comfortable to carry without sacrificing playing time for size. Remember that a well-designed heavy battery pack can be easier to carry than a badly designed light one, depending on how it connects to the CD player and how it rests against your body. Also weigh the number of hours of play the pack will provide against the number of batteries that it consumes. If you expect to spend long hours away from home, you may simply want the longest playing pack, regardless of its size or weight. And although rechargable batteries are a greater initial expense, they can pay for themselves after only a few rechargings. You will pay a penalty since they often reduce playing time, but again, after a period of recharging they are again ready to go. The recharging period varies depending on the type of rechargable battery. Look for those with quick recharging times so that you can spend less time waiting and more time listening to your machine. Finally, a few players have ac-to-dc converters built into them and do not require a separate converter to plug into a wall outlet. This is an advantage if you wish to use them at home and do not wish to purchase a separate converter box.

Comfort and Convenience Features

I mentioned comfort before, and indeed, this is an important consideration when buying a player. If the unit has odd angles or buttons and straps that protrude uncomfortably when it is carried around, you will not find it convenient to carry for long periods of time. This is particularly true of battery packs since they often fit onto their players in unusual manners. You may also wish to consider the player's shape if you plan to mount it in your car. One player may fit onto a particular spot with no problem, while another's controls or outputs may be obscured by a panel, lip, or depression. If you are going to mount the player under the dash, it is imperative that discs can be inserted and removed easily and that all the controls are within easy reach while you are driving. Keep in mind that a compact disc player should not be exposed to extreme heat or sun, so mounting the unit on top of the dash can be trouble on a sunny day. Your CDs will fare no better when heated to extreme temperatures, so you may wish to buy a player that will fit under the dash rather than on top of it. Another feature to check is the headphone output. Is it enough to drive a pair of headphones to the levels to which you are used to listening? And if you plan to hook up a second set of headphones, will their combined impedence be too low for the unit to drive adequately? If the unit does not have a balance control, you will be stuck with whatever relative listening levels are preset at the factory or recorded onto a particular disc.

SINGLE, MULTI, PORTABLE: WHICH TYPE IS BEST?

All these are things that you should think about before you decide to buy a particular player. And certaintly, you should decide which of the many features that are available on portable players you will really use and need. If you plan to use the player in your home as well as on the road, you may want as many of the same features as are available on home units. If it is only going to be used away from home, you may miss some features. As with any type of disc player, you should choose the one that best suits your needs, wants, and wallet.

CD PLAYERS FOR THE CAR

If you are like most people, once you have purchased a disc player you will begin to amass a collection of discs. After spending large sums of money on such a collection, you will want to enjoy each disc as often as possible. If you are a commuter or do much traveling, a disc player may eventually find its way into a permanent spot in your car. There are a variety of players designed for in- or under-dash initallation. Some play only discs; others double as radio tuner and amplifier. Like the portable players, these units are rugged and designed for the harsh environment of the automobile.

The Different Types of Car Players

There are a few classes of car players. Some, like home units, are strictly disc players. They provide no means for amplification which can drive your car's speakers. Like a home player, they require a separate amplifier to take their line-level signals and transform them into speaker-level outputs. Some car stereo receivers have inputs that accept such line levels, while others do not. If you already have a stereo in your car and it does not have such inputs, you will need more than just the player to play CDs. Conversely, if your present car stereo does have such inputs, you need only connect these lines to the disc player's output to realize a working system.

If you end up needing a separate amplifier for your player, you may consider purchasing a car disc player with a built-in amplifier. Like a car receiver, this unit will require no external electronics to power-up a set of speakers. Indeed, many such disc players are integrated into a receiver design, providing a tuner to pick up radio broadcasts as well as an amplifier. The front panel of such machines can be quite crowded and you will find that many buttons do double duty as both disc player and tuner controls. Unfortunately, there seem to be no car players that handle cassette tapes as well as CDs, so if you have many tapes that you play in your car, you will need a separate deck for them. This will put you into the same position that you were originally in with a disc player without an amplifier.

How Do Car Players Work?

Like car tape machines, car CD players are designed so that the discs are inserted into a slot in the front of the unit. A motor grasps the disc when it is inserted and pulls it into the body of the player. From there, operation is the same as for any other type of player. Some players require that you first encase the disc in a special cartridge before placing it into the slot. This method has both advantages and disadvantages. An encased disc is protected from physical damage as well as fingerprints and dirt. This is quite an advantage in the auto environment, as most cars are far from immaculate even when they are vacuumed and cleaned often. The disadvantage is that it can become a hassle to load and unload the discs whenever they are to be moved from the home to the car. One cannot simply grab a few discs off of the stereo cabinet and toss them onto the front seat or pop them into the car player. The discs must be taken from their jewel boxes and placed individually into the car disc holders. And if you wish to have a number of discs handy for automotive use, you must buy a supply of disc holders, which adds to the already high price of compact discs. Still, this method can save your discs from harm, so you must weigh the safety factor against that of convenience.

Remotely Controlled Car Players

Car players are available with remote controls. This may seem a strange idea, as in order to use the player you must be within arm's reach of it. Such controls can be mounted on the steering wheel hub or close to eye level so that you need not take your eyes off the road to adjust the stereo. Perhaps the ultimate remotely controlled player is one that fits in the trunk of your car. One manufacturer provides such a unit which holds a number of discs in a cartridge located inside the trunk. Only a small, unobtrusive remote control is located inside the cab, and this controls the disc changer and all of its functions. As a bonus, multidisc cartridges are interchangeable between home and car players of the same manufacturer, so the same cartridge that you use in your living room can be popped out and transported into the car player. As you might expect, this luxury does not come cheaply, but a trunk-mounted multidisc player is convenient and its absence from the dashboard area is a great theft deterrent.

Ergonomic Considerations for Car Players

If you opt for the in-dash rather than the remote or trunk-mounted player, be certain that you will be able to operate the player without being distracted from the road. This translates into an easy-to-operate and logically thought out front panel, one that you can use without pressing long sequences of buttons or reading tiny print on a small front panel. The last thing that you want to find yourself doing is plowing into a telephone pole because you had to take your eyes off the road to adjust a disc player.

Upgrading Your Car's Stereo System

While we are still on the subject of car players, remember that CDs will require more power and better speakers than tape or radio if you wish to experience their full potential. The dynamic range of these machines will certainly be enough to drive the average car stereo amplifier and speakers into destruction. This means that you will either have to curb your listening levels or upgrade your present system to meet the demands of the compact disc medium. If you do hear distortions while playing your discs at a high level, chances are that you are damaging some component in your stereo system. The only remedy for this is to locate the weak link or links in the system and upgrade them accordingly. This can translate into better speakers, a stouter amplifier that can deliver greater amounts of power, and even separate speaker components to handle high, mid, low, and ultralow frequencies.

Disc and Player Care

Discs that will spend much of their lives in your car will require special attention. We have already discussed some of the potential hazards that discs face outside the home. But remember that a car player will spend all of its time in a harsh environment. Take care how and where you mount the player. If it is an in-dash model, remember that a dashboard can become extremely hot when beaten down upon by the sun. My own cassette deck gets so hot in the summer that it literally destroys tapes if I try to play them before the dash has a chance to cool down, and the inside of the deck is too hot to touch without incurring some painful burns. The same can happen inside a disc player that is mounted high up in a car's dash. Never leave a disc inside the player on a hot and sunny day, as you may find that both the disc and the player have molded themselves together upon your return. It is probably a good idea to let the player cool before you pop a disc into it, as both the player's internal mechanisms and the disc will be adversely affected by operating them while they are hot. The same is true for cold weather, as discs can crack and belts and pulleys will squeal when they are operated at very low temperatures. If you think that a steering wheel is too hot or cold to grasp, chances are that your discs will feel the same way about their player.

Ruggedness and Theft Deterrence

Finally, remember that car disc players will be subjected to more bumps and jolts than any other type of CD player. This means that you should buy a rugged, well-constructed player with very good error-correction capabilities if you expect to get much use or life out of the player. Also note that car stereos are high on the hit list for many thieves, and car CD players top this list. You may want to install your player so that it can easily be removed and locked in the trunk or taken with you when you leave the car. There are many such installation kits; consider using them if you wish to remain a car disc player owner for very long.

THE FINAL CHOICE

It would seem, ultimately, that the player you choose depends not only on its sound, but also on its features. A good-sounding player that is difficult to operate may not be as pleasureful to own as a slightly inferior sounding, easy-to-use machine. If the error correction on one machine is particularly good, you will not find yourself removing a disc in the middle of a song because a spec of dirt caused a mistrack. This may or may not justify spending a little more money on the unit or sacrificing one feature for the sake of another. Just keep in mind that the cost of a CD player can be quite large, as can the accumulated value of all the discs that you will buy in the future. After only a few months of disc ownership, you may accumulate a substantial number of CDs, and you will want to enjoy them from the standpoints of both musicality and convenience. This type of monetary investment warrants a similar investment of your time in researching and picking out a suitable player. The great number of models that are available on the market guarantee that there is one which suits your exact needs. You need only take the time to find it.

9

THE ELECTRICAL OPERATION OF A COMPACT DISC PLAYER

Until now, we have attempted to look at the internal workings of the compact disc player in as nontechnical terms as possible. Block diagrams have been used to map out the flow of data or sound from analog to digital and back again to analog. Although the theory of the digital system has been discussed, as well as some points of its implementation, we have yet to get our hands dirty and probe the resistors and microcircuits of a player to see how they work and what they do. In this chapter we do just that. The reason that this section has come so late in the book is that it is not intended for everyone. Some of you may not care how a clock regeneration circuit works, or how integrated circuits are used to control a laser beam's intensity. If you have a little knowledge of how electric circuits work, or are wondering about how electronics are used to control the many functions of a compact disc player, you will find that information here. In this section we discuss exactly how those block diagrams perform their functions, and how they interact with each other. We take a look at specific microchips and see what functions they perform, and see why some are so well engineered that they can take the place of many predecessors. The workings of a laser pickup and its associated components are discussed from the pickup mechanism through to focusing and preamplification. We trace the flow of data through the player and see how clock regeneration, disc speed control, and a number of other functions are accomplished. The brains of a compact disc player, the microprocessor control, are examined, as are some of the circuits that control the player's display and error correction. As with any such dissection, not all of the circuits will be the same for every player on the market. Some use one chip, whereas others use several; many may use multiple devices, whereas others implement only one. The mechanisms for tracking and servo control also vary between manufacturers, but regardless of the exact electrical implementation, all attempt to attain the same basic goals. For this reason the circuits and implementations contained herein will be an accurate guide to any compact disc player, requiring small adjustments for particular models and manufacturers.

THE LASER PICKUP AND ASSOCIATED CIRCUITRY

In Chapter 6 we unveiled some of the workings of the laser pickup. Remember that a beam of light is transmitted through a series of lenses, and the reflected beam is used to correct the focus, beam intensity, and the tracking of the compact disc's surface. Since these elements mark the beginning of the transformation of pits and lands in a plastic disc into music, they are the logical processes for us to begin with.

The Laser Diode: An Unfocused Light Source

The laser beam begins its life inside a laser diode. The diode is a semiconductor device that works on the same principle as the *light-emitting diode* (LED), which is so popular in electronic watches and games. When electricity passes through the diode, its electrons are stimulated and give off light. The difference between an LED and a laser diode is that the frequency and spectrum of light is different in each. The intensity of the output of the laser diode is controlled electrically by feedback from several circuits (Figure 9.1).

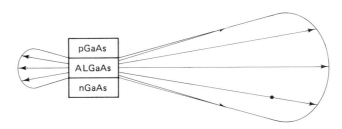

Figure 9.1   Laser diode. (Courtesy of NAP Consumer Electronics Corp.)

Collimator and Objective Lenses:
Focusing the Laser Beam

When a laser beam exits the diode, it is not focused, and left to its own devices would diverge and become useless. It is therefore focused by a lens whose function is to turn the divergent beams into a parallel beam. This lens is called a *collimator* (Figure 9.2). The collimator bends the light inward by a specified angle until the exiting beam is an almost completely parallel one. This beam can travel a large distance before diverging, and so can be focused easily onto a disc. The parallel beam then passes through another lens whose distance from the spinning disc can be varied. Because the beam is parallel between the two lenses, the distance between them is immaterial. This is true because the way a lens focuses light is based on the angle at which the light enters the lens, not on the distance it traveled in getting to the lens. This is why a magnifying glass can focus a light bulb's light which may be just a few feet from the lens as well as it can light from the sun, which is 93 million miles away. If the laser beam were not parallel, the intensity of the beam incident on the disc would vary as the distance

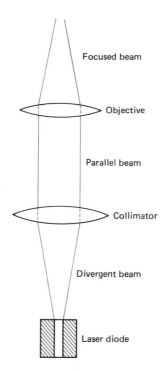

Focused beam

Objective

Parallel beam

Collimator

Divergent beam

Laser diode

Figure 9.2   The collimator lens turns the divergent laser beam into a parallel beam, which is then focused by the objective lens.

between the two lenses changed. The distance between the second lens, called the *objective lens*, is continuously monitored and adjusted so that the laser beam forms a sharp spot on the disc. When the focused beam hits the metallic backside of the disc, it is reflected back through the objective and collimator lenses along its original path. This reflected beam is diverted from reaching the laser diode by a prism that lays between the laser diode and the collimator. This prism serves two functions. The first is to alter the path of the reflected beam. This is accomplished by placing a half-silvered surface inside the prism. Like the surface of a one-way mirror, light can pass from the laser through the prism but not from the collimator to the laser. Instead, the return beam is reflected at a 90° angle to its original direction, so that it falls upon the surface of a light-sensitive photodiode. The prism also splits this reflected beam into two beams, each of which falls on separate parts of the photodiode (Figure 9.3). The position of these beams depends on how well the laser and lenses are aligned with the surface of the compact disc, as well as on the focus of the beam.

Photodiodes: Sensing the Laser's Light

The two beams of light then strike two pairs of photodiodes. The electrical current emanating from these devices is proportional to the amount of light striking them, so if the beams are not properly focused and aligned, the output of either one or both diodes will be affected. It is the

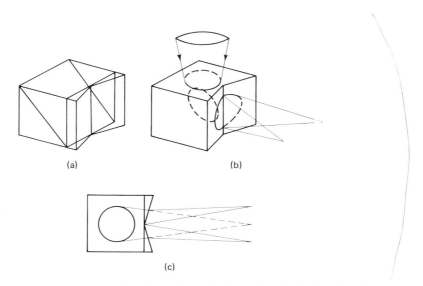

(a)   (b)

(c)

Figure 9.3 Splitting prism (a). The reflected beam is diverted by a half-silvered surface and split into two separate beams on its way to the photodiode (b). Top view of the prism (c). (Courtesy of NAP Consumer Electronics Corp.)

voltage from these units that is used to control the positioning of the tracking assembly. If the beam is focused correctly, as in Figure 9.4a, the amount of light falling on each pair of diodes will be equal. This means that the amount of current emanating from them will also be equal. The current from each photodiode is summed by a differential amplifier whose output is relative to the difference between the two currents. The difference amplifier is like an electronic balance. If current 2 is greater than current 1, the amplifier will produce a negative voltage at its output. If current 1 is greater than 2, a positive voltage will result. In Figure 9.4a the main beam is focused, so that the summer's output is zero. In Figure 9.4b, the beam is out of focus because the objective lens is too close to the disc, so the amplifier's output is positive. Figure 9.4c shows just the opposite situation. As noted, each bank of photodiodes consists of a pair of diodes, not a single one. Also, the intensity of the reflected beam depends on whether it passes through a

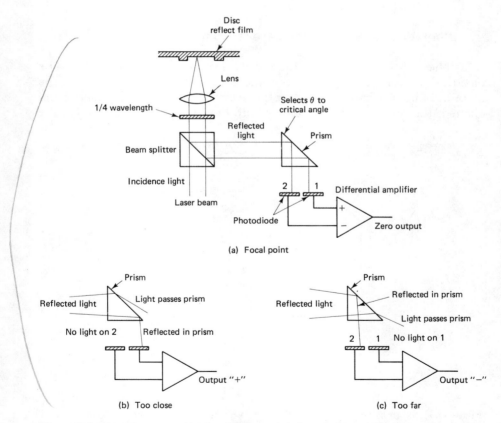

Figure 9.4 Focusing correction showing three situations: in focus (a), too close (b), and too far (c). (Courtesy of Yamaha Electronics Corporation, USA.)

pit or a land. When it hits a land, it is nearly completely reflected back on its original path, while hitting a pit causes less light to be reflected. The output of the four diodes is summed not only for tracking purposes, but also to assess the intensity of the reflected laser beam, and hence determine whether a pit or land is focused upon.

It is also necessary to determine whether or not the laser spot is impinging on the center of the compact disc's track rather than to one side or the other. This is also accomplished via a summing of the diodes. One problem which occurs is that as the laser pickup ages, the spot it casts may become eccentrically shaped, that is, deviate from a perfectly round spot. Left uncorrected, this would tend to cause the pickup to offset to one side of the track and introduce an offset into the voltage which is produced by the photodiodes. This off-center condition is unacceptable, so the position of the pickup arm is modulated by a 600-Hz sine wave. The sine wave causes the more or less radially stationary arm to swing back and forth in a scanning motion. The amplitude of this swing is quite small, approximately ±0.05 micrometer. The spot will be on center sometime during this swing, so the output voltage from the photodiodes will contain an oscillating component at 600 Hz. The amplitude of the component increases as the spot moves farther from the center of the track, and its sign changes from positive to negative depending on which side of the track the beam hits. This signal is averaged over time and this average dc value is used to correct for an out-of-round or off-center beam (Figure 9.5).

Laser Intensity: Maintaining the Brightness of the Beam

Finally, the output intensity of the laser diode must be maintained in some manner, for it, too, will change with both temperature and age. A monitor diode is used for this purpose (Figure 9.6). Some of the light which

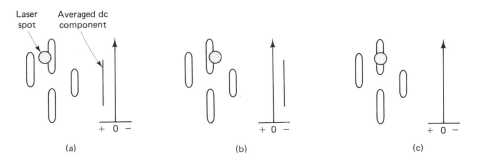

Figure 9.5 An out-of-round or off-center laser spot causes an average dc component in swing of the optical assembly. If the beam is off center to the left, a positive component appears (a). A right off-center condition causes a negative component (b). This signal can be used to modify the positioning of the optical assembly until no dc component remains (c).

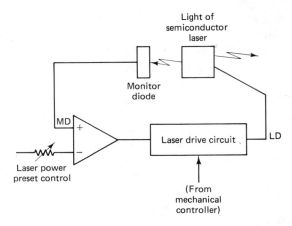

Figure 9.6 Monitor diode and laser drive circuitry. The monitor diode's output is compared to a reference voltage, then used to regulate the output of the laser drive circuit. (Courtesy of Yamaha Electronics Corporation, USA.)

initially emanates from the laser is diverted to the monitor diode, which itself is simply a photodiode. The ouput from this device is fed into one input of a difference amplifier. The other input is fixed to a constant, predetermined value which corresponds to the correct laser diode intensity. The output of the amplifier controls another circuit, called the *laser drive circuit*. This, in turn, controls the amount of current fed to the laser diode, thereby closing the feedback loop. If the output of the laser increases, the monitor diode's output increases and the voltage at the positive input of the difference amplifier becomes greater than the reference voltage. This signals the laser drive circuit to decrease the amount of current to the laser diode. If the laser diodes ouput falls, the output of the difference amplifier swings negative, signaling the the drive circuit to increase the amount of current to the laser diode. In this manner a constant light intensity can be maintained, so that the light falling on the photodiodes is dependent on the surface characteristics of the disc rather than an unsteady laser intensity. If no such correction were made, the light hitting the photodiodes would vary not only because of pits and lands, but also because of the variations in the laser diode circuit. This could cause the pits and lands to be read incorrectly by the optical assembly.

The Optical Assembly: Maintaining Alignment Between the Components

In order for corrections to be made after the tracking signals have been obtained, there must be some mechanism to move both the laser assembly and its components relative to the disc and each other. The laser, lenses, and photodiodes are collectively called the *optical pickup* (Figure 9.7).

These are mounted on an arm much like the tonearm of a turntable. A motor moves the arm into various positions and is controlled by some of the signals which we have just discussed. The objective lens must also move in and out relative to the collimator, so it is mounted to a coil and magnet assembly which is used to control its linear motion with respect to the disc's surface. The signals that are derived from the photodiodes are sent to an amplifier, then an actuator, which converts these signals into pulses which can control the movement of the motor or magnets. These signals, combined with others derived from the front-panel buttons, programming information, and the digital data itself, are used to position the optical assembly and control the tracking of the compact disc.

DATA-HANDLING CIRCUITRY

Zero-Crossing Detector: Determining the Pit and Land Transitions

Once the optical pickup is under way and tracking, a stream of data will emerge that must be processed. After emerging from the photodiodes,

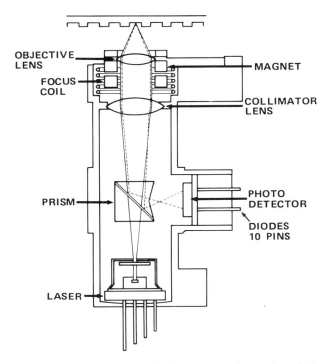

Figure 9.7 Optical pickup unit showing the lenses, prism, laser, photodiode, and magnetic focusing ring. (Courtesy of NAP Consumer Electronics Corp.)

the electrical pulses are converted into an eye pattern. The zero crossings of this eye pattern are used to mark the transitions between pits and lands. It is these transitions which determine the value of various channel bits. The crossings are detected by a device called a *zero-crossing detector*. This is yet another differential amplifier which is set to detect when the eye pattern's voltage crosses a reference level of zero volts. What emerges from this detector are the actual channel bits which were encoded so long ago. The zero-crossing detector is pictured in Figure 9.8.

Clock Regeneration: Synchronizing the System

A clock signal must be derived from these channel bits to control the operation of the demodulator, memory buffer, error-correction circuitry, demultiplexer, disc motor speed controller, and the digital-to-analog converter. The clock regenerator is basically one big feedback loop (Figure 9.9). Signals are compared to each other and adjustments are constantly made to both the phase and period of the outputted clock signal.

A frequency-to-voltage converter is used to get a rough approximation of the clock frequency. Since the frequency at which the clock should oscillate is a known quantity, it can be used as a first approximation to the correct frequency. This frequency is known because the data rate at which information was encoded on the disc is the same for all compact discs. The rate at which they should be read off the disc is the same frequency, so this can be used as a first approximation. This frequency is fine tuned by comparing the position at which the transitions in the data occur to where the transitions in the rough clock approximation occur. If the clock is locked onto the correct frequency, these transitions will occur at the same time. Any difference in the transitions is detected by the phase detector and used to modulate the output of a voltage-controlled oscillator. As its name indicates, the VCO oscillates or produces a square wave of a particular frequency which depends on the two input voltages from the frequency-to-voltage converter and the phase comparator. The clock exiting the VCO is

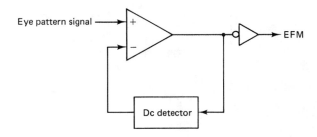

Figure 9.8 A zero-crossing detector is used to extract the transitions between pits and lands from the output of the photodiodes. (Courtesy of Yamaha Electronics Corporation, USA.)

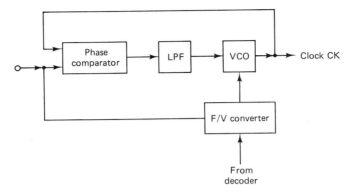

Figure 9.9 A phase-locked loop is used to extract a clock from the EFM transitions. (Courtesy of Yamaha Electronics Corporation, USA.)

used as an input to the phase comparator, which again checks it against a known frequency. In this way the feedback loop is closed. The clock that emanates from the VCO must be very accurate, as it is used to control the 4.32-Mbps stream which is encoded on the compact disc.

Demodulation: Reversing the EFM Process

Once a system clock has been regenerated from the channel bits, the bits are ready for demodulation back into data bits. Recall that data undergo eight-to-fourteen modulation (EFM) before they are encoded on the disc's surface. The demodulator is a look-up table whose input is the stream of channel bits and whose output is a stream of data bits. The input is matched to the correct output inside the demodulator. This output contains not only the multiplexed audio data, but also error-correction and synchronization bits. The frame synchronization bits are identifed and stripped off the outgoing stream. These synchronization bits are necessary so that the beginning and ending of a frame can be marked and identified and also so that the correct portion of channel bits are used for the fourteen-to-eight demodulation. In this way, frames can be identified and decoded in a single stage. The audio data and error correction bits exit the demodulator, all of which have yet to be demultiplexed and decoded back into their original 16-bit PCM forms. The demodulator also provides a signal which indicates the beginning and ending points of each frame as well as a bit that signals where the beginning of each track occurs. The latter bit is used by the control logic to position the optical pickup at the correct point over the beginning of a track on the disc as well as signal the beginning of the subcode information. When a search for a particular selection is in progress, this bit is monitored and the subcode information is used to determine if the correct track has been accessed.

FIFO Buffer: Getting Rid of Wow and Flutter

From the demodulator, the data now travel into a memory device called a *first-in, first-out buffer* (FIFO). The FIFO is an electronic memory which works much like a paper cup dispenser. Bits stream in at the input, or top of the FIFO, and fall immediately to the output, or bottom of the FIFO. So the first bit that is input to the FIFO is also the first one available at its output, hence the name FIFO (Figure 9.10). The FIFO buffer can hold a large number of data bits, so if there is a deficiency of bits because the disc is read too slowly, the FIFO can be drained of bits while a correction to the turntable speed is made. If too many bits avalanche at the FIFO's input, it can absorb and store these bits while a controller slows down the turntable. Since data can be clocked out of the FIFO at a constant speed regardless of the speed at which they are input, data will flow out of the FIFO at a constant rate. The system clock that was recovered from the bit stream is used to clock data out of the FIFO. This buffer is one reason that wow and flutter figures for a compact disc player are so low. For although there may be physical wow and flutter of the turntable's speed, they are buffered by the FIFO and electronically obliterated. The only wow and flutter that will occur are those caused by irregularities in the system clock.

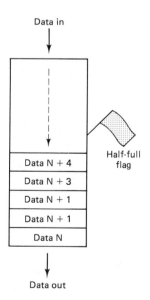

Figure 9.10   First-in, first-out buffer, or FIFO. Data appearing at the FIFO's input fall immediately to the top of the stack. Data at the output of the FIFO can be clocked out independently of the data coming into the FIFO.

Error Correction: Implementing it in Hardware

From the FIFO, data bits, still in a serial form, are passed onto an error-correcting device. This device works with another memory device which once again buffers data. The purpose of this buffer, called a *random-access memory* (RAM), is to hold several words of data while they are deinterleaved. You will remember that the audio information was scrambled in time, or multiplexed, before its conversion into channel bits. The RAM stores a large number of bits which can be accessed so that the original stream of bits can be reconstructed. When the RAM is half full, it sets a bit which indicates to the servo drive controller that the motor is spinning the disc at the correct rate. The rotational speed of the motor is directly related to the number of bits per second which are read off the disc. If the RAM drops below half full, indicating a deficiency of bits, a similar signal is sent which tells the motor controller to speed up the rotation speed until the RAM is again half full. If the RAM fills above the halfway point, indicating that too many bits persecond are being read from the disc, the motor controller is signaled to slow down the rotation speed. This action, combined with the action of the FIFO, eliminates wow and flutter almost totally (Figure 9.11). The RAM is accessed by the error-correction circuitry, which checks the parity bits and determines if an error has occurred. If one has, the CIRC code is used to correct it. Occasionally, an error will occur which is too severe even for the CIRC coding to correct. This is a rare occurrence, as a stream of data about 4000 bits long can be wiped out before the error correction fails. When such a failure does occur, the audio signal must be either muted or replaced by a linear interpolation.

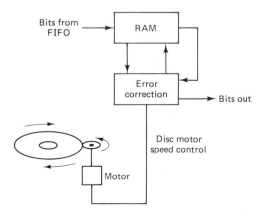

Figure 9.11 The disc motor's speed is controlled by signals from the error-correction circuitry and the RAM. If the RAM fills above halfway, the motor is slowed. If it drops below half full, the motor is speeded up.

Muting and Interpolation: Covering up when Error Correction Fails

From the error correction section, data bits are passed to a muting or interpolating section. If no errors have occurred or if the errors have been corrected, this section merely passes on the data without change. If an error has occurred, a signal is passed along with the data which marks them as bad. If possible, this stage performs a linear interpolation of the previous and next symbols and inserts this average value in the place of the erroneous bits. If consecutive errors have occurred, the output of the player must be muted until good data are again detected. Also, when a search for a particular track is in progress, the output of the player must be muted, so this signal serves a double purpose.

Digital Filtering and D/A Conversion: Turning Bits into Sounds

If the data from the error correcting section were good, the data are separated into left- and right-channel components, and if digital filtering is used, passed on to that stage. The digital filter applies the algorithm which we discussed in Chapter 3. Each symbol is passed through a series of stages which multiply it by a filter coefficient and then sum it with a number of the previous products. The left- and right-channel data are pipelined through separate, although identical filters, and emerge ready to be applied to the digital-to-analog converter. If a single converter is used, first the left, then the right channel will be D/A'd. Switching is accomplished by a multiplexer which alternates clocking the left- and right-channel data into the D/A. If dual D/As are used, the data are clocked into them simultaneously, and the analog conversion takes place at the same time for both channels. The signal, now analog, is passed through a low-pass filter bank and is then amplified and output to the rear panel of the player (Figure 9.12).

CONTROLLING THE PLAYER'S MANY FUNCTIONS

Disc Motor Servo: Controlling the Speed of the Disc

A phonograph is a constant-radial-velocity device. That means that regardless of the position of the tone arm, the record spins at $33\frac{1}{3}$ rpm. At the outside of the record the velocity of the groove is much higher than at the center. If you were to stretch out the record groove into a straight line, you would find that the speed of this groove, called the *linear velocity*, decreased as the record was played. This occurs because the circumference of one rotation in a groove at the inner part of the record is shorter than at the

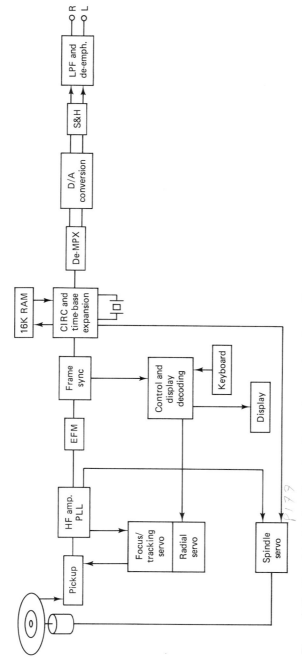

Figure 9.12 Complete data handling, decoding, and conversion scheme. [Courtesy of Pioneer Electronics (USA) Inc.]

outer edge. Because the frequency response of a record is dependent on the velocity of the groove, this response will change from the record's center to its middle. The compact disc is a constant-linear-velocity device. This implies that the velocity of the pits and lands as they pass by the laser optical assembly is held constant. This also means that the rotational speed of the disc, the speed at which it spins around, depends on the position of the tracking arm in relation to the disc's center. When the arm is positioned over the outside of the disc, the rotational speed is relatively low. At 2.25 in. from the disc's center, a track is about 14.14 in. around, while it is only about 12.55 in. around at 2 in. from the center (Figure 9.13). As the arm tracks from the center, the rotational speed is decreased so that the linear velocity of the track remains the same. So unlike record player's turntables, which are often quartz locked to a specific frequency, the rotational speed of a disc player is constantly changing. Under normal circumstances, this quantity is controlled by monitoring the output of the RAM as well as the clock period.

Microcomputer Controller: The Player's Electronic Brain

Some disc players use separate circuits to control many of the aforementioned functions. Others use more sophisticated methods. The brains behind this activity is sometimes a microprocessor. This is simply a microchip or set of microchips which are able to execute some simple commands and react to input data, much like the microprocessor of a computer does. The microprocessor that is contained in a compact disc player is, however, much simpler than that of an actual computer, but its capabilities are more than adequate for the job for which it is intended. A

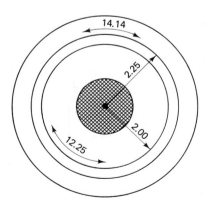

Figure 9.13   The circumference at 2 in. from the disc's center is 12.25 in., while it is 14.14 in. at 2.25 in. from the center. This means that the disc must revolve more slowly as the outer tracks are read so that a constant linear velocity can be maintained.

typical setup is depicted in Figure 9.14. As you can see, this particular compact disc player uses two microprocessors to control just about all of the tasks associated with decoding a disc.

CPU-2 controls the disc player's interface to the outside world. It monitors all of the buttons that affect the player's operation, such as the open/close, play, and other functions. When a key is pressed it signals CPU-1 to perform some function, such as to skip to another track or fast scan the disc. It also controls the display panel of the player and sends these commands, which indicate the track, expired time, or other such information. The two CPUs talk to each other over a connection called a *data bus*. As its name implies, the data bus carries information in between the two central processing units.

The other processor, CPU-1, controls signal processing and mechanical functions. Information from the decoder is sent to the CPU, which makes a decision as to whether or not the data should be muted or interpolated or if they are good. Signals from the photodiodes are also passed to this CPU so that it can control tracking, focusing, and the disc's rotational speed. The CPU has a set of instructions that it executes when the player is powered-up. These instructions may tell the CPU to check if the disc drawer is open, and shut it if it is, or to check for a disc in the tray and play it if one is found. The processors may perform quick test of various parts of the player to determine if they are working, and report an error condition if one is found.

The CPUs tie together all the components of a disc player. Each subsystem acts autonomously under certain conditions and is subservient to other systems at times. The laser control circuits sometimes regulate the optical assembly, while the CPUs can act to control both these circuits. Similarly, the disc drive motor is controlled sometimes by signals from the RAM and sometimes, such as during spin-up or shutoff, by orders from the CPU. The CPUs determine which system has priority over another and often regulate these priorities by checking the condition of each system against a program of possible conditions. The designers of the disc player must take into account every possible scenario and conflict that may arise involving the subsystems of the disc player, and program the CPU such that it can handle every possibility. This is part of the flexibility of the compact disc player, for its attributes are limited only by the imagination and capabilities of its designers.

MECHANICAL ADJUSTMENTS

There a number of adjustments that can be made to a compact disc player when it acts erratically. Some involve testing and adjusting the electronics, others require the replacement of parts, and some just require that the

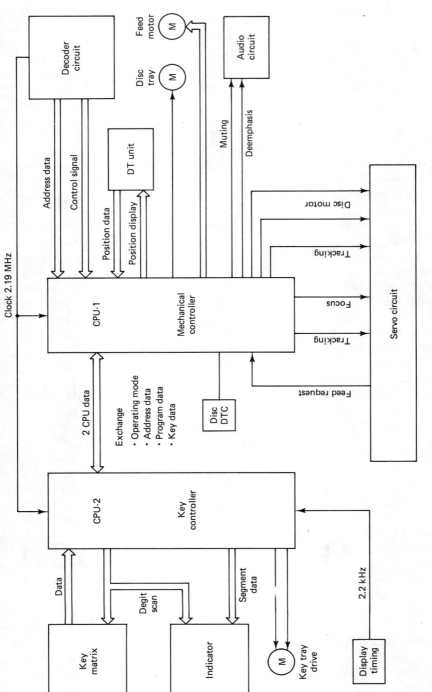

Figure 9.14 Outline of the microcomputer control for a disc player. CPUs 1 and 2 control many functions, including display, front-panel inputs, tracking, focusing, and others. (Courtesy of Yamaha Electronics Corporation, USA.)

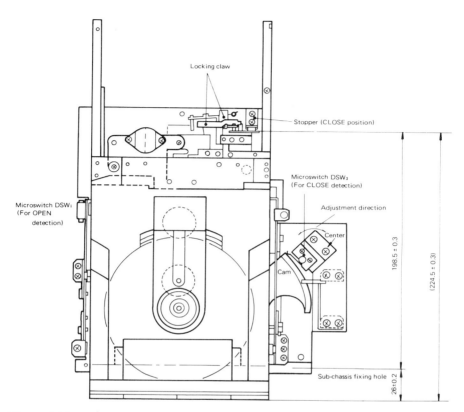

Figure 9.15 Disc drawer showing microswitches, spindle, and disc tray motor and clamp. (Courtesy of Yamaha Electronics Corporation, USA.)

correct screw be turned. One common problem is with the disc tray (Figure 9.15). If the disc tray sticks or acts strangely, it may not be aligned correctly with the opening in the player's front panel. There are a number of screws situated around the tray which can be used to position it correctly. There is also a microswitch which is depressed when the tray is fully seated inside the player, and there may be one that is actuated when the tray is fully opened. If these become misaligned, the player may not be able to tell when the tray is opened or closed. These switches are also adjustable. When the disc tray is closed, it may be held shut by a lever or cam. If this fails to make contact with the tray, the disc will not align correctly when it is played. Similarly, if the lever does not release the tray smoothly, the drawer will stick. If the tray has become jammed, there is a possibility that the tray motor has burned out or its gears have been stripped. This problem cannot be cured by adjustment, but rather, warrants replacement.

If the drawer functions correctly and the player is still erratic, the clamp that holds the disc may be out of alignment. This can cause the disc to slip while it is being spun or to wobble as it turns. The gears that drive the disc from the motor can wear out or strip, as can the motor itself. Finally, the optical pickup can lose its alignment and become canted to one direction or be too far from the disc to focus properly. This type of adjustment requires that the eye pattern as well as several other signals be monitored while the adjustments are performed. Adjustment of the voltage-controlled oscillator, focusing circuit, and laser diode output require specialized equipment and specification as well as a keen knowledge of electronics. Such things as the tracking circuit and output level involve testing and adjusting components on the circuit boards themselves.

Although the procedures for making these adjustments are not difficult, they are impossible without the correct tools, information, and training. For these reasons, all the aforementioned adjustments should be left to trained service people and should not be attempted by the casual owner.

CONCLUSIONS

The disc player as a whole is a combination of mechanical and electronic systems. Although this can be said of many consumer products on today's market, the disc player differs in that it embodies some of the most sophisticated aspects of both. Miniature laser diodes and optoisolators are relatively new devices, as are cheap digital-to-analog converters. Many of the disc player's chips have been combined so that there now exist special-purpose chips which, when hooked together, form the basis of an inexpensive yet technologically advanced machine. This sometimes belies the fact that inside these few chips are literally tens of thousands of transistors, the function of each of which has been painstakingly thought out and implemented in silicon. Even the simplest circuits are complex when considered from this level. Luckily, most of us need never bother with the details contained in this chapter, but it is interesting to see how modern advances have made possible a new era in the audio field.

10

ACCESSORIES AND CARING FOR COMPACT DISCS AND PLAYERS

Evaluating, understanding, and buying a compact disc player are only a few of the things you need to know about them. Ownership of a disc player involves more than knowing how it works. In fact, knowing about the inside of a player does not help you care for its outside. Discs, too, need special care from time to time, as they can become dirty, scratched, or warped if handled incorrectly. In this chapter we learn about some of the do's and don'ts of disc handling. We'll see how and where to store discs, how to take care of them, and how to take care of your disc player. To help compact disc player owners to take care of their investment, a number of companies have introduced accessories tailored to that purpose. Everything from disc storage modules to disc cleaning devices are available from these sources, as are a host of products that claim to better the sound and performance of disc players. There are also a number of handy converters, carriers, and other accessories that may be considered useful, and we investigate what is available on the market.

CARING FOR YOUR PLAYER

At first it may seem that the compact disc player requires no care at all. You simply pop a disc into it, press a few buttons, and let the player do the rest. For the most part, this is true, but there are a few things that you may wish to note.

Keep Your Player Away from the Elements

If you have a home player, the first thing that you should do is make sure that you have placed it in a good location. If you place it on top of a table, is it in direct sunlight? As most players have black finishes, they will absorb heat from the sun and may heat to well above room temperature. Even in an air-conditioned environment, a metal case can become quite hot and possibly damage the internal components. Leaving a player in the sun will not only hurt the electronics by overheating them, but may also warp internal rubber and plastic parts such as vibration dampers, bushings, and even the optical pickup arm and disc tray. If you leave a disc in the player, it may warp and become useless if heated to high enough temperatures. In short, do not put a player in direct sunlight unless you want trouble. This is even more true for portable players, as they are sometimes left on a car's dashboard or outside in the sun. The car environment is perhaps the worst for a portable CD player, as the air temperature inside the car will rise while the sun heats the player's casing, causing a doubly bad environment. If you must leave a portable player outside or in your car, either place it under a car seat or under a shirt or bag so as not to expose it to direct sunlight. Wind, dirt, and moisture are as destructive as heat, so your player should not be exposed to these elements either. In the home, this means that you should not put a player near an open window if that will expose it to outside dirt and dust. If the player is kept in a particularly smoky room, be aware that such smoke can enter the player and deposit itself on the optical parts of the machine, causing them to perform less efficiently. Dirt such as that produced in a workshop can become airborne and enter the player, as can dust that settles on the player's outer surface. If you have a portable player, it will probably experience all of the aforementioned elements. When possible, keep the player shielded from these, as they are all potentially destructive. Do not expose the unit to rain or dust storms, and if you use it at the beach, keep it as isolated as possible from the sand and spray. These can corrode the outside of the player as well as its inside. If your unit has a remote control, keeping the remote unit clean will keep dirt and grease from interfering in its transmission and aid it in performing satisfactorily.

Cleaning the Player

A good idea is to clean the outside of a disc player, either home or portable, on a regular basis. This removes dust and dirt which can find their way into the player or damage the unit's appearance. Be careful never to use chemicals that might damage the player's finish. The manufacturer will usually recommend a safe cleaning method for a particular model, and this should be adhered to, as it will usually provide the best results. If you must use a cleaner not recommended by the manufacturer, experiment with it on a small area in an inconspicuous place on the player to determine if it will or will not harm the finish.

Vibrations and How to Stop Them

While you are considering where to place your player, remember that it is sensitive to vibrations. Putting the player on an unsturdy table will only amplify the effects of footsteps, slamming doors, and passing trucks, so the base should be as stable as possible. If you place the unit near or on a speaker, then as the musical intensity increases, so will the vibrations that are transmitted to the chassis. This can cause the player to mistrack or introduce errors into the bit stream. Finally, most manufacturers will tell you not to stack items on top of a player, as this can distort the shape of the chassis and cause the components which are fixed to the chassis to lose their alignment. Stacking components onto a disc player may also cause its vibration-absorbing feet to become crushed or distorted, thereby decreasing their effectiveness.

Powering Your Player

One thing that people never seem to consider is which electrical outlet to plug a player into. One possibility is the back of a receiver or amplifier. These units sometimes have outlets in their chassis which make handy points to power up your other components. These outlets come in two varieties, switched and unswitched. *Switched* means that when the power is turned off to the receiver or amplifier through its power switch, power is also shut off to the switched outlet. This type of outlet is most often used with preamplifiers, tape decks, and graphic equalizers. An *unswitched* outlet is one that stays on as long as the receiver or amplifier is plugged into the wall outlet. The main power switch has no effect on this outlet. This outlet is normally reserved for a turntable, since it is a bad practice to shut power off to this device while the turntable is rotating and the needle is in contact with the record. Either type of outlet is suited for use with a CD player. Before you plug a disc player or any component into the switched or unswitched outlet, make certain that you will not exceed the maximum power capacity of that outlet. This maximum rating is usually marked next to the outlet in the owner's manual of the component. Simply look up the maximum power consumption of the disc player on its back panel or in the owner's manual, and make sure that that quantity is less than the maximum of the outlet.

If the player is not going to be plugged into a receiver, a wall outlet is your next choice. The first thing you should check is that there are no noisy devices on the same circuit as the player. A refrigerator or washer/dryer will often cause voltage spikes when they are turned on and off. These spikes travel along the electrical wiring of your house and can damage a player or cause noise at its output. They do this by overloading the internal circuitry of the player and blowing out either fuses or internal components, or by passing noise in through the power supplies. You have no doubt heard such pops and clicks over a radio or stereo or have observed the effects of a vacuum cleaner which causes interference in a television's picture. If you are serious about protecting a player from noise spikes, you can buy a box that fits between the player's power cord and the electrical outlet and will filter out such spikes. More on that later. It is also a good idea to unplug your disc player, or, for that matter, any sensitive electronic unit, whenever there is an electrical storm in the area. A lightning strike can send a massive pulse through electrical lines which can damage a player even if it is not turned on. The strike need not be a direct one, as electricity in the air will cause voltage surges in your home's wiring. Even a surge protector can be overloaded under these conditions, in which case both the protector and your disc player could be zapped simultaneously.

CARING FOR COMPACT DISCS

Compact discs are not indestructible. You cannot step on them, use them as a Frisbee, and clean them with gasoline and still expect them to play well. They are made of plastic, very strong plastic to be sure, but they still must be treated with the same care that you would show a record album or tape. Discs become dirty for many reasons and so must be cleaned. They must be stored and handled, played, and transported. All of these operations subject discs to possible damage, but there are some rules of thumb to adhere to which can lessen the probability of such damage.

The Compact Disc's Enemies

To begin, what goes for CD players goes for the discs as well. They should never be exposed to extreme heat or placed in direct sunlight. Discs are made of a polycarbonate plastic. This type of plastic begins to soften at temperatures between 200 and 230°F. Unfortunately, discs can warp at temperatures below this threshold, and can be affected by such temperatures. Leaving a disc near a fireplace or on top of a radiator is a definite mistake, as is letting one bake on top of a car's dashboard or in its trunk. This kind of abuse will severely shorten the life of a compact disc. Extreme cold is as hazardous to a disc as is extreme heat. In particular, leaving a disc outside on a cold winter's night can cause it to crack or cloud, ruining the disc. Taking a disc from one temperature extreme to another can also damage it. Taking a hot disc, such as one that has been sitting in the sun, and placing it in a disc player can induce a warp that might not have occurred if the disc had been allowed to cool before it was played. Similarly, a disc that has been cooled down to a freezing temperature should be allowed to come up to room temperature before it is used in a player. Not only can such thermal shock damage the disc, but moving a disc from cold to heat can cause moisture to condense on the surface of the disc, moisture which is then spun off the disc and into the player.

Dust, dirt, and grease have to be the number one enemies of the entire CD system. Not only can they damage a player, but they can destroy a disc at the same time. Like any plastic, the surface of a compact disc is subject to scratches. A few such scratches are not bad, as they can be corrected by the player. But when enough scratches accumulate, the player cannot correct the errors which they induce and the disc can no longer be enjoyed. Like a skipping record, the disc player will have to be advanced manually when the bad section of disc is encountered.

The first rule of disc care is to store discs where they will not be subjected to dirt. Keep them in their case when not playing them, for this is perhaps the best way to keep dirt from impinging on them. Also be sure to keep the disc cases, called jewel boxes, clean, so that when a disc is inserted into one, it will not pick up any dirt. When you do handle a disc, hold it by its outside edges, just as you would a vinyl record. You may also place your finger in the middle hole of the disc and hold it that way. Jewel boxes are made so that you need not handle the disc's surface when removing the disc. Take advantage of this ability. The same care should be taken when you place in or remove a disc from the disc drawer.

Cleaning a Disc

No matter how well you treat your discs, they will become dirty. If the disc is not dirty enough to cause an audible error to occur while it is playing, the best advice is to leave it alone. Cleaning a disc can be a destructive process. That is because dirt laying on the disc's surface can be ground into the plastic in the act of cleaning. So although the dirt is removed, scratches will remain, and they cannot be removed. If the disc becomes dirty enough to warrant cleaning, you will have to use a cloth or cleaner. Before you try cleaning the disc with a cloth, there is one thing that you might try. Cans of compressed air can be bought at many department or specialty stores. These can often be used to blow dust and dirt off the disc, making further cleaning unnecessary. At worst, they will remove superficial dirt so that further cleansing is less troublesome and destructive. If you must use a cloth to clean the disc, there are a few rules to follow. The first is never to clean a disc with a dry rag or cloth. This will inevitably leave scratches in the disc, since the cloth will merely grind the dirt into the disc. Always moisten the cloth with some type of liquid before using it to wipe the disc. The next rule is not to use strong cleansers such as benzene or volatile solvents such as paint thinners. These can cloud or soften the plastic or take the label right off. Some cleansers will turn plastic into a gummy goo, so avoid any cleanser that you are not sure of. If you are going to use such a cleanser, try it out on a disc that you are not too fond of and expect the worst. Many products are available which claim that they are safe for use on compact discs. These liquids are formulated so as not to harm the disc's surface. This type of product should be used to clean the disc, or you can use distilled water or a nonvolatile cleanser such as denatured alcohol. When cleaning a disc, always wipe from the middle of the disc out toward the center. Never wipe across the face of the disc or in a circular motion. Wiping in an outward direction will prevent scratches from causing errors in a number of consecutive bits. Wiping the disc in a circular motion will cause scratches across the face of the disc which can wipe out many consecutive bits, thereby causing an error that cannot be corrected. There are devices on the market specifically designed to clean compact discs. Some of these use the correct method of cleansing and some do not. Stay away from units that do not clean the disc by wiping it along its radius. These can only damage your discs in the long term.

TROUBLESHOOTING PROBLEMS

When a compact disc player malfunctions, there is very little in the way of service that an untrained person can do. Unlike a tape deck, there are no heads or capstans to clean, nor can you check for a worn stylus or incorrect antiskate pressure as with a turntable. All of the inner electronics are unservicable without the correct training and equipment, something that few of us have. There is also the optical section to contend with, and this, if damaged, is usually replaced rather than repaired. So aside from the aforementioned preventive measures, there is little to do when a player will not operate. Before you send a player off for service or take it back to your dealer, there are a number of things that you might check for that could masquerade as serious problems (Table 10.1).

Problems with the Player's Output

The most common thing to go wrong with a player is that it has no output (Table 10.1a). This can be the fault of a number of systems. The laser diode might burn out, the photodiode could be damaged, or the digital or analog sections of the player may have been zapped by static electricity or have simply died for an unknown reason. The disc may not sound as if it is spinning when inside the player, or the disc drawer itself may become jammed. Alternatively, the player's lack of output may be caused by a very trivial matter. The first thing to check when the disc player does not play is the rear-panel connections. As most players have only one output, this is a

TABLE   10.1   Disc Player Problems

Possible Cause	Check	Cure
a. *Symptom:* No output		
1. Incorrect cable connections	Check input and output connections against those in the owner's manual	Correct connections
2. Amplifier or receiver not switched to CD input	Check front panel switches	Switch to CD input
3. Bad CD player	Connect a different source, such as a tape or phono, to CD input	Service CD player
4. Bad amplifier	Same as (3)	Service amplifier
5. Bad cable	Substitute a cable from a working source	Replace cable
b. *Symptom:* One channel out		
1. Bad amplifier channel	Switch cables at amplifier	If the same channel is still out, service the amplifier
2. Bad CD channel	Same as (1)	If a different channel is out, proceed to (3)
3. Bad cable	Switch cables at CD player	If same channel is out, replace the cable. If a different channel is out, service the CD player
c. *Symptom:* Disc tray jammed		
1. Disc not seated correctly	Open drawer and check the disc	Reseat disc
2. Disc upside down	Same as (1)	Flip the disc over
3. Foreign object in player	Check inside the player (if the warranty allows); first make certain that the player is unplugged	Dislodge object or remove disc

simple matter. The output from the left channel should go into the left channel input of the receiver or amplifier, and the right-channel output should plug into the right-channel input. If the player has digital outputs, be sure not to swap these for the audio lines.

If these connections are correct, check that the amplifier is switched so that the CD player is its source. Often, a number of components will be connected to an amplifier to act as its source, so although the CD player may be playing its disc, the selector switch may be set for a different input, such as a record player or tape deck. If the volume control is turned up sufficiently, the CD's signal may leak into the other channels, so you may actually hear the CD player at a much reduced volume. Setting the selector switch so that it matches the correct source will solve this problem.

The next step is to check if the problem is in the amplifier rather than in the disc player. To do this, first disconnect the disc player from the amplifier. Now connect another source, such as a tape deck, to the one occupied previously by the CD machine. If the problem was in the amplifier, this source will not work either. If the problem was not in the amplifier, the source will work normally. If you ascertain that the amplifier is all right, then another component may be at fault. The cable that connects the CD player to the player may be bad, so switch this with a good set of cables. If sound returns with the new set, the problem is in the old cables, not in the disc player.

What to Do If One Channel Is Out

Occasionally, only one channel of the player will work (Table 10.1b). In this case the first thing to do is switch the left and right channels of the CD player where they connect to the amplifier. If the same channel plays as before they were switched, the problem is in the amplifier, not in the player. If, conversely, the opposite channel comes to life, the amplifier is all right and the problem is with the player. Again, you must check the cables to make certain that they are functioning. To do this, switch the cables where they exit the CD player, not where they exit the amplifier. If the opposite channel goes out, the fault is in the cable, not in the player. If the same channel stays out, the player has a problem.

What Can You Do About a Jammed Disc Drawer?

Even though the disc player does not produce an output, it is not necessarily the time to call in the service department. It is entirely possible that a disc may sit incorrectly inside the disc tray, and so although there is no output, there is not necessarily a service problem (Table 10.1c). If the disc is not put flat into the disc tray, when the tray attempts to close, one of two things will happen. The most probable is that the player will reject the tray until the disc is placed onto it in the correct manner. The disc tray may also jam, in which case it should be gently nudged outward until it releases the disc. Alternatively, the tray may slide into the player but the spindle will be unable to grasp the disc, so the tray will remain shut but the disc will not spin. There will be no signal at the player's output, and this can often be mistaken for a malfunctioning electronic section. One way to tell whether or not the disc is spinning is to check the elapsed time indicator. If it shows that the disc is playing, chances are that the disc tray is not the problem. Since the LED display of most players functions differently when the disc is in play than when it is not, this may be a clue as to whether or not the disc is seated correctly. If you believe that the disc is jammed, open the disc drawer and reseat the disc. Also make certain that the disc has not been placed into the tray upside down. Most players will accept the disc in this position, but they will be unable to scan it for information. If a disc is unusually dirty, the player will again be unable to scan it and will show the same symptoms as those of an upside down or jammed disc.

Foreign Objects Inside the Chassis

There is also a possibility that some foreign object has entered the player and is obstructing the optical pickup or other mechanisms. With the player unplugged, it is often possible to take off the cover to the player's chassis and visually inspect the inside of the player. Since this action may void your warranty, you may wish to consult that document before turning any screws. If there are no foreign objects inside the player, close the cover, as there is nothing else inside that you can service. If a disc has become jammed inside the player, the only way to free it may be by removing the top cover and freeing it manually. If you do open up the player, make certain that it is first unplugged and that it will present no electrical hazard. Again, you may wish to have an authorized service person perform this service for you, as it is possible to do more damage than good by opening up the player.

COMPACT DISC ACCESSORIES

If your pocketbook is not depleted after having spent several hundred dollars for a disc player and a dozen or more dollars per disc, you can empty it further by spending your money on compact disc accessories. There are dozens of companies producing hundreds of products for the CD owner, all of which claim to make that ownership a more pleasurable or musical experience. There are units made to store CDs, clean them, and catalog them. There are cleaners for the inside and outside of your player, as well as covers, tables, cabinets, remote controls, and adapters which hook onto and around the compact disc player. some of these accessories are for show, some are merely convenient, and a few are quite handy.

CD Cleaners

The most common accessory is the compact disc cleaner. As you will find out, discs do get dirty and do require cleaning. Compact disc cleaners perform this cleansing function. There are two types of cleaners: good ones and bad ones. The good ones are those that clean the disc radially, from the center outward. The bad ones are those that sweep across the disc's surface. The only way to tell which category a cleaner falls into is to pick it up and examine it. Just about all of the cleaning devices require that you drop a disc into them, close a cover, and then turn a crank to spin either the disc, cleaning pad, or both simultaneously. Some cleaners may take more muscle than others to operate, and some may have a geared crank which can make this process both faster and easier. Many cleaners come with a brush which is used to remove superficial dust and dirt before further cleaning is performed. Make certain that such brushes will not scratch the clear plastic of the disc, and always use the brush before resorting to the rotational cleansing method.

If the pads that wipe the disc are not replaceable or cannot be cleaned, then after a period of time you will just be grinding old dirt into new discs when you attempt to clean them. The type of pads that are used in cleaning devices varies, as does the type of fluid that is used to lubricate the pad and loosen dirt on the disc. As stated before, a caustic cleanser can ruin a disc, so be sure to use the fluid that comes with the cleaner. Other types can damage either the cleansing pad or the disc itself. If you intend to clean a large number of discs regularly or are not fond of cranking, there are a few motorized disc cleaners on the market. Although these devices can be quite expensive, they can also be a great convenience if you own a large number of discs. There are a few cleansing systems that do not use the crank or motorized method. These come with a cleaning pad that is moistened and then used to scrub the disc. The disc is placed upside down on a flat surface or pad, and then the cleaning pad is moved back and forth on the disc. Although a bit less complex than the crank method, there is no reason that such cleaning devices should work any less efficiently than their more complex counterparts. The best advice when using a disc cleaner is to use it only when absolutely necessary, and then only in the prescribed manner with a clean pad and the correct fluid.

Disc Storage Devices

The most common way to store compact discs is in the now familiar jewel box. Although these can be difficult to open and shut, and extraction of the disc is sometimes difficult, they are the standard of the industry. These cases protect the disc from physical damage and dirt and hold information about the album which is normally found on a record or tape jacket. There are a number of sources for empty jewel boxes should one become damaged. Most record stores that carry compact discs also have such products. If you are not fond of the jewel box, there are other methods to store compact discs. If you have a portable or car player, carrying discs in their jewel boxes may be too bulky a method. If so, there are disc albums and sleeves that address this problem (Figure 10.1). The disc sleeve is a pocket of plastic much like the sleeve of a 45-rpm record. The disc album is a hinged collection of these sleeves which is protected by a soft cover, much like a photo album. While such systems may save space, they do not afford the discs as great a factor of protection as do other carrying methods. If dirt enters the disc sleeve, it can rub against the disc surface and cause permanent scratches. It also provides less physical protection should a disc be dropped or have something dropped on it, for there is but a flexible layer of plastic between the disc and its demise. In situations where it is completely impractical to carry discs in their jewel boxes, the disc sleeve is better than no protection at all.

Once you have owned a disc player for any length of time, you will probably find that storing the discs, even in their jewel boxes, is a cumbersome task. It is hard to keep discs organized if you have no good place to store them, so several manufacturers have stepped in with disc storage units. Like the units that house audio or video cassettes, those for compact discs are tailored to the disc's case width and depth. Some units store the discs in a carousel, making for easy access in a confined space. Others take the drawer approach, putting the discs inside their own cabinet with pull-out drawers. Other housings may simply be an appropriately sized rectangular box inside which you can place a number of discs, while some manufacturers produce glass-doored, bronze-hinged-and-trimmed cases which perform much the same function. Stackable units are handy since as

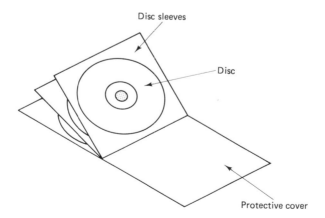

Figure 10.1 Disc album.

your disc collection grows, you need not outgrow a disc cabinet. Simply adding a stack-on cabinet to the previous one doubles its disc capacity. This feature is also available on some carousel models. If you plan to stack a number of cabinets, you may prefer that they interlock so as not to tip one over inadvertently. Some models lock together both horizontally and vertically so that you can expand the cabinet in all directions. There are also those that can be wall mounted. Some cabinets have a spring-loaded plate behind each compact disc jewel box which can eject the box an inch or so when a lever is depressed. These types of cabinets stack discs very close to each other since you need not be able to grasp a case edge to remove it—you need only eject it. These cabinets are more compact than most other designs. There are also a few manufacturers who produce compact disc furniture which consists of tables and bookshelves specifically tailored to compact disc storage. If you have enough discs to fill such a piece of furniture, the price tag of the cabinet will probably seem small compared to the value of its contents. If you are on the go, consider buying a compact disc carrying case. Like those that hold cassette tapes, these cases are usually appropriately shaped vinyl cases with plastic handles for portability.

Car Stereo Adapters

Many buyers who purchase portable compact disc players intend to use them in their cars as well. Unfortunately, not every portable disc player has the appropriate connectors for auto use, and often the car stereo system has no inputs that can accept an external source such as disc player. Even if all the connectors do match, it is often difficult to rewire the car stereo so that the disc player can be integrated into the car's environment. As with many such shortcomings, these are addressed by the manufacturers of CD accessories. There are a number of disc player adapters suited for car use. Their aim is to provide a link between the disc player and the car stereo's amplifier and speakers. Some units merely convert the output of the disc player's headphone outputs to a level suited to the preamp inputs of a car stereo receiver. Unfortunately, not many car stereo receivers have such inputs as standard, and so this type of adapter is useful only for a limited number of car stereo units. Another type of converter uses the headphone output of a disc player, but converts it into a format that can be input through the antenna lead which connects to the car stereo. In effect, such a device frequency modulates the CD player's output just the way a FM radio station broadcasts voice and music over the air waves. The output of this adapter is connected to the antenna input of the receiver either directly or through a Y-type connector (Figure 10.2). The Y connector allows you to choose either the CD or RF antenna input, much like many selector boxes allow a television to switch between a VCR or live transmission. This method can bandlimit the output of the CD since the FM broadcast's

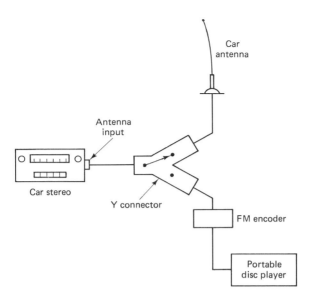

Figure 10.2 An FM encoder allows a portable disc player to play through the antenna lead of a car stereo. The Y connector chooses between the car antenna and the disc player.

bandwidth may not be as wide as that of the disc player. There is also the possibility that the signal-to-noise ratio of the FM modulator and other such specifications will not match those of the disc player, and so may degrade the player's output. Since the car is an unusually noisy environment and few car stereos can match the musical quality of the compact disc medium, this degradation in sound will occur anyway.

If such a system does not appeal to you, there are yet other ways to pipe CD music into your car. One manufacturer produces an adapter that plugs both into the CD player's headphone outputs and a car stereo's tape deck. The output of the CD player becomes an input to the car stereo through the magnetic head of the tape deck (Figure 10.3). In essence, the converter makes the car stereo think that the CD player is a cassette tape. This system suffers from the same shortcomings as those of the FM system: Its bandwidth and other specifications may not equal those of the CD players. In particular, few cassette decks that are meant for car mobile applications have much of a frequency response beyond 12 or 14 kHz. And because some tape decks respond better to one type of cassette than to another, the adapter may not match the best cassette type in terms of frequency response and signal-to-noise ratio. Conversely, if you are satisfied with the sound that emanates from the tape player, you will probably not find fault with a well-engineered CD-to-cassette deck converter.

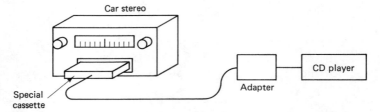

Figure 10.3   An adapter and special cassette allow a portable disc player to play through the tape head of a car stereo.

A final converter type plays the CD's output over the car's speakers, not through the receiver, but through the car's electrical system. Such units take the headphone output of the disc player, amplify it, then shoot it through your car's electrical system via the cigarette lighter plug. This type of system can provide only monaural amplification, so the sound emanating from your car's speakers will be not stereo, but mono. Such a system is also very susceptible to spurious noise emanating from other points in your car's electrical system.

Consolidating Your Remote Controls

Many disc players come with remote controls. Others have the capability for remote control, but the remote controller must be purchased separately from the original disc player. Although an option such as remote control is convenient, often a house contains many remotely controlled devices, such as a television, VCR, or stereo components. Normally, each one of these requires its own separate controller. Since many such devices look the same, it can be a chore in itself to pick the right controller for a particular appliance, and it is certainly unseemly to have lots of remote controls laying about the coffee table. Lately, some manufacturers have begun to integrate all their components so that they can all be controlled by one remote unit. If you buy a brand X television, stereo, and VCR, there may be a single brand X remote control to handle all their functions. If, however, you own several different brands of electronics, you will need a more flexible remote controller. There are a few remotes on the market which actually learn from other remote units so that they can perform their functions. Such a unit can control several brands of equipment. This works only with infrared remotes which use light, rather than a cable, to transmit their controls.

Special Cabling for Disc Players

The increased frequency response of the compact disc player manifests itself not only in the quality of stereo components which are necessary to back it up, but also in the quality of interconnecting cables that one uses to hook up such components. Some cables are designed to mask the effects of crosstalk between themselves and other cables, and to pass audio signals with a minimum amount of distortion. They often have gold-plated connectors to ensure good electrical conductivity between components, and they are shielded to eliminate spurious emanations. If you own an average stereo, the chances are that you will not be able to tell the difference between these cables and ordinary connectors. If, however, you own a top-of-the-line system and want to squeeze the best possible sound out of it, you may well consider purchasing such cables. Besides interconnecting cables, there are also some very high quality speaker cables on the market which incorporate the same design principles as the interconnect. Such cables can handle the high frequencies and currents associated with the compact disc system's very large dynamic range. Again, if your amplifier or speakers are not able to match the quality of your disc player, an investment in high-quality cabling will not produce significant results. Conversely, if you own a high-powered or top-quality stereo system, premium cables can have a significant and beneficial effect.

Disc Dampers

The compact disc is a relatively light object. It is held in place inside the disc player by a spindle that spins it at between 200 and 500 revolutions per minute. Because the disc is so light, it has very little rotational momentum, meaning that its speed is stabilized only by the corrective action of the disc player's electronic circuitry. Discs are also sensitive to vibrations because of their light weight. These conditions were taken into account when the compact disc system was initially conceived, and there are many corrective measures incorporated into modern players which address these areas. In the continual search for better performance, some aftermarket manufacturers have developed so-called disc dampers or stabilizers, which attempt to reduce the disc's susceptibility to vibration and rotational speed imbalance. The dampers are shaped exactly the same as the compact disc itself, but are made of metal. They are placed on top of the compact disc and this sandwich is inserted into the disc drawer as usual. Their manufacturers claim that the added weight and stability aid in the tracking of the disc, and so promote overall better sound. If you plan to try a disc stabilizer, be forewarned that they effectively increase the overall weight of the compact disc, so that the disc drive motor must work harder in order to accelerate and decelerate the disc. Since such changes in the rotational speed of the disc occur normally, the disc stabilizer can actually hinder the disc player during such periods. Reports indicate that disc dampers can improve the player's sound quality, but the effects they have on the overall reliability and wear of the player's drive components are as yet unknown. One manufacturer produces two types of stabilizers of differing weights and recommends the heavier stabilizer only for players that are able to handle its higher weight, indicating that perhaps disc stabilizers do put a strain on the player's mechanism.

Disc Protectors

If you are concerned about the label of your CD becoming scratched or damaged, there are transparent mats which affix to the label side of the CD to form a protective barrier against dirt and physical damage. The label is only part of the disc that is not protected by a layer of plastic; the metallic coating of the disc is under such a layer. Never use such a protector on the bottom side of the disc, for its refractive index as well as that of the glue used to hold it on differs from that of the CD material. This, combined with tiny pockets of air that could be trapped between the protector and the disc, will cause errors when the disc is tracked by the laser pickup.

Isolation Feet

The compact disc player is vulnerable to vibrations transmitted through the surface on which it rests. Some players have specially designed feet that buffer the player from the table or shelf on which it rests. If your player has no such feet or you feel that they are inadequate, you may choose to replace them. There are many such replacement feet available, most of which were originally designed for use with turntables. They work equally well with CD players. If you find that the slamming of a door or other such occurrences causes your player to mistrack, better isolation feet may alleviate the problem. Some feet produce a shock absorber–like action, actually riding on a cushion of air, whereas others consist simply of large soft rubber or foam discs which absorb vibrations in a similar manner.

Which Accessories Do You Need?

Like the good capitalists that they are, manufacturers of disc accessories are continuously trying to convince the public that their products are indispensable. Most of the products we have examined here fall into the class of add-on's, things that are used to fine tune your system. Some will provide audible gains, while others will prolong your system's usefulness or extend its capabilities. Some manufacturers claim that their products make up for deficiencies in disc or disc player faults. Remember that these same people sometimes have no experience with digital audio, but rather call on other skills or beliefs as the basis for these claims. You, the buyer, must sort out the useful accessories from the useless or potentially destructive ones. For although most accessories do address some real need or deficiency, a few simply create their own problems. At best, such accessories will merely increase the bulk of your audio investment; at worst, they will reduce the life of a system.

11

COMPACT DISC TRIVIA

The compact disc system is one of the biggest things to happen to the audio industry since the invention of the record player. Entire industries have begun to grow in both disc and player manufacturing. Today, dozens of disc-pressing plants are opening around the United States and Japan, and dozens more are in the planning stages. All of this effort is not directed simply toward the compact audio disc effort, but also toward discs that store information suited for use by computers. These compact discs are called CD ROMs, and they are beginning to play and ever-increasing role in the electronics and computer industry. There are also a number of digital recorders and players on the market that use magnetic tape to encode music and information digitally. The bits stored on these tapes are derived in much the same way as for compact discs, but because the bits are stored on tape, they can be both recorded and played back over and over again. There is also a trend toward putting video images on compact discs, which, much like a music video, could augment the music. Finally, the disc player itself is constantly undergoing redesigns that improve both its capabilities and sound. Many of these endeavors are products of new technological gains which a few years ago would have seemed unlikely to have made such a great impact on everyday life. Today, these new products, although as yet not standardized, are finding their way into business, scientific, defense, and home markets. The compact disc itself may some day be as much of a relic as cylindrical records, yet today it is one of the fastest-growing commodities and industries.

HOW DISCS ARE MADE

There are many processes involved in the manufacture of a compact disc. A plant that can perform all of these processes and produce compact discs costs more than $20 million, accounting for the relatively high price of discs. In the previous pages we have seen how the information encoded on discs is modulated and encoded until it is ready to be transferred into pits and lands on the surface of a disc. Here, we will examine the physical processes which go into producing a finished disc.

Formatting, The First Step

The first step in producing a disc is to format it so that it conforms physically to the CD standard. The audio samples, as well as subcode data, must be readied for transition to the disc medium. First, information about the music is compiled and stored in a disc directory. This directory, much like the table of contents of a book, holds information about the length of each selection, its starting and ending positions on the disc, the total number of tracks on the disc, and other such housekeeping information. Once this directory is constructed, the information is stored on a digital tape so that it can be played into a mastering machine (Figure 11.1). The digital tape also holds the digital forms of whatever music is to be encoded on the disc. At this point, no error correction has been added to the samples, but all of the subcode information has been recorded on the tape. Although there are eight digital channels devoted to subcode information, only two are used at present, leaving four for future endeavors such as adding video images to CDs.

Creating the Master

After this first tape has been made, the master disc is ready to be formed. A master is the prototype after which all other discs will be patterned. You can imagine that such a disc must be absolutely flawless; otherwise, the tens of thousands of discs that are made from it will be defective. To achieve this nearly total perfection, the master disc, a circular piece of glass in the shape of a compact disc, must contain no physical flaws.

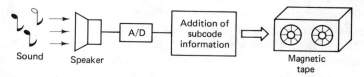

Figure 11.1 First step in constructing a compact disc. Audio data are digitized and placed onto a magnetic tape, along with subcode information.

This is achieved by forming the disc in a dust- and dirt-free environment called a *clean room*. Such a room is free of airborne and sedentary contaminants. Anyone that enters the clean room must wear special superclean overalls, face masks, hair covering, gloves, and special boots. The entrance to the clean room is an airlock in which dozens of tiny jets of air blow dust and dirt off the person's body, contaminants which are then sucked out of the airlock by strong fans. Needless to say, smoking is strictly prohibited in such an environment, and even the lint from a facial tissue could devastate the cleanliness of the environment. The reason for such stringent measures is the microscopic size of the pits and lands that are cut in the disc, and the inevitable multiplication of errors should a piece of dust or dirt land on an unprotected master disc. Even a mild case of dandruff can ruin an entire batch of discs, and an uncontrolled sneeze can be similarly disastrous. The air inside the clean room is constantly filtered to remove any contaminants that make it past these stringent safeguards.

The glass used to make the master disc, called *float glass*, is formed in a superclean environment. It is created by pouring absolutely pure molten glass onto a liquid in a circular tank (Figure 11.2). As the glass cools, it forms an optically pure bubble-free disc. This disc is then polished until its surface is completely flat and smooth, with no surface irregularities such as dips, waves, or pits. The disc is then tested with a laser to confirm that no irregularities exist and that no air bubbles were trapped during the forming process. Next, the disc is coated with a *photoresist* material on one side of its surface, and then baked in an oven until the photoresist is cured. Photoresist is a chemical that forms an enamel on top of the disc's surface. When exposed to light, the photoresist can be selectively dissolved through a chemical process. During the coating process, the thickness of the photoresist is monitored by a laser to make certain that the depth of the photoresist

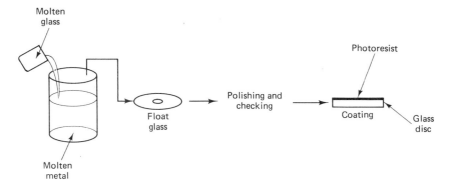

Figure 11.2 Float glass is made by pouring molten glass onto a liquid metal. A disc is removed, shaped, polished and cleaned, and then inspected and coated with a photoresist material.

stays within a predetermined limit. If the photoresist is not applied correctly, it will have an uneven depth and will have to be removed from the glass substrate, then reapplied.

Cutting a Master Disc

The blank master disc is transported to the mastering machine (Figure 11.3), which will inscribe the pattern of pits and lands that will eventually be read by the disc player's laser. The magnetic tape serves as the input to this machine, but all of the error correction, framing, and interleaving is done on the fly by the mastering machine. As each selection is read, it is separated into frames, then interleaved. The CIRC coding process is performed on it, and finally, it is modulated using the eight-to-fourteen modulation method. All of this is done by electronics in the mastering machine, just as the reverse is done when a CD is read. The spinning disc is rotated at a constant linear velocity, which translates into a rotational velocity of between 200 and 500 rpm. As the disc spins, a laser that is focused on the disc is modulated by the bit stream so that it turns on and off to coincide with the EFM transitions. The laser light changes the composition of the photoresist material when it strikes the disc's surface. Another laser is used to focus the cutting laser and and track the disc. The frequency and intensity of light that it emits does not affect the photoresist material and so, unlike the cutting laser, it does not cut pits into the material. The laser assembly moves across the surface of the disc, tracking and cutting in the same manner that the optical assembly of the disc player will read the disc when the time comes for playback.

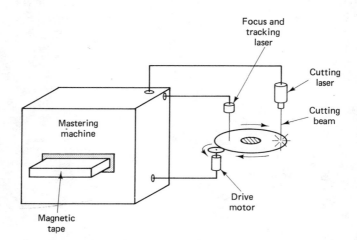

Figure 11.3 The mastering machine, driven by the magnetic tape, etches the photores material with one laser and checks tracking and focusing with another.

Developing the Master and Further Reproduction

After the disc has been burned in this manner, it is transported to a developing tank, where it is washed with an etching solution (Figure 11.4). The etching solution removes the part of the photoresist that was exposed to light, leaving the unexposed material untouched. Left in the solution long enough, the photoresist would eventually dissolve, so as soon as the etching solution reaches the underlying glass surface, the disc is removed and cleansed of all residual solutions. This master is used to make a metal disc called the "father," which is a negative of the original glass master. By depositing a metal on the surface of the glass master through the process of electroplating, this nickel negative is formed. One more disc must be made, which is the negative of the father disc and an exact duplicate of the glass master. This metal "mother" disc is used to press out a number of discs which will be used as masters to reproduce the final, salable, production discs.

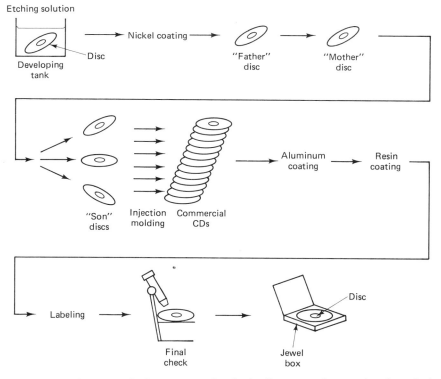

Figure 11.4 The exposed photoresist is dissolved off in an etching tank, after which a number of master discs are formed. Commercial discs are injection moulded, coated with aluminum, and protected with resin before the label is silkscreened on and the disc is shipped.

Pressing Out Commercial CDs

A pressing machine is used to copy the production masters over to the polycarbonate discs, which will be coated with aluminum and sold. The "son" discs are placed in pressing molds which are injected with molten polycarbonate plastic, a cousin of plexiglass. The plastic is extremely pure, like everything in the compact disc pressing process, and is left to cool before the mold is separated and the disc is removed to make room for the next one. The pressing process takes but a fraction of a minute to perform, and after molding, the disc is checked again with a laser to ensure that no bubbles or impurities have become embedded inside the disc. Its flatness is also checked, and a small percentage of the discs are rejected because of such flaws.

Coating and Labeling the Disc

The next step in the compact disc's long journey to the record store is aluminum coating. The disc must be coated with a reflective material so that the laser in your player will have a return beam to sense and process. Discs are coated by vaporizing aluminum and condensing the vaporized mist on their surfaces. A film approximately 75 nanometers thick is deposited on the discs, after which the discs are again inspected for pinholes or uneven coatings. The disc, now almost playable, is protected with an acrylic resin which is deposited on top of the aluminum coating. This keeps the aluminum from being scratched and protects the surface from exposure to the elements. The disc's label will be sprayed on over this resin in a silkscreening process and then cured in ultraviolet light. Every completed disc is tested for errors on a high-speed disc reader. Those that have a few correctable errors are passed and packaged into the familiar jewel box. Those that have too many errors to be corrected by the CIRC code, as well as those discs that are borderline, are rejected and thrown on the scrap heap. Other machines perform a final check on the physical parameters of the disc, such as its roundness, flatness, and the evenness of its surface (Figure 11.5). The sheer number of discs that do not make it past this involved process of checks, as well as the elaborate processes and facilities that are necessary to produce discs successfully, are the major reasons for the CD's high prices and sometimes limited availability. With more and better plants opening every day, these shortcomings may soon be on the wane.

CD ROMs

The compact disc medium is geared toward information storage and retrieval. For the audio industry, this translates into the recording and

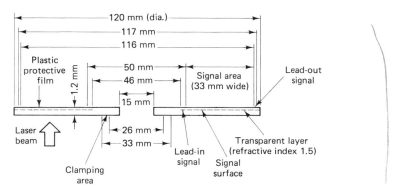

Figure 11.5 Physical parameters of a compact disc. [Courtesy of Pioneer Electronics (USA), Inc.]

replaying of music. But CDs can store any type of information, as long as it is encoded into binary streams of 1's and 0's. Computers store information in just this form, and anything that can be stored on the written page can be transferred to a computer. The average home computer can store from 10 to 40 million bytes of information. By comparison, a printed page translates into roughly 3000 bytes. A CD can store nearly 600 million bytes of information, 15 times as many as a computer's disk drive. It is for this reason that industry has begun to develop and market the compact disc read-only memory (CD ROM). As you may gather, the one disadvantage that CDs have is that they cannot be randomly written to and read from. In this sense they will never replace the more versatile computer disk drive, called a *hard disk*. On the other hand, there are many applications in which there is a great deal of information that must be recorded and accessed on a regular basis, information that is not constantly changing and being updated. Dictionaries and encyclopedias are two such examples, as are training and repair manuals, and technical or financial databases. Imagine an entire law or medical library contained on but a few thin discs, all indexed and cross-referenced, and available at the touch of a button. Pictures and sound can also be inscribed onto the CD ROM, so interactive tutorials in which a student can interact and learn can be contained on disc. These are all applications where a mass of information that would overwhelm a normal storage system could be handled easily by a single disc. It is the disc's portability which causes a worry—that an entire library could be lost or stolen because the discs can be so easily concealed. And with the cost of many technical libraries ranging into the thousands of dollars, how much should one charge for a few discs containing the same material? Cannot such material be copied via computer without the publisher's permission? These are some of the questions that arise regarding the CD ROM.

CD ROM Format

The audio disc and CD ROM differ in several respects. Although to look at them you would perceive no physical difference, there are differences in the way that information is organized onto the disc and presented to the outside world. When an audio disc is read and an error is detected, that error will be corrected by muting or linear interpolation if the error correction cannot completely correct it. This is not good enough for the CD ROM medium, for such an error may contain vital statistical information such as the population of a city or total assets of a corporation. For this reason, CD ROMs utilize more powerful error correction than do audio discs—in fact, correcting errors thousands of times better than the CIRC code used for audio discs. As you might expect, data are not formatted in the same manner for the different media, so an audio CD cannot be read by a CD ROM drive, or vice versa, unless the players are specifically designed as dual-purpose machines.

CD ROM Players

Another difference is not in the discs themselves but in the players. Audio players D/A convert their full output, while that of a CD ROM is still digital, but in parallel form. Also, CD ROM drives must have very fast seek times to keep up with the information demands of a computer. An audio player, conversely, may have a several-second delay between the time a selection is requested and when it begins to play.

Standardization Among ROM Manufacturers

One of the major obstacles facing the acceptance of CD ROM into the commercial world is its lack of standardization. Each year, new standards for the way information is encoded and set up on a disc are introduced, sometimes obsoleting old standards, sometimes merely clouding the waters as to which standard is best. Until a uniform standard, such as that for audio discs, can be agreed upon, it appear that each manufacturer will go with their own proprietary standard. This could have the effect of making one manufacturer's discs not usable on another's system, thereby negating a great deal of the appeal of the disc medium. With the cost of mastering a new disc at about $4000, it seems ridiculous that different masters of the same information need to be made to run on various systems utilizing differing disc drives. The fact that CD ROM is here to stay is evidenced by the ever-increasing number of drives available on the market. When and if they will be standardized is not known.

MAGNETO-OPTICAL DISCS

One of the drawbacks of compact discs is that they are a read-only device; they cannot be recorded upon, except through the original mastering process. This is not necessarily bad, for records are read-only and they seem to have done rather well in the past. There is an emerging product, called the *magneto-optical disc* (MOD), which addresses this matter, for MODs can be both read from and written to. Like optical discs, MODS use laser light to read the rotating surface of a disc which has the same physical shape of a CD. Unlike CDs, the reflected light is modulated not by the depressions in the disc's surface, but by shifts in the reflected light's polarization because of magnetic fluctuations. A MOD is made by first cutting a magnetic material into the shape of a CD, much like the magnetic media inside a computer's floppy disc. The medium is magnetized by heating a tiny area of the disc with a laser, then applying a tightly focused magnetic field to this area so that the electrical charges on the disc's surface are polarized. The result is a very small, well-defined, polarized area of charge whose physical analog is the pit of a CD. When a scanning laser hits this spot, the reflected light will be oriented in a slightly different manner than had it hit a nonpolarized section of the disc. This shift can be detected, and transitions from polarized to nonpolarized sections may be interpreted as easily as those from pits to lands. The good part about all of this is that unlike conventional tape recorders and players of both the analog and digital variety, the magnetic surface is never touched by a tape head, drive motor, or capstans, so the wear associated with these devices is nonexistent in the MOD recorder/player. Like other tape decks, MODs can be erased and recorded over and over again, each one holding over an hour of music. Like CDs, each MOD will contain a section devoted to directory information and addressing, and will come sandwiched between protective plastics plates. Since both compact discs and MODs are read in similar manners, it will be possible to fabricate MOD machines that can also play standard CDs, although your present player probably will not be able to handle a MOD.

DIGITAL AUDIO TAPE

Optical discs are not the only medium that can handle digital recordings. As we saw before, the magnetic tape that feeds a disc mastering machine is digitally encoded. In fact, digital recording using reel-to-reel tapes has been around for quite a few years. Such recorders have usually been bulky, noisy, and expensive machines such as those employed for mainframe computers. Lately, the taping process has been refined and the mechanisms miniaturized so that digital taping is now possible in the home as well as the studio.

The digitization process used for *digital audio tape* (DAT) is the same as for the CD. Unlike discs, however, the binary information is recorded onto the tape by a magnetic head that contacts the surface of the tape in much the same way that a videocassette recorder works. The difference is that the recorder need recognize only two values, the binary 1 and 0, rather than trying to accommodate an analog signal. This is good, because small amounts of noise will not affect the values of these binary numbers as they would an analog voltage. The bad part is that the bandwidth of such a binary stream is immense, especially when one considers the limited bandwidth of most tape recorders. This means that the tapes used in a digital recorder must be of higher quality than regular audio tapes and the recorder itself must be both complex and bandwidth efficient.

The Recording Process

Enter the two major contenders for the DAT market, R-DAT and S-DAT. Like the Beta and VHS standards for videocassette recorders, these two standards are competing for what may eventually be a one-recorder market. The basic idea of both recorder types is this. Magnetic tape consists of particles that reside on its surface. These particles are polar, like a common bar-shaped magnet, and their positions can be reoriented by applying a magnetic field to them. The particles hold their orientation when the field is removed. Because the particles themselves generate a field, their orientation can be read by a tape head as it contacts the surface of the tape. As more particles are packed onto a tape, the resolution of the tape increases, and it can record with a higher fidelity, that is, a wider bandwidth. A point comes, however, when so many particles are packed onto a tape that they begin to attract and repel each other independently of how they are oriented by the passing magnetic field. When this happens, the tape demagnetizes itself and becomes unusable. There is a maximum information density that can be packed onto a magnetic tape—between 20,000 and 30,000 bits per inch. Consider now that the serial stream which is recorded on a CD runs at around 2 million bits per second before EFM, and you will soon see that a tape would need to run at around 80 in. per second to accommodate such a bit rate. By comparison, a regular cassette recorder runs at $1\frac{7}{8}$ in. per second. You can see that this type of recording is not going to work very well for digital recording.

The answer to this problem comes in the form of a process called *perpendicular recording*. Rather than orient the magnetic particles horizontally, along the surface of the tape, why not orient them vertically, perpendicular to the surface? Now more particles can be packed in the same space without inducing self-demagnetization, and the information density of the tape increases because there are more particles per inch of tape (Figure 11.6). In fact, such a method can increase the information density

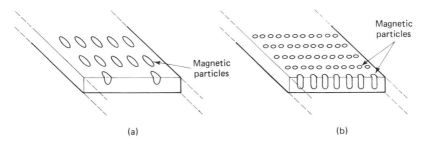

Figure 11.6 Cross section of a strip of magnetic tape. In low-density tapes, magnetic particles are aligned horizontally along the surface of the tape (a). High-density tapes have particles that are aligned vertically into the tape's surface (b).

by a factor of 10, 20, or more, to over 200,000 bits per inch. This brings the tape speed down to a livable and mechanically feasible range, one that can be implemented in a home unit.

R-DAT and S-DAT

A question arises: After constructing the perfect magnetic tape, how do we record information on that tape? We have already settled on the idea of recording digital information, binary 1's and 0's, rather than the original analog signal, but the design of the recorder has as much to do with the tape's bandwidth as with the tape itself. There are two predominant trends in DAT recorder design, the stationary head (S-DAT) and the rotary head (R-DAT) (Figure 11.7). The stationary head design is similar to that of an ordinary cassette deck's head. Tape is drawn past the magnetic head, which imparts a magnetic orientation to the particles of the tape corresponding to binary bits. A drawback of the S-DAT recorder is that in order to achieve a small cassette size, it is necessary for such a recorder to record multiple

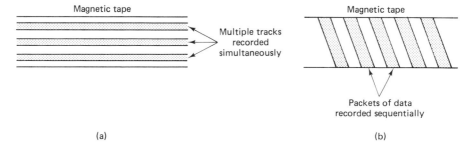

Figure 11.7 S-DAT recorders place several tracks of information along the length of a tape (a). R-DAT recorders place packets of information diagonally along the width of a tape (b).

tracks on a section of tape, much like the old eight-track systems. This would necessitate that very precise alignment be maintained between the tape and the tape head, so the complexity and cost of the system increases. This is not necessarily a crippling problem, but it is one that must be overcome by design engineers if they wish to construct a portable S-DAT machine.

R-DAT borrows some ideas from the video recorder field. Video recorders use a recording head mounted on a rotating drum. The tape is drawn across the drum more slowly than it would be in a stationary head design, but since the head is rotating, the effective tape speed is quite high. Also, rather than record tracks along the length of the tape, they are recorded diagonally across the width of the tape. Each diagonal swath is a small packet of information; they are simply not continuous in the way that a track along the tapes length is. The R-DAT approach is also a complex endeavor, but the design of rotary head recorders is well established in the VCR arena.

Trends in the DAT Market

At the present time, it appears that R-DAT recorders will be the preference of the consumer market. Because rotating-head technology is already in use in VCRs, the development of R-DAT recorders is already firmly established. There are a number of standards for R-DAT, and the types of sampling, recording, and playback varies from machine to machine. The basic feature that should be available on all R-DAT machines is 16-bit quantization with a 48 kHz sampling rate. This means that you can record audio at this sampling rate, then play back the tape on any R-DAT recorder. Note, though, that even though R-DAT recorders will supply an input for digital information, and many CD players have a digital output, you will be unable to record your CD because of the mismatch in sampling rates. It is also rumored that all prerecorded digital audio tapes, such as those that you will be able to buy in record stores, will be copy protected so that you will be able to play them, but will not be able to record them to another digital tape. The eventual selling price of digital tapes and recorders is difficult to project. As with any new product, prices at this time are still quite high, just as they were when CD players originally hit the market. Whether or not digital audio tape recorders will catch on as well as CDs is a question that will only be answered by time. It appears, however, that manufacturers have made a firm commitment to DAT, so you can expect to see recorders available in more and more locations.

FUTURE TRENDS IN DIGITAL AUDIO

The compact disc is still quite young. Today we are seeing digital technology being utilized in new ways for exciting new products. Soon the digital recorder will be as common as the cassette recorder is today. Computers will be employing CD ROM drives to access huge databases of information, and the audio disc may well contain both video images and music. Like any new product, the compact disc player is being improved as quickly as manufacturers can get the changes integrated into their production lines. So what could be next?

Improvements in the CD Player

There are some improvements still to be made to the CD player, some of which may benefit the system's overall sound, some of which are just gimmicks. Already available on the market are players employing 18-bit dual analog-to-digital converters with quadruple oversampling. So what else can be done to these machines? In the future we will probably see players that can handle CDs with video images as well as interface to computers to drive CD ROMs. If MODs catch on, there will be players to handle such discs, and perhaps players that can ingest all types of CDs just as many turntables handle LPs, 45's, and 78's. The video disc market is far from dead, and in fact there are already players that accept both audio CDs and video discs. In the area of digital audio tape recorders, a single standard will have to emerge. Perhaps the proponents of this medium will allow their recorders to tape compact discs; but it is more likely that these two media will be mutually exclusive. No doubt some "black boxes" will become available to interface DATs and CDs so that the needs of the audio consumer will be satisfied. Certainly, the price of discs will begin to decrease as more manufacturing plants are built in the United States and abroad, and as other industries begin to take advantage of compact disc technology for information storage and retrieval. The price of CD players has plummeted since their introduction, and this trend should continue to make better-quality players available at ever lower prices.

Digital Sound Processors

Some of the greatest gains will be realized not in digital recorders, be they tape or disc, but in digital sound processors. A *digital sound processor* is a machine that takes an audio signal, either analog or already digitized, and shapes it with digital filters. Graphic equalizers are available today which use analog filters to compensate for the uneven frequency responses of amplifiers, speakers, and even a room's acoustics. Delay boxes can make a regular listening room sound like a concert hall or put the listener in the middle of an orchestra. Digital sound processors will do these things and more, but the contrast between them and their analog counterparts will be as great as between records and CDs. Because these processors will use digital filters and delays to modify sound, they will not be inhibited by the imperfections and limits inherent in analog components. Already there has appeared a digital sound processor which an emulate the acoustic characteristics of a number of concert halls, turning even a modest living room into a digital Carnegie Hall. Future machines will also have the ability to clean up dirty-sounding records or tapes, compress and expand music for recording, and in general will far surpass conventional equalizers, delay boxes, and other sound-modifying devices.

A Digital Future

In all, the future of the compact disc, and indeed, digital sound in general, seems bright. We are at the beginning of a new era in music, just as innovative and exciting as was the introduction of the record player or the first reel-to-reel tape deck. Technology, visible in so many areas of everyday existence, has gained another foothold in our homes. Like any new product, the compact disc has been misunderstood and misrepresented, but when the power is turned on and a disc begins to play, there is no question but that this is a miraculous and innovative piece of audio gear.

GLOSSARY

aliasing The phenomenon whereby frequencies above half the Nyquist frequency will fold down across that point and interact with the components in the audio band. A significant problem in digital audio.

amplitude The maximum value of a wave or function.

amplitude modulation The process whereby an audio signal modulates the amplitude of a carrier wave so that it can be transmitted over the air waves.

analog-to-digital converter An electronic device that converts an analog waveform into a digital sample. For compact digital audio, an analog waveform is converted into 16-bit-wide binary numbers. Two types of A/D converters are the integrating converter and successive-approximation converter.

AND gate A type of digital logic circuit. It consists of two inputs and a single output. The output is high if and only if both the inputs are high.

attenuate To decrease the amplitude or power of a signal or frequency band.

bandpass filter A filter that passes a narrow range of frequencies while attenuating those above and below the band.

Bessel filter A filter that introduces little phase shift in its roll-off region.

binary numbering A number system based on powers of 2 rather than powers of 10 as in the decimal system. There are only two possible values for a binary digit, 1 or 0.

bit A single binary digit, either 1 or 0. The bit is the basis of all digital systems.

block code An encoding scheme used to formulate error correction bits from a number of data bits.

burst error An error that occurs in a digital medium. Such an error can cause large numbers of consecutive bits to be misread. The cause of a burst error may be dirt, grease, or scratches on the surface of a disc, or an imperfection that occurred during the manufacturing process.

byte A unit of information consisting of 8 binary bits.

capacitor A charge storage device that holds a voltage applied across its terminals. Capacitors of differing values charge and discharge at differing rates.

CD ROM Compact disc read-only memory. The CD ROM is a type of CD which is used to store digital information geared toward use in computers rather than in audio gear. The CD ROM, like the audio disc, holds approximately 600 million bytes of information, the equivalent of 200,000 written pages of text.

channel separation *See* stereo separation.

CIRC Cross-interleaved Reed–Solomon code. An error correcting linear block code used to multiplex and encode frames of digital data before it undergoes further modulation and is cut into the compact disc. The CIRC used on compact discs can correct a burst error of nearly 400 bits.

clock A digital signal, often a square wave, which maintains a constant frequency and is used to control the synchronization and operation of various other electronic devices.

collimator A lens that focuses a divergent beam of light into a parallel beam.

compact disc A circular disc made up of polycarbonate plastic upon which are engraved pits that store digital information. The compact disc can hold approximately 75 minutes of audio information, which equates to 4,800,000,000 binary bits of data.

companding A process that increases the number of quantization levels available to encode low-level inputs, and decreases the number of levels for large-scale inputs. This tends to keep the average S/N ratio equal for both small- and large-scale inputs.

comparator An electronic device whose output is proportional to the two voltages applied to its inputs.

CRCC Cyclic redundancy check code. Used to identify frames that contain errors when they are read from the compact disc.

CVSD Continuously variable slope delta modulation. A type of delta modulation whose step size is varied depending on how well the input matches the output.

dc Direct current. Refers to a signal that does not vary with time, but rather, remains at a fixed amplitude.

decibel A unit of comparison based on the ratio between the power of two quantities. It is a system based on logarithmic, rather than linear progression. The ratio in decibels of two quantities, Q_1, and Q_2, is defined as $[10 \times \log(Q_1/Q_2)]$.

decoder A device that takes an encoded signal or data stream and returns it to its state before encoding.

digital filter A filtering operation, such as low pass, which is performed on the digital samples of an analog waveform rather than on the analog wave itself.

digital-to-analog converter An electronic device that converts a binary number into an analog voltage. Converters used in digital audio applications range from 14 to 18 bits wide on their inputs.

disc changer A compact disc player that can access and hold several discs at one time.

discontinuity A sudden change in the value of a function or wave, such as the change in amplitude from one step of a staircase waveform to the next step.

distortion A destructive change in the value of an analog waveform. *See* total harmonic distortion; intermodulation distortion; quantization.

dither A small amount of noise which is added to the input of an analog-to-digital converter. Dither reduces the amount of destructive distortion that occurs when a low-level input is present.

dynamic range The ratio beween the maximum and minimum sound levels that can be recorded upon a medium. Usually expressed in decibels.

EFM Eight-to-fourteen modulation. The process whereby 8 data bits are encoded into 14 channel bits so that the number of transitions needed to encode the data is minimized.

Exclusive-OR gate A logic gate whose output is high if one, but not both, of its inputs are high.

eye height A measure of the quality of a transmission channel.

eye pattern The pattern that results from the amplified output of a the photodiode as the laser beam tracks a compact disc's surface.

FIFO First-in, first-out buffer. An electronic memory device. The first data word passed into the FIFO is the first data word that is available at its output.

filter A device or process that attenuates or amplifies certain frequencies.

floating-point converter An A/D converter that takes an analog input and converts it into an exponent and a mantissa rather than a straight binary or two's-complement number.

flutter The high-frequency oscillations in the rotational speed of a turntable or any rotating platter.

folding *See* aliasing.

frame A stream of bits that are grouped into sections of equal length in preparation for encoding or multiplexing.

frequency modulation The process whereby an audio wave modulates the frequency of a high-frequency carrier wave so that the audio information can be transmitted over the air waves.

frequency response A measure of the effect that a sound amplification or reproduction device has on its source. All audio components change the relationship between the original power distribution of frequencies and the distribution after the input is amplified or reproduced. Frequency response is usually expressed as the maximum deviation in decibels over a certain range, such as ± 3 dB from 20 Hz to 20 kHz.

Gaussian A probabilistic distribution with a characteristic bell-shaped curve.

Gaussian noise Noise that spans the entire audio spectrum whose power at any frequency follows a Gaussian distribution.

guard band A band between frequency spectra or modulated data which prevents information from one spectrum from leaking into adjacent spectra.

Hamming distance A measure of the efficiency of an error-correcting code. Defined as the number of digits that one binary code word differs from another code word. The Hamming distance between 0100 and 1011 is four, since all the binary places differ from each other.

hard disk A magnetic storage device used by computers. A hard disc may store from 5 to 400 megabytes of data, depending on its design.

hardware The electrical components of an electronic device, such as microchips, capacitors, wires, and resistors.

Hertz (Hz) A measure of the frequency of a signal, defined as the inverse of the time for one complete cycle. A 10-Hz sine wave takes a¹ of a second to complete a full cycle.

high A digital logic state that equates to the binary 1.

high-pass filter   A filter that passes high frequencies while attenuating low frequencies.

initialization   Occurs when a CD is loaded into a player. The directory data of the disc are read so that the position and length of tracks can be stored and referenced by the player.

interleaving   The process of taking the consecutive bits of a frame of data and spreading them out in time to reduce the damaging capability of a burst error. Akin to shuffling a deck of cards in an ordered fashion.

intermodulation distortion   The distortion that arises from mixing different frequencies in the analog components of an amplifier or preamplifier. The product of intermodulation distortion bears no relationship to the original audio signal, and is similar to the effect that aliasing has on a signal.

interpolation   A process whereby several samples are averaged together in order to come up with an approximation to a lost sample's value.

inverter   A digital logic gate whose output is the opposite of its input.

isolated circuitry   Electronic circuitry which has been separated into subsections so that noise does not propagate from one section to the next.

jitter   A random change in the phase of the digital clock which governs the working of the compact disc player. Jitter can cause errors in the acquisition and processing of a digital stream of data as they are read from the CD.

kilohertz (KHz)   1000 hertz, or 1000 cycles per second.

land   The section of a track on a compact disc which is at the same level as the surface, rather than impressed, as is a pit.

laser   A coherent light source which produces a pure beam of light at a prescribed wavelength rather than the complete spectrum of light which emanates from the sun or a household light bulb. Acronym for Light Amplification by the Stimulated Emission of Radiation.

laser diode   A semiconductor device that produces laser light whose intensity is a function of the current applied to its input.

line level   The voltage appearing at the output of a source audio component such as a CD player, tape deck, or turntable, as opposed to the output of an amplifier or microphone. Usually on the order of a few volts.

lissajous pattern   The pattern that arises on an oscilloscope when its time, or X axis, is swept by one channel of a disc player and its amplitude, or Y axis, is controlled by the other channel.

low A digital logic state that corresponds to a binary 0.

low-pass filter A filter that passes low frequencies and attenuates high frequencies. Used on the input stage of a digital recorder before analog-to-digital conversion and on the output stage of a digital player after digital-to-analog conversion.

LSI Large-scale integrated circuit. A microchip that contains several hundred logic gates which perform complex functions. Reduces the amount of chips and power necessary to realize a function, such as error correction.

megahertz (MHz) 1,000,000 hertz.

merging bits Bits used to string channel bits together so that they do not violate the minimum pit spacing.

microsecond (μs) 1/1,000,000 of a second.

millisecond (ms) 1/1000 of a second.

MOD Magneto-optical disc. A disc made of magnetic material which can be both written to and read from. It is read with a laser much like a CD, but is encoded with magnetically charged particles rather than pits and lands.

monitor diode A photodiode whose output is proportional to the intensity of the laser diode's beam. It is used to keep the laser's output at a constant light intensity.

nanosecond (ns) 1/1,000,000,000 of a second.

noise A signal that is unrelated to the original signal applied to a system, which results from unwanted side effects of that system.

noise shaper A circuit that subtracts out the average noise value of a signal in order to increase the signal-to-noise ratio of the system.

Nyquist sampling frequency A sampling frequency that is twice the highest-frequency component of an audio signal. The Nyquist sampling theorem says that by sampling at this frequency, the original frequency band can be reproduced completely and accurately.

objective lens A lens that takes a parallel beam of light and focuses it on a surface.

optical assembly The section of a compact disc player that houses the lenses, prism, photodiodes, laser, and focusing apparatus.

oscilloscope An electronic instrument that displays the amplitude of a wave as it varies with time.

overload The condition experienced by a delta modulator when its output waveform cannot match its input waveform. This is caused by either an incorrectly chosen step size or sampling frequency.

oversampling The process whereby the noise in a signal is spread out over a wider frequency band than the original audio band, so that the signal-to-noise ratio can be increased. Allows the use of D/A converters with less accuracy, and low-pass filters with gentler roll-off regions. An alternative meaning is taking more samples of a waveform than its bandwidth warrants.

parity bit A bit which is chosen such that it keeps the number of binary 1's in a row or column of a block code at either an even or odd number.

passband The region of a filter in which all frequencies are not attenuated, but rather are passed without significant changes.

PCM Pulse-code modulation. A type of modulation that converts an analog value into a discrete digital sample using some type of binary notation.

phase shift A skewing of the time relationships between different frequency components of the same audio signal. Similar to the effect of placing a speaker's tweeter far behind the woofer, so that the high- and low-frequency sounds reach the listener at different times.

photodiode A light-sensitive electronic device whose output voltage is proportional to the amount of light that impinges on its surface.

pit A depression in the surface of a compact disc.

printed circuit board A fiberglass board manufactured so that it contains electrical interconnections and receptacles for electronic devices such as chips, resistors, capacitors, and the like. This decreases the amount of labor that is necessary to construct a circuit board.

prism A block of glass shaped such that it diverts a beam of light from its initial path without changing the shape of the beam.

quantization The process whereby an infinite number of analog values are mapped into a finite number of digital values. Quantization results in the addition of noise because the original value of a signal is almost never preserved, but rather is mapped to the nearest available quantization level. A 16-bit analog-to-digital converter contains 65,000 quantization levels.

RAM Random-access memory. An electronic storage device that holds data in storage until the data are requested by another device. Unlike a FIFO, any group of data can be accessed at any time, regardless of the time at which it was put into storage.

random error A patternless error that wipes out bits without regard to their positioning in a data stream.

R-DAT Rotary head digital audio tape recorder. A type of DAT recorder that uses a rotating magnetic head to increase the effective tape speed of a cassette. It recording mechanism functions much like that of a videocassette recorder.

redundant coding A type of coding in which data are encoded several times by different methods rather than by a single encoder.

resistor An electrical device that resists the flow of current through its body. The resistor dissipates voltage in the form of heat according to the equation: voltage = current × resistance ($V = I \times R$).

RF Radio frequency. The frequency at which radio transmissions such as AM or FM travel through the air.

ringing The ripple that occurs in the normally flat portions of a sine wave which arises because of intermodulation and harmonic distortion or aliasing.

ripple The amount of deviation from perfectly flat of a filter's band regions or in the response of a flat portion of a wave or transfer function.

roll-off The region of a low-pass filter between the passband and cutoff region.

sample-and-hold A circuit that holds the value of an analog signal while the A/D converter performs its function. The circuit samples the analog signal at regular intervals and holds that value until the next sampling interval. Can be realized in hardware with a few simple components.

sampling frequency The rate at which a digital system converts an analog signal into digital samples. This frequency is 44.1 kHz for the compact disc.

S-DAT Stationary head digital audio tape recorder. A type of DAT recorder which records several tracks of information in parallel along the length of a cassette tape.

signal-to-noise ratio The ratio between the highest level of audio signal to the largest possible amount of noise that can enter the system. Usually expressed in decibels.

spectrum A range of frequencies.

spectrum analyzer A device that plots the strength of individual components of a frequency spectrum and displays the plot on a fluorescent screen.

spurious noise Noise introduced into an electronic circuit because of its interaction with neighboring circuitry.

square wave A signal with a constant frequency which assumes only two possible values, each of which are equal in length.

staircase waveform The input to an A/D converter and the output of a D/A converter after the sample-and-hold. This PAM waveform is a sampled analog signal whose discontinuities give it its characteristic staircase appearance.

step/stepsize The value of a single quantization unit of an analog-to-digital converter.

stereo separation A figure that has to do with the amount of signal that leaks between the right and left channels of an audio device.

stopband The region of a filter in which all frequencies are significantly attenuated.

stylus The portion of a turntable's arm that contacts the groove of the record and transmits these vibrations so that they can be converted into electrical impulses.

subcode The portion of which is encoded on a compact disc and holds information about the track number, length, position, and other nonaudio data.

summer A circuit whose output is the sum of the weighted values of voltages that appear at its input.

synchronization bits Bits that are tagged onto a frame of data so that its beginning and ending points can be determined.

total harmonic distortion The ratio of the power of a fundamental frequency as measured at the output of an audio component versus the total power of all the harmonics in the frequency band at the output of the system.

trace A line of conductive material that resides on a printed circuit board and connects the devices on that board.

track A single musical selection on a compact disc.

tri-beam laser A laser pickup that splits a single laser beam into three separate spots to control the reading, tracking, and focusing of a compact disc.

volt The basic unit of electrical measurement.

voltmeter An electronic instrument that displays the voltage of a signal in either numerical or scalar form.

watt A unit of electrical power.

wow The low-frequency oscillation in the rotational speed of a turntable or any rotating platter.

XOR *See* Exclusive-OR gate.

INDEX